NAVIGATING YOUR RELATIONSHIP

NAVIGATING YOUR RELATIONSHIP:

A Voyage for Couples

H. LAURENCE SCHWAB, M.F.T.

Two Harbors Press
Minneapolis, MN

Two Harbors Press
322 First Avenue N, 5th floor
Minneapolis, MN 55401
612.455.2293
www.TwoHarborsPress.com

This publication is designed to provide accurate and authorita-
tive information in regard to the subject matter covered. It is
sold with the understanding that the publisher and author are
not engaged in rendering a substitute for psychological or other
professional services. If expert assistance or counseling is needed, the services of a competent professional should be sought.
To protect privacy, all patient names have been changed.

ISBN-13: 978-1-63413-395-1
LCCN: 2015903022

Distributed by Itasca Books

Book Design by Sophie Chi

Printed in the United States of America

Dedication

I dedicate this work to my
immediate family:
first and foremost my wife, Linda;
and also
Emily, Jeremy, Laurel, Jon, Heather, Chase,
Nancy, David, Annie, Peter, Charlie, and David

Thank you for all you have taught me. It can,
indeed, take a village.

Praise for
Navigating Your Relationship: A Voyage for Couples

This is a practical, systemically oriented guide that couples and clinicians working with couples will find helpful in navigating the complex, often turbulent, waters of intimate relationships. Through his creative use of metaphor- building and steering a boat- Schwab targets significant aspects of relationships, such as defining each partner's limits of responsibility, viewing intimacy as a celebration of differences, accepting our own vulnerability, and bringing personal integrity to our interactions in the present. The focus on viewing challenges and conflicts as opportunities to experiment with new skills and remaining open to new ways of thinking is a refreshing shift from the conventional way of looking at human behavior in terms of fixed realities and pathology.

- **John Brendler**, MSW, ACSW, LMFT, family and
marital therapist, and founder of *Building Bridges*,
a multidisciplinary, holistic healing context in Media, PA
- Co-author of *Madness, Chaos, and Violence:
Therapy with Families at the Brink.*
- Teacher, leader of supervision groups, and
international seminar leader in family therapy.
- Recognized expert in dealing with dangerous
symptoms, destructive relationships,
and families in serious trouble.

NAVIGATING YOUR RELATIONSHIP:

A Voyage for Couples

CONTENTS

**At the Tipping Point – Kaleidoscope as Truth –
Baseball as a Guide – STRAND —The Wrong Voice**

If you listen to your partner, he or she will behave better toward you. You can learn to slow down the pace, not compete, and be fascinated by another perspective.

Planets – Moving Toward the Middle of the Boat

You have predictable, selfish tendencies that are important to embrace and understand. They just aren't the same as your partner's. If you think you can have it all your way, think again.

The Gumball Theory – The Power Within – Fishing for Control – What Can We Get Under Control?

Diplomacy is the art of letting someone else have it *your* way. Let's admit we need things to feel like they are under control and make better choices about what we can control.

Feeling Small AND Looking Big

It is normal, and crazy, for *both* of you to feel small and look big at the same time. If you get this distortion under control for yourself, you'll be even more attractive and desirable to your partner.

What kind of "garbage" are you carrying around, anyway? What makes you think the way you think and behave the way you behave? Is there an elegant way to explore yourself and still have dignity and integrity?

Is anyone steering the boat? It's easier to know whether you feel like a captain than it is to know whether the co-captain feels the same way. How do you find out how well you are doing at navigating this boat?

What if we have just brought too much anxiety and fear on board with us and it isn't helping that we are on a boat?

How is it that women so often feel abandoned and men so often feel attacked (or slimed)? What makes us react to sliming by retreating and react to abandonment by sliming? Does fairness matter more to us than our dignity and our ability to work together? Perhaps a better understanding of injustice and power can help.

Handling Ambiguity – Handling Change

What if we can learn to handle unpredictable weather on the high seas? How are we going to handle the change? What happens next?

Getting Honest With Yourself – It's Over . . . The "Tearable" Marriage: Considering Children's Needs – Responsible Co-Parenting – Getting to Know Yourself

Is there ever a time to abandon ship and start over, despite the obvious costs? How does that happen, and are there ways to make the process less painful, especially for the children?

Growth – Climbing the Steps –Both/And

On a boat, our relationships and families can be very confusing and we can get lost in the fog. This is actually an opportunity. What does it take to seize the opportunity to take care of our selves and those around us?

Taking the opportunity for a final "interlude," let's step back again from the voyage and see what it looks like from a distance.

28: Integrity: Being A Pendulum 269

What Sports Teach – Golf – The Pendulum – Integrity and the Dialectic

The sports that we play, in addition to sailing, offer plentiful examples of ways to handle awkward stressful moments with your partner. The goal for both captains, really, is a personal integrity that feels balanced, even on a boat.

29: Reaching the Lighthouse and the Harbor 280

Defining Change – The Power of Blending – The Basics – Feeling Small AND Looking Big

How do we know that we've reached our goal? What does that look like and feel like? What will have changed about us? Will we know it when we see it?

PREFACE

A Voyage of Growth and Learning

This book offers the two of you an opportunity to take a voyage. During this voyage, you will be encouraged to consider surprising images and intuitively sensible truths about intimate partnerships.

> A great deal of our meaning in life comes from the reflections that we give each other, and the meaning we generate out of that. When we're not paying attention to each other, we wind up hurting each other, causing each other pain that could be very easily rectified with a drop or two of moment-to-moment nonjudgmental awareness.
>
> - Jon Kabat-Zinn
> *author of Full Catastrophe Living*

The room was crackling with tension and silence. Julie and Josh sat uncomfortably in my office, having just described to me the course of their currently disappointing and frustrating relationship.

I asked Julie, "How big do you feel when Josh interrupts you?" and she promptly answered that she felt about as small as a worm. "How big does Josh look at that moment?" I asked. "He's gigantic. He's always dismissing my thoughts and feelings." I turned to Josh and asked, "How big to do you feel when she just keeps talking?" and without hesitation he stated that he felt like a piece of dirt. "How big does Julie look at that moment?" I asked. "She's enormous. I don't know what to do. I don't know how to make her happy and she doesn't hear me."

Sound familiar? What I told this couple is that, although it doesn't make any sense, both people are big and small at the same time, and this confusing distortion happens all the time.

Now that I've been working with couples and families for nearly thirty years, I have an array of stories and visual devices that give comfort to my visitors. From garbage to gumballs, from fishing to baseball to soccer, from kaleidoscopes to Slinkys to Venetian blinds, I create a variety of stimulating visual experiences that are intended to interrupt and redirect the automatic and familiar behaviors that are connected to emotional cues. I will be sharing many of my favorite interventions in this book.

As you read this book, you will be taking a journey on a boat, just like the couples that bring their problems to me do. In exploring your relationship with your partner, you will discover how small you *feel* and how big you *look* at the same time, and how confusing that is. I hope you will embrace the complexity of relating and get more comfortable with who you are and how your relationship works. Hopefully, you can see this as a growth opportunity, and experience the satisfaction of developing more self-control as a way of creating a better intimate relationship with your partner.

This journey will offer you an unusual set of metaphors

and analogies that constantly simplify your relationship in an optimistic and clinically helpful way. You will each be accountable for the way you handle *your* tipping point and be responsible for the behavior you use to keep from feeling worse when the boat feels tippy to you. You will be taught memorable tools that will help you communicate under duress, and become more comfortable with the familiar discomforts that lead to conflict and disconnection, giving you a better chance to short circuit the patterns that have led you to seek help from a book.

There are many books intended to help you, and this one will, hopefully, teach you that the dynamics that are driving you crazy are actually quite normal, and the solutions are not too complicated. You can find the strength and talent in yourself to improve your relationship, be a strong and attractive partner, advocate for your wishes, and navigate the shoals by absorbing these intriguing ideas and putting them into action as teammates who pull together on a voyage.

Using the best ideas that have been developed in the field of marriage and family therapy, you can become more adept at connecting your feelings to your thoughts and actions, more aware of motivations and reactions that are grounded in your family of origin, and more of an expert about who you really are. You will be prompted to catch yourself and be "more than a squirrel," claim "your gumball," handle "being in a swamp," and "feel like a captain" of your relationship boat, and you will be gently reminded many times that *both* of you may be feeling small *and* looking big.

One of the risks you are taking as you read this book is that one of you will change and the other will need to respond to change in a healthy way. You may even find your own reactions to change surprising. Sometimes the whole idea of change is daunting. Even though the journey will take some twists and turns, and sometimes require you to stretch your imagination or your tolerance for mixed metaphors, the stories, advice, analogies, and original concepts are all intended to make your relationship voyage much more pleasant, meaningful, and long-lasting.

Among other things, I have used my family background of artists and caregivers to create original tools for you, just as you might gravitate to the work your parents did. I believe that certain principles matter, and I try to incorporate them into my work. The worth and dignity of each person matters. Speaking the truth matters. Our independence and interdependence matter. The journey matters as much as the destination. Early in my journey I found that "The Kingdom of God is within you. You need only to claim it," and that matters. I happen to think that this concept transcends religion, and embraces the remarkable variety of personal narratives and religious beliefs that exists. Whatever your history is, you are welcome here.

This book is the product of my family history, days spent on a sailboat as a child, the different careers I have pursued, and distinctive experiences I have had. It is a privilege to treat couples, and to have them share their private truths with me, and in return I offer all of the creativity and mindful presence I can muster from my self.

When a couple comes to my office, I need to know how they tell their story, and I need them to know that I don't have magical skills. I tell them that we are going to talk to each other and seek changes, but that I am not a magician. I tell couples to look again in the Yellow Pages or on the Internet if magic is what they want. I do something else.

What I can do is listen with authenticity. As I was trained in Contextual Family Therapy, I can say that I use "multidirected partiality." In other words, as an "authentic listener," I am partial to both partners in multiple ways that move the process forward. I try to listen in that way, actively giving credit to each person's truth as I hear it. I also explain that I am focused on treating their relationship (the space in between them that also connects them). I admit to couples that it is an occupational hazard that I may annoy both of them so much that they agree with each other that I wasn't favoring either person when they felt they were clearly "right." If this book becomes challenging in some way for you, go ahead and blame me if you need to.

The various boat-themed chapter headings are intended to suggest a journey, using as touchstones the experience of being on a boat, while addressing emotional realities that emerge whether you are on a boat or not, and offering solutions that urge you to have your feet firmly on the ground. On or off the boat, I will keep the process sounding simple, by encouraging you to understand how much having things under control matters, how it may be enough to be more aware of your co-captain, or how when we sound like third graders we simply have an opportunity to grow. Later in the book, I will offer concepts that help with specific family issues (like the growth of a teenager, or infidelity, or other challenges that build up over time), but, first, we will focus on being a couple.

Enjoy the journey.

1

Getting on the Boat

To begin this journey, you and your partner learn that you are
on a boat and that it matters how you handle tippiness when
there are two captains on the boat.

> If you are certain, then you are a prisoner of
> the known. When you embrace uncertainty,
> and include intention and detachment, then
> the most improbable happens. That's what we
> call a miracle.
>
> - Deepak Chopra, M.D.
> author of *Ageless Body,*
> *Timeless Mind*

"I have this theory that couples are on boats," I say
unexpectedly to a couple that has just met me for the first
time and spilled out their story. I really don't know what
they'll think. I barely know them and they are trusting me to
understand their shared emotional climate.

When couples visit me for the first time, they're likely
to be experiencing deep uncertainty. Wishing and once

believing that they could work out problems for themselves, they suddenly find themselves dependent on a total stranger who will somehow do things with them that they'd hoped to be able to do for themselves. They don't know how therapy will work, whether it will work, what it will ultimately cost, or what mysterious demands it will make on them. Yet, something has convinced them that they need to make this complicated and daring journey and talk to me about very personal things in the presence of their partner.

On top of the uncertainty, there is disappointment. I vividly remember attending a conference workshop about couples, where all of the therapists in the room were distracted by great weather, a fun lunch break near great restaurants, and the freedom of being away from their offices while collecting further education credits. The presenter tried and tried to get our attention, but without much success. Finally, he asked a single question that went something like this: "What is the most common emotion about their partnership that couples are experiencing when they begin therapy as a couple?"

Here was a roomful of perhaps eighty therapists from all over the country. I imagine the *average* therapist in the room had twenty years of experience with couples. We began to answer the question about what couples were experiencing emotionally about their partnerships. Thoughtful and experienced answers gradually began to cascade and echo around the room as we began to pay attention, but, actually, they were all the same answer. There was really only one answer offered to this carefully crafted question: *disappointment*. I realized that I was thinking of that answer, too. As it turned out, that was exactly what the presenter expected us all to say.

What does this mean? This means it is natural and predictable for you to have wonderful *expectations* for your marriage. After all, you can't have disappointment without expectations. Unfortunately, expectations rarely match up with reality, especially over time. It is understandable and normal that, over time, couples experience something different from their special expectations for their relationships—and that both members feel disappointed.

Once I have heard both versions of the story that brought the couple in to see me, I often suggest that they are on a boat.

The Boat

It has dawned on me that I have been hearing narratives from couples that parallel my experience of sailboats. My theory is that when you met and fell in love and it was juicy and sexy and charged, you didn't know you were building a boat. You see, my father loved sailboats and, after twenty-five years trapped in a stifling corporate job, he and a friend decided to start a business building beautiful ocean-racing yachts. Because I was about twelve years old, I just figured this was what fathers did, and it seemed perfectly ordinary to walk around the huge construction space and find all of these people just loving their jobs. I assumed everyone loved their jobs. What did I know? It turns out these workers were like couples falling in love: full of energy, joy, and hope—perhaps high on the fumes from the varnish or the new sails—certain that this would be a special boat, better than any boat anyone had sailed on before.

As couples, I think we usually start out on this kind of high. We believe we have the right partner and that we know how to do a great job of being married and parenting. *We'll do it better than our parents, right?* But nobody tells us we are building a boat. Most of us wouldn't choose to build a boat! Instead, we imagine we're building a cozy, safe nest, where we will listen to each other and adore each other and it will be quiet and protected and everything will feel under control—the kind of climate couples seek when they visit my office. We need to believe this. We need this *expectation*, and, yes, we might need to be a little bit high. It helps us build the boat, and it drives us to jump onboard.

I remember the launchings of the boats my dad's company built. There was champagne and dancing and everyone made promises about winning races and making more boats and being successful and happy. It was somehow sacred, just like a wedding where we make promises about success, having fun, staying on the boat, staying safe, supporting each other, and being faithful to the dream. Usually, even couples who haven't had a formal launching have made this kind of promise when making a commitment to be together.

But, think for a minute. Wouldn't your mind work differently on a boat? If you knew that—instead of a cozy little nest—you had built a boat, invested in a boat, jumped on the boat, and were sailing the boat yourselves, while promising that you would make the journey memorable and safe, would you still be as intoxicated as you were while building the boat, or would other kinds of thoughts take over? If you knew you were going to be going on a voyage, wouldn't you instead ask "Where are we going? What's the weather like? Do we have enough supplies? What if the boat gets tippy? Who's in charge? Will it leak? Are we safe?" This is a very different mental and emotional experience from the more exciting building of the boat.

Couples often describe and share this unexpected shift when they tell me their story. They don't know how or why their experience changed so dramatically, but when we start discussing boats they do find it easy to describe the way they would start to think if they were on a boat and responsible for its success and safety. When I tell them that they are sailing the boat, not just having a fun ride in the sun, there's a pause, and then a less playful, more measured, weighty response about safety or direction, responsibility, or accountability that illustrates how much more seriously they are thinking.

Maybe it is important to imagine what it is like on a boat, and to accept that you build them and leap onto them—planning to keep your promise that nothing will go wrong. Maybe your minds just shift into a different gear once you are on a boat. We all have this gear, just waiting to kick in when we act on a serious decision and start an important journey.

I remember my father's pretty ordinary sailboat. It wasn't an ocean-racing yacht. I now realize that I didn't invite my friends or enjoy the day when I was a young teenager and still went sailing most summer weekends with my parents. I see now that I was tuned out, not really there. We would sail to an island for a picnic, but I don't remember the island at all. I know it was an island on a lake full of sailboats, but I have no real picture of it in my head. I was switched off, like many of the people who visit me with their partners.

To me, boating was complicated and overwhelming and since I couldn't get out of my obligation to be on the boat, I just put myself in neutral. Actually, I do vividly remember the unusual damp smell of the fiberglass boat, and the rhythmic tapping sound of the water hitting the front of the boat. But that's all. I was functioning on a pretty primitive level. Most importantly, I also remember that I suddenly became very present when the boat felt tippy. When the boat was tipping, I really was there. I took immediate action, and moved to *balance* the boat. At that tipping point, I responded to the same feelings of vulnerability and danger that also motivate our behavior in our relationships.

What if you and your partner each brought half of the boat with you? Each of you carries with you your gender, your family, your personal history, your career, your sexuality, and your expectations, and somehow you have created a supposedly leak-proof craft with another person with all of their qualities. It's pretty exciting to see all the different pieces come together when you are building the boat. Once you are on the boat, though, the same differences make the boat feel tippy, like your partner is having it *their* way.

It feels like the boat is tipping away from you when your partner behaves in a surprising, unwanted, or unfamiliar way, compared to what you expected or felt you needed. When this happens, it doesn't feel familiar, and it may not feel safe or controlled enough. If that is the way it feels, you could easily keep the promise you made at the launching, and move away from the middle of the boat, toward *your own side*, to keep it from tipping over. It's as if the thought of both of you behaving the same way seems so extreme, that you exaggerate your *opposite* response. We react and respond for the sake of the boat. *In fact, you promised that you would at your launching. Remember assuring your partner that the boat won't tip over?* But, your movement toward your side of the boat feels uncomfortable to your partner, for they feel as though the boat is now tipping away from them, and they move away, too, toward their edge of the boat, in order to rebalance it. *They promised, too.* Moving to my own side to balance things out is what I did on my dad's boat, and that's what I hear couples indicate they are doing with their actions.

When the boat gets tippier and tippier, the somewhat different person you couldn't resist becomes someone who surprises and confuses you. They seem to be a danger to your comfort and don't seem to be the person you chose, who seemed so safe and delightful. Now this person seems like a caricature of the person you fell in love with. You become disillusioned. Those poetic silences you used to love seem different, more negative. Those clever asides seem personal and pointed. Those kindnesses seem less sincere and less frequent.

If we are honest with ourselves, we realize that we, too, are becoming a caricature of the person our partner fell in love with. Both of us are exaggerating our differences, in order to keep the boat balanced. We do this with our behavior. We behave in opposite ways—for the boat.

Ebenezer and Florence, who you will meet again, often experience the most common, and most puzzling, play of opposites. For instance, Eb will have something important to say to Flo, but she'll feel interrupted or that her space is being invaded, and she will withdraw instead of talking to Eb. Eb will respond by trying harder to get Flo's attention, and Flo will withdraw even more because she is feeling pressured. Eb will eventually be afraid that Flo is mad at him, and pursue her even harder for an explanation or reassurance. Flo will eventually be afraid of being crushed by Eb's pressure and withdraw even more. Pursuing and withdrawing are *opposite* behaviors and Eb and Flo are exaggerating them, hoping to keep the boat from tipping over.

Maybe you are a couple who do another version of this dance, with one of you getting louder while the other grows more silent, or one of you doing more tasks while the other does fewer. There are many ways to try to keep the boat from capsizing. Consider the ways you may act for the boat: one of you may be expansive and the other shrinking, one may begin to do things faster and the other to do things more and more slowly, or one may get tighter (more rigid) and the other looser (easy going) as things get tippy. Have you considered what your particular opposites are?

How Many Captains on this Boat?

A relationship can be like a pretty unusual and challenging boat. It can be tippy on one side and not the other. The weather can be terrible on one side and not the other. I innocently ask couples how many captains there should be on their boat. After a lot of squirming, their eventual answer is that there need to be *two captains*, and I agree emphatically. There must be two captains on today's relationship boats. Somehow, both people need to feel like captains. This may not have been as clear to your parents, many of whom relied on a single captain, but you are navigating new waters, and it may seem at times as if you are pioneers. This is not a normal boat. Sharing the captain role is tricky, kind of crazy, and sometimes just not "fair"! It requires teamwork, patience, listening, and collaboration.

It will be helpful for both of you, as captains, to learn about your own emotional tipping points, and be able to catch yourselves as you slip from any sensitive, charged moment into your automatic, reactive behavior that makes the boat even tippier for the other captain.

There will inevitably be *tension* on the boat when it tips, and you can learn to handle that tension better—for the boat. That was your *best intention* anyway when the boat felt tippy, right? You promised. This new kind of boat safety is more considerate, more collaborative, and develops *care*fully, with less urgency. The best treatment that I know of for relationship seasickness is talking and listening. As a professional talker and listener, I naturally believe that these skills can help captains feel strong, competent, and safe. I help people reduce tension on their boats by talking and listening, and I think you can do this, too.

Here is a possible "takeaway" from this chapter:

CAPTAIN'S LOG

You didn't expect to be on a boat. It can be complicated and disappointing.

2

Being A Captain Who Communicates

The best seasickness medicine is communication that reduces tension. Some intriguing recommendations help you talk about yourself and listen to your partner with less defensiveness.

> Love doesn't consist in gazing at each other. It consists in looking outward in the same direction.
>
> - Antoine de Saint-Exupéry
> author of *The Little Prince*

"We just don't communicate . . . We used to have more patience and understand each other better . . . I want to feel like I'm being heard . . . We're both stubborn . . . I really think I'm right!"

These are familiar words from the couples that visit my office. Over and over again, I hear that communication is frustrating and becoming toxic when it used to be enjoyable and comforting. When I ask these couples what they want, they often tell me: "We want to communicate better."

When you leave your comfort zone and begin a relationship voyage as a co-captain, the seas can feel pretty rough. Your once-exhilarating voyage now feels disappointing, uncomfortable, and much too tense. Communicating the way you are trying to communicate doesn't seem to help, but you feel that it *should.* You might agree that the best seasickness remedy is better communication, but you may not know what "better communication" really is. Let's set a goal as co-captains to create balanced and transparent communication that reduces tension. To keep it simple, let's concentrate on how you talk—and how you listen.

Eb and Flo

Words inspire us, but they also paralyze us. Consider Eb and Flo again, a typical couple on a sailboat. Eb assumes he is the captain of the boat and tells Flo that the children need to be more disciplined. As Flo pictures a family of scared, compliant people with Eb in charge, she responds by setting *fewer* limits on the kids. "The kids need to be treated with more respect and consideration," she says.

But Eb, who pictures a chaotic family with no rules, counters that following rules shows that children respect their parents and provides order. He becomes more agitated about being ignored and defied by his family. Now Flo pictures a family living in an angry climate and tries to make it sunnier, advising Eb to "try to chill out." Eb hears Flo's response as a statement that he is wrong and being yelled at. "Get real!" he snaps.

Flo hears, in Eb's response, that she is unimportant and being dismissed, and so she withdraws some of the comforts and rewards of being a couple (ranging from simple kindnesses to sexual favors). Eb interprets this as a clear sign that he isn't desirable or adequate and decides it isn't worth even trying to communicate anymore. Flo retreats with resentment to her job or hobbies or the children or friendships or perhaps an addiction, and Eb retreats in anger to his career or watching TV sports or perhaps pornography on the Internet. They become two captains moving in opposite directions on the boat—because they said they would—and then exaggerating their responses on the way to mutual withdrawal. They are not hearing each other and each is not speaking a language that the other understands. It is a frustrating and toxic situation, definitely not enjoyable and comforting. When asked about the source of their trouble, Eb and Flo easily agree: it is a failure to communicate.

Rules of Engagement

It turns out there is an established and useful theory about how to communicate well. I learned how to teach this theory some fifteen years ago in a workshop led by Bernard Guerney, founder of the National Institute of Relationship Enhancement, and I've used his method ever since.

This is a tool for your toolbox that will reduce tension. The resulting conversation will be unusual, maybe even odd. (Feel free to say it was my idea!) It will not be a useful conversation for making decisions or even settling an argument. The resulting conversation's specific purpose is to lower *tension* so that you will feel more connected to each other and be more able to settle your differences.

Before you get into the conversation, I'm going to make some rules. So you might as well get ready to handle any difficulty you have with following rules if you'd like to experience a calmer and safer relationship.

Begin by remembering that you and your partner are both captains on this unexpectedly complicated and crazy boat. Not surprisingly, you will experience "tippiness," or a sense that the boat is *not under control. Either captain* may feel the tippiness, and either captain is entitled to request a conversation. This is not a contest or a sport or a game—and it is not some kind of test to see who can tolerate the most tippiness.

After the request for a conversation has been made, the other captain must agree to talk about the situation, for the sake of the boat. Remember, either captain can request the conversation, and the other captain must agree to talk—for the sake of the boat you built together.

Before starting this conversation, it may be best to break off hostilities, wait twenty minutes or whatever it takes, so that you will both start in a calmer and more more productive state, or you may need to schedule the conversation for a time when you are both free of work or children or any other demands on your time and energy. Make an arrangement to talk in a quiet space where you can be near each other, look at each other, and hear each other well, so that you can give yourselves the best chance for success.

A few tips:

1) You are an expert on yourself, period. If you are behaving like an expert about your partner, it is speculation, even if you have lots of evidence. Use your curiosity, not your certainty.

2) You'll get more satisfaction out of this exercise if your partner does well. Help him or her follow the rules well. Encourage them.

3) This is a slow, deliberate process, and that is what makes it intimate. If you respond too quickly, you will probably miss something. Take your time.

4) The goal of the exercise is to reduce tension. Keep that in mind when you are measuring how well you are doing.

So, what are the rules, then?

The *captain who felt the tippiness starts the conversation*, because he or she has something specific to talk about.

The speaker always tries to follow *Rule #1:*

Talk about yourself with authority. Describe your feelings and thoughts accurately and honestly. Don't talk about the other person. This is often called an "I statement."

The partner listens and follows *Rule #2:*

Don't defend yourself. Try to repeat or reflect back what your partner is telling you. Don't try to fix the problem. Listening will be enough. This is often called "active (or reflective) listening."

When the speaker has been listened to and feels understood, you follow *Rule #3:*

Switch. The reward for listening is that you now get to claim your perception of the situation and be listened to by your partner. The speaker becomes the listener, and the listener becomes the speaker.

Switch back and forth, rewarding each other for listening while helping each other speak clearly and listen well. Follow this pattern of listening and speaking until you have reduced tension as much as you can for now.

If you are concentrating on how to describe your own feelings and thoughts, and holding yourself accountable for them, you are developing self-awareness. With self-awareness, you will be able to make yourself more understandable to your partner, because you will know what you are talking about, not just because you need their attention.

If you are careful not to make your own interpretations, nor to distort your partner's feelings or thoughts, you will be developing empathy. With empathy, you can openly offer your insights about your partner's desires, motives, and feelings, because you are curious about them, not because you think your partner is wrong and you are right.

How to Follow the Rules

This is a very intimate and unpredictable conversation, so you may need some help to prepare for it. It may help to try to attain a particular frame of mind.

Rule #1 is challenging because you are revealing a lot about yourself without knowing the outcome. I recommend that you imagine you are deciding to have sex for *the first time* with your partner. Take the risk to initiate verbal foreplay without knowing how it will turn out. You need to be revealing and vulnerable, even though you don't know how well either of you will perform or whether it will be very satisfying. You could wake up the next morning and wonder what you'd been thinking. Nonetheless, keeping your clothes on and avoiding this opportunity could cost you too much. Think of the intimacy and fulfillment you could be missing if you back off. Then, once you realize you are both vulnerable to what lies ahead, move into the conversation.

Rule #2 is challenging because it is natural and familiar to defend yourself. Your brain is ready to come up with answers, excuses, and explanations, but it is impossible to do that and listen at the same time. I recommend that you imagine that you are *playing soccer*. With apologies to soccer fans, there is only one rule that makes soccer difficult (which explains why children in every country find it an easy game to pick up). That rule is that you can't touch the ball with your hands. When your partner is speaking, even if they are wonderful at following Rule #1, it will feel as though the ball is coming straight at you, *hard!* To listen and really acknowledge and validate what they are saying, you need to get your hands out of the way, even though the ball could hurt you. If you master this rule, you can stay on the team. You have not committed a foul. You have not interrupted the game by being too defensive.

Most importantly perhaps, you get the ball if you listen well! Let the ball hit you. Be at least as good at this as the little kids in Brazil, England, Spain, or South Africa who can dream of glory, and wealth, if they can just keep their hands out of the way.

You'll be rewarded for listening by having your turn to talk. The exercise will not go well if you are in a hurry or interrupt or decide that rules are not for you. You have an opportunity to collaborate by using what your partner hears as a chance to edit what you are saying so it is closer to what you mean. Or, you have a chance to delay your hot reaction to what your partner is saying by listening and making sure you hear them accurately, before gathering and describing your own thoughts and emotions about what you are experiencing. Once you have taken the time to listen, you will be more thoughtful and careful about what you say about yourself.

When you are making your "I statement," be careful and accurate about what you are saying. You want to be understood.

When you are using "active listening," listen respectfully and accurately. When it is your chance to speak, you don't want to come across as dismissive, angry, sarcastic, or uninterested. Slow down and be authentic about this. It matters.

This is a way to build a bridge between you because you can hold yourself and each other accountable for words and actions that you have discussed in a private way. This is an introduction to a refreshing, authentic—perhaps completely new—kind of intimacy.

This kind of intimate, give-and-take conversation works. It really does reduce tension. That's because it matters to all of us to feel understood. It matters to be able to speak our truth. This is the value-added part of having built a boat. This is a way to feel more like a captain.

CAPTAIN'S LOG

When the boat feels tippy, you are both entitled to say your side *and* have your side heard.

3

The Other Side of the Boat

If you listen to your partner, he or she will behave better toward you. You can learn to slow down the pace, not compete, and become fascinated by your partner's perspective.

> Sacred partnership is a rich and deep friendship between equals that brings us sanctuary, soul growth, and sizzle.
>
> - Sue Patton Thoele
> author of *The Women's Book of Courage*

I am constantly struck by the courage of couples who commit to working on their problems. It is incredibly bold and challenging to consistently put yourself on the other side of the boat, and to develop intense curiosity about another person who was not born and raised on a boat that would feel familiar to you. It takes courage to become two captains.

I'm reminded of a day I was building some IKEA furniture with my daughter, and the fun we had with the directions that said, "you need to be two people." It sounds really funny, but that's what I ask couples to do.

You may be wondering if it is worth the effort to develop the skills needed to be two captains. What if I could persuade you that following the rules we discussed in the last chapter would make you even more attractive and desirable to your partner? I am suggesting that, if you try this approach, your partner will relax and behave better toward you—and you will do the same for your partner. A relaxed, engaged person is a more desirable person. That's how it works.

At the Tipping Point

First, you need to identify a familiar tipping point that creates tension or tippiness on your boat. For most couples, the tipping point has something to do with sex, money, in-laws, the house, your jobs, or the children. The tension associated with these issues need not be surprising. This is predictable and reliable. It is important to immerse yourself in the emotional climate of that kind of moment to get the most out of this chapter. We will keep returning to these tipping points and their familiar feelings of helplessness, frustration, powerlessness, and disappointment.

I have done an experiment with couples for several years that illustrates how important the rules of communication are. As you consider your own tipping point (or points), ask yourself these questions:

- What is the difference between the way I typically feel at my tipping point and the way I'd feel if my partner had acknowledged and *validated* my perspective by telling me what they heard me say and what they understood me to mean?
- Can I describe how I would feel differently at that tipping point?
- If I experienced this difference, how would my behavior toward my partner change?

I have offered these questions to more than 200 couples. Remarkably, *every person*—whether they were newlyweds or long-married, rich or poor, highly educated or not, male or female, gay or straight, young or old, regardless of religion or culture or politics—has answered the same way. Every person tells me that they would feel *calmer, happier, and more secure* if they felt listened to, and that in response they would behave more positively toward their partner—which is often exactly the behavior that their partner has been craving.

What an elegant possibility. If you listen well to your partner, your partner will behave better toward you. That's what everyone says. What a deal! Let me repeat what this experiment proves:

If you listen well, they'll behave better.

Everyone has said so. They'll feel better—and that will change their behavior.

Kaleidoscope as Truth

There really are at least two sides to every story, and your story isn't any different.

I remember vividly my first day of graduate school, when one of my professors proclaimed that everything we thought was true about our family relationships was really a distortion. I have come to see that it is sensible to see partnerships as a mix of deeply held distortions.

Once again, let's revisit whatever you have decided is a familiar emotional tipping point, and use a tool I have been introduced to. Imagine for a moment a "wedding kaleidoscope," which is a two-ended scope that you can both peer through at the same time. I use one in my office.

I ask couples to imagine their stressful issue and, while doing so, describe what they are seeing through the two-ended kaleidoscope. I tell them they are both looking at the same array of beautiful pebbles and I just want to know what they see. Inevitably, partners make a major effort to try to agree on what the pebbles look like, but they simply can't. I ask them what they are going to do about this conflict.

I usually offer this passage (that comes with the kaleidoscope), which offers hope:

> This is a marriage of two kaleidoscopes blended into one. Each side reflects a different kaleidoscopic image.
>
> As a metaphor for marriage or partnership it demonstrates that two people can view the same subject at the same time while each perceives a uniquely different vision. The partners can rejoice in the knowledge that their diverse perspectives will enrich their shared experiences.

Your differing views about the pebbles in the kaleidoscope are actually as close to agreement as you're likely to get as a couple. You each have genuinely different perspectives. As hard as you try to agree, they'll still look different to you. How could it be any other way? You are from different families and have had different lives. The really important thing is how you choose to respond to *not* agreeing. You have lots of options. Do you take command and say that the way you see the pebbles is "right"? Do you capitulate to your partner and decide that you just can't see things clearly or that it is better to avoid conflict? Do you belittle your partner because they can't see what you see? Do you just give up because you feel helpless or confused?

What are you going to do *with the kaleidoscope?*

Here is another option: You can *carefully and gently turn the kaleidoscope around* so you can see what your partner has been seeing, slowly, without disrupting it. This takes real *curiosity*, empathy, and love. This response benefits both of you. When couples do this well, I hear the delight when partners find that the other person meant what they were saying and that both ends are beautiful in their own way.

Hopefully, these exercises make you very aware of how vulnerable you are to behaving in a way that tips the boat for you partner at your own tipping point, triggering an emotional response from them. (I'm sure you can imagine a discussion of the kaleidoscope images which sounds like: "What do you mean you see a yellow flower? It's a green turtle kind of thing! Why do you always insist on seeing things that aren't there?") What you may be finding out is that it's all too easy to find the other person's tipping point, and that it's become a habit for you to trigger responses in them that make you feel superior.

It is a better choice for you, as a co-captain, to place yourself firmly on your partner's side of the boat and take a look at the boat from there. You may need to learn to use parts of yourself that you are not accustomed to using at tense moments—curiosity, patience, perspective, and empathy.

Baseball as a Guide

Sometimes it is hard to tolerate this mix of kaleidoscopic perceptions, and it feels more like a battle for control with both of you determined to win. Here is another scenario that will help you catch yourselves in your familiar interactions:

Imagine for a moment that you are experiencing that familiar emotional tipping point. This time, however, you have a baseball in your hand, while your partner has a baseball bat.

What do you *usually do* at this "tippy" moment? Even if you rarely think about baseball, hang in there. If you had a baseball, what would you do? What would your intention be?

I get a variety of responses to these questions, and very few of them are good for your relationship boat. A very common response is to try to hit one's partner in the head with the ball. A slightly less destructive response is to try to strike your partner out. That's safer, but humiliating, and defeating your partner is definitely not good for the boat, especially if there are children on it. Some people say they will issue a base on balls and let their partner get to first base. That is a way of neither hitting nor humiliating the partner that gives them a place to go. But it's also a mild form of disengagement and avoidance. Others say they would completely disengage and just throw the ball into the crowd or just drop it and walk away. All of these are recipes for eventual loneliness and isolation.

It is actually a trick question. Remember, I only said you had a baseball in your hands. I didn't say you were competing in a baseball game. Most couples automatically place themselves in the game as opponents—or enemies. It is that easy to see a relationship that way.

If it's not an actual contest, and your partner is not your opponent, there is a possible response that is good for the boat: You can have batting practice with your teammate. You can still enjoy the exertion and satisfaction of throwing the ball and the challenge of throwing it skillfully, but now you are throwing it *so your partner can become better at hitting it*. Your throw needs to have some edge to it, so that it will help them handle complex and tippy situations, but the intention is for them to manage the situation well and hit the ball. At your tipping point, you need to behave with these goals in mind. It is an art.

STRAND—The Wrong Voice

To truly take charge of tippy moments, it is important to notice your own voice. It may be hard to hear it, but it may sound like this:

Sarcastic
Thoughtless
Resentful
Angry
Negative
Dismissive

Try to remember that your partner has to live with the way you sound. Would you want to be around your own voice? Try to be aware of the impact you are making on the other side of the boat, or the other end of the kaleidoscope.

To make positive changes in your relationship, you need to use your imagination and your curiosity in ways that initially may not seem fair to you. When you were building the boat and promising to protect it from danger, you didn't know that it would require you to use these generous and delicate qualities at the most important moments. If you can speak and listen well, throw batting practice, and gently turn the kaleidoscope around with genuine curiosity, you will be using your personal resources in a way that helps you sustain your relationship. Who knew that navigating a boat would be this challenging?

Just as you need to remember that if you play soccer well (with empathy for the other captain) you will get the ball, it is important to recall that you have not given up your position as a captain, nor minimized the importance of the weather on your own side of the boat. You are behaving with greater flexibility and compassion for the sake of the boat—the precious, fragile vessel that is your partnership.

CAPTAIN'S LOG
If you listen well, the other person will behave better.

4

Your Side of the Boat

You have predictable, selfish tendencies that are important to embrace and understand. They just aren't the same as your partner's. If you think you can have it all your way, think again.

> Honor your own complexity.
>
> Mark Gerzon
> author of *Coming
> Into Our Own*

So, what is the weather on your side of the boat, exactly? If your partner can be so sure about what they are seeing and feeling, you probably are, too. What makes us so sure of ourselves, even when we don't like tension and conflict?

There are many sciences to choose from in the quest to understand people better. You might choose geology or political science or sociology as a determining factor. I've visited many in my journey (history, economics, politics, philosophy, sociology, communication studies, science, and theology) but they have all led me back comfortably to psychology. If we want to understand ourselves and our surroundings, it is important to explore how our emotions lead to our behaviors, how our history informs our presence, and how we make sense of our discomforts and distortions. Something happens to us when we are surprised or challenged that makes us choose certainty and reaction, sometimes regardless of the consequences. What we sense and feel drives us to use fundamental intuitive responses in order to avoid danger, or change, or a more upsetting experience.

Planets

I am only one of many who think about these things and write about them. For instance, John Gray has famously written *Men Are from Mars, Women Are from Venus*. As many of you know, that book's intention is to help us to better understand our differences. Let's assume, for the moment, that the planet where you develop your sensibilities determines how you find comfort, how you handle discomfort, what is important to you, how you know things are safe, what has meaning, and ultimately how to act if you feel action is needed.

When I am working with a couple, I refer to this idea, which I have mangled in a sexually explicit way to make a point about our sensibilities. (I apologize in advance for the graphic nature of my ideas, as occasionally couples are uncomfortable when I'm being so bold. Actually, I don't use any profane language, but I do make my point in an unmistakable—and hopefully memorable—way, and couples don't seem to mind. Do notice the hand gestures I am describing. You've been warned.)

You see, on a boat, when it feels tippy, we are responding to *tension*, pure and simple. We have the capacity to warn ourselves that something feels wrong and needs our attention, so we feel tense. This uncomfortable feeling is so natural, reliable, and universal, that it happens all the time—wherever you happen to come from. As we have discussed, if we do something about tension without consideration for our partner, our behavior may well make their side of the boat feel tippy, and things will escalate.

If men and women come from different places, then in a woman's place there's plenty of tension and everyone has a circular sensibility between their legs (I want you to use your imagination while I spin my arm around in circles like I'm winding something up). To deal with tension, women prefer to talk, to process their feelings, to look at things from many directions, to listen, focus on the senses and intuition, to pay personal attention to everyone's emotions, and to engage in a relational process until tension goes away. It's circular, and it works.

In that other place, where men find their bearings, there's plenty of tension, and everyone has a straight line sensibility between their legs (I want you to use your imagination while I move my arm up and down like I'm chopping something or my arm's having an erection). To deal with tension, men prefer to fix things, create distance from emotions, push things away, cut things off, ignore things, put things behind them, use logic to explain situations, or stop anything stressful in order to reduce tension. For men, it's all about straight lines, and it works.

What is your goal, in terms of your emotions, when you resort to your natural sensibility to reduce tension? What is it you want, emotionally, for you and your partner?

I believe that if I asked this question exactly the right way, everyone, from either starting point, would answer the same way: People want peace, security, safety, fairness, and a sense that things are under control.

People from the two places described above meet each other on Earth and build boats, and there is tension. Both feel they know how to handle it, and give it a try. Both have brought their tension-reducing gift from their original place for just such a moment. Both are startled by the other person's response, get frustrated, and decide that their own method is failing. The sense of failure is what leads to the boat getting tippier.

So let's imagine a normal moment of conflict here on Earth, when the boat is at its tipping point. One of you tries to fix it in a grandiose, linear, and final way, while one of you wants to process it and discuss it in a circular way. Neither approach feels like it is working, and both people get frustrated. That's right. You have brought this wonderful gift to Earth that you know will help when there is tension, and it is not working.

What is that like when your sensibility (remember the arm gestures: chopping and spinning) isn't working?
What happens to the amount of tension you are feeling?

Nobody misses this one. You are *more tense* when your cherished sensibility doesn't work. What are you likely to do about that? Well, if you have learned one successful way to reduce tension and there is more tension, you just do what you learned to do—but even more (bigger arm gestures). This begins to look a lot like poor Eb and Flo on the boat, each exaggerating their way of keeping the boat from tipping over, and feeling they need to do it as quickly and directly as possible, but triggering just as exaggerated a response from the other.

If you could catch yourself at your tipping point and recognize the risk of making the boat tippier, how

would you handle this obvious difference between your sensibilities?

Just for fun, why not remember how marvelous it is that the other person has what they have between their legs, and how desirable and wonderful that is when you are having sex. You want your partner to have what they have between their legs when you are private and intimate. Let them have it and use it. Appreciate it. Get curious about it. Enjoy it.

Keep what you have and keep expressing it, but in ways that remember the other person has what they have, just as you would in enjoyable foreplay. Any couple can play along. Who is harder or softer? Who pushes and who receives? Who gives and who takes? When you enjoy each other, what is the effect of the other person on your anxiety and stress?

What the other person offers helps to make you calmer and more satisfied. Perhaps this is another way to remember there is a co-captain, or that you can throw batting practice, or that there is another equally clear way of seeing the pebbles in the kaleidoscope.

Maybe these fundamental differences are *combined* constantly and we need to enjoy straight lines and circles when they come together. Computers only really understand zeroes *and* ones, right? Don't we use circles *and* arrows all the time? Isn't it a good idea to check in with both sensibilities? Circles and lines both work, but they work even better when they are in balance—or they are having intercourse.

It is remarkable how relieved people feel when their point of view is called a "sensibility." Consider your reaction. What is it like when your intuitive response is treated as a natural process and a way of *taking care of yourself?* My visitors' typical reflections include: "Of course that is what I do," or "That's my map. I've never known anything else." It's all part of how you are made, and you will see as we take this journey that you can be who you are *and* make choices that keep the boat afloat.

Maybe we are just insecure enough that our first priority is to take care of ourselves in all kinds of ways that have fancy names (denial, projection, intellectualization, rationalization), making sure we avoid pain or shame or embarrassment. Maybe all of these things work really well, except that they can be toxic (or just create tippiness) in relationships.

Take heart. There is hope. There are ways you are already wired to handle this boat. The force that pushes you to combine yourself with someone very different from you and build a boat is very powerful. Let's go with the flow. Remember that automatic gut reaction to the boat tipping away from you? What if you can use that same reaction to gain closeness with your partner?

Moving Toward the Middle of the Boat

It stands to reason that if we move away from the center of the boat when it is tipping away from us, we will move toward the center of the boat when it is tipping toward us—for the boat. All we need to do is identify the opposites in our behaviors (silence and talking, pursuing and avoiding, speeding up and slowing down, taking the lead and falling behind, etc.) and catch ourselves doing it. Theoretically, if we catch ourselves and do something more like what our partner usually does, making the boat tip in the direction of *their* usual behavior will make them behave more like the way we usually behave, because they will also want to balance that tippy feeling. It's worth a try, right? Do this as teammates, discussing your different opposite responses and trying the other person's approach to tension. Don't worry. There is a limit. You won't end up being from their planet, or their family, or their history.

Now you are really trying something new and different. In

fact, we are redefining intimacy. The more you take command of your side of the boat, address the importance of tension, express your needs, listen to your partner as a dignified and important co-captain, collaborate, and take care of yourself, the more intimacy you will have.

My goal is to have you get used to a tippy boat with two sides and two captains, and discover a new kind of animated and mature intimacy based on both of you being distinct individuals. Sex therapist David Schnarch calls this desirable state "differentiation." As a couple, it is your differences and uniqueness that drive you to deeper connection, not being a blob of undifferentiated goo in the middle of the boat. The more you are aware of yourself and the more responsibility you take for your distinct self, the more desirable you will be, the less needy you will be, and the more intimacy you will experience.

CAPTAIN'S LOG

We respond to increased tension in predictable ways that *increase* tension.

5

Self-Control: Be More
Than a Squirrel!

Diplomacy is the art of letting someone else have it *your* way.
Let's admit we need things to feel like they are under control
and make better choices about what we can control.

> . . . Was it a nut that lured you down,
> Or did you seek a mate to love,
> Gray, sleek and agile as yourself
> A tempting sight, seen from above?
>
> So down you came, an innocent,
> To chase and play upon the ground
> Trusting, unwitting and harmless,
> Till squashed by drivers homeward bound. . . .
>
> - Mark Hopkins

Briefly back on land, perhaps it seems obvious that I wouldn't
offer psychotherapy to squirrels, but as a clinician I am making
an important distinction.

Imagine that you are a squirrel in the road and you feel

the familiar tension we've been identifying. Your partner is coming down the road, and you react as though he or she is a truck. Squirrels, thankfully, notice when a truck is coming, in much the same way that a crocodile notices something is wrong and either attacks an intruder or slinks away. But, a squirrel sometimes doesn't quite know which to do: attack the truck or run away. What we have in common with squirrels and crocodiles is that we do have a primitive reptilian brain that tells us a truck is coming and quickly warns us, as we need it to, of terrible danger. Fortunately, our rational brain usually catches up moments later and can choose to argue with the reptilian part of our brain and work out a reasoned response.

So, the first reason I work with people, not squirrels, is that we have more brain. We are able to consider whether it is really a truck coming toward us, and therefore whether we should be standing in the road. We can also learn from other scary moments on the road. Most importantly, we can talk to the driver of the vehicle about where he or she is driving and how fast. Is he or she really intending to run us over?

As you might imagine, I have also decided to refuse to treat a squirrel that comes in and says that he or she can't stand the pain and embarrassment of jumping up and down in the road in confusion when it feels like a truck is coming. I'm a professional caretaker who could be sucked into trying to keep a squirrel from experiencing uncomfortable feelings. If I took the bait, gave the squirrel intensive treatment, and somehow succeeded in helping the squirrel eliminate their anxiety and discomfort, I'd be liable for malpractice, because the squirrel would probably get run over by a truck and its family could realize that I had somehow anaesthetized their loved one and sue me. Hence, it is a doubly-bad idea for me to treat squirrels. For people, I don't try to *eliminate* distress and negative feelings. Those feelings are needed and they can be managed.

I do encourage the people I treat to handle their distress by using more of their brains. I am often heard encouraging others to "be more than a squirrel!"

The Gumball Theory

Perhaps it will help to see both of you as gumballs.

No, really . . .

Let me back up a bit. Garrison Keillor, who has long produced and hosted a show on National Public Radio called *A Prairie Home Companion*, once made an amusing and concise comment about religious differences by offering a global explanation for our individuality that I've found helpful. He suggested that, when a couple gets pregnant, a great big gumball machine up in the sky rattles around and spills out a gumball for the baby, that we may think of as a "soul" or a "self" or an "essence." Each of us gets one. (Clearly, our gumballs are small, unique, colorful, powerful, and fragile.) As Keillor implies, the notion of a distinct human essence is present in every religion, whether your particular flavor of religion calls it a soul or a self or something else. In this world of healing, you might think of it as your personality, your way of being, or your self.

This got me thinking about how we spend our developing years creating a cushion (or warning system) around our gumball so that it won't get hurt, especially if we think we can control something about the way we have been hurt. This cushion becomes an important part of our life's work. When we plunge into having a partner and building our boat, we experience all kinds of intimate and personal threats to the gumball we have so carefully protected. We can't allow our gumball to get hurt. It is our core.

One thing that happens to couples, I've found, is that these cushions take up more room on the boat than we expected.

If there isn't room for one of the partners to just react, behave, have ideas, make mistakes, and so on, then each little movement hits the cushion of the other person. If we think that our cushion *IS* our gumball, then each time the cushion gets hit, we think it is our gumball being threatened, and we react with our primitive brains—just like the squirrel in the road.

We need to know *the difference between our cushion and our gumball.* When our cushion gets shaken or squeezed or pushed, we need to react the way we do when the alarm clock goes off in the morning. When that happens, we realize that it's not a smoke alarm or other indicator of peril, and we wake up, get cleaned up, put on our face and our clothes, and begin to deal with the normal confusing disappointing and unfair tension of relating all day. We'd all rather be dreaming, of course. We don't want our warning system to be triggered. Yet, we can pull ourselves together pretty well in the morning. The alarm clock is a normal, daily occurrence, so we shouldn't be surprised by it.

On the other hand, we need to know when something really is endangering our gumball—and to speak up for ourselves. When we're confronted with a real gumball issue, it is time to set off a fire alarm, and that is a different reaction.

I'll illustrate with a story about Dan, a football player who attended a men's group that I was running. I didn't know his wife, but I did know that they'd worked through a lot of their issues and that Dan was generally a wise, supportive voice in the group.

One week, my co-therapist and I hadn't really checked in with everyone at the beginning of the session and instead had just followed the energy in the room, until there were about five minutes left. Our solid football player suddenly revealed that things were not going well for him. He was truly distressed, because his wife and daughter had blamed his parenting style for a conflict they were having. It was a topic worthy of discussion, but we were all ready to go home, it was late at night, and we all needed the bathroom, so it was not a good moment for a long healing conversation. As he asked for help and sounded helpless, all I could think of to suggest was to say "*ouch*" to his family. Each time he countered me—looking surprised that I would give him such simple, seemingly useless, advice—and told me why it wouldn't work, I simply repeated myself: "Say 'ouch!'" Time ran out and everyone headed for home.

I soon realized that I had suggested something quite radical to Dan. How on earth could a guy who'd been told all his life that pain didn't really hurt, that in order to be tough he couldn't admit pain, and that he needed to get back in the game—someone who had reached the pinnacle of playing in the NFL in part by denying pain—possibly make any sense of that advice, or be able to act on it?

Essentially, I was saying that Dan had shown real resilience in dealing with issues that set off the alarm around his gumball, but somehow, this was different. This was not a cushion issue. This was gumball stuff—an issue that threatened Dan's very essence. He needed to say that his gumball was hurt, stand his ground, and claim his needs. I hoped he could do it.

I didn't need to wait long to find out. Dan came into the next session and bubbled with appreciation at the simple idea that he needed to say that something *hurt*. He had told his family that their words about him hurt and that he was confused and bewildered. His family had listened. I told him I was very impressed by his courage and strength in this new endeavor of personal growth and relational skill. And we were all reminded that toughness occurs in different ways.

The Power Within

I was one of those radical young people in 1970 who wanted to transform our society when I was eighteen. Incredibly, I was at a school that decided our senior class should find something educational to do for the spring term, away from school, and then just come back and graduate. Maybe they were afraid we would burn something down, or take over a building or something.

Anyway, I entered the world of a theater group on Cape Cod that was performing progressive and challenging plays at churches all over New England throughout the spring and then at our Cape Cod theater that summer. One of these plays, written by a Methodist minister named Dick Waters, was called *The Son of Man*, and was set in a church sanctuary, featuring the return of Jesus Christ to talk to a congregation.

To this day, one of the lines spoken by the character Jesus stays with me. "The kingdom of God is within you; you need only to claim it," he would blurt out at the congregation that had not really met his expectations or really heard him. He was not satisfied with the people of the church or the ministers or the politicians in his audience. This Jesus felt that nobody had really understood that his gospel was about self-discovery and empowerment, not about building churches or holding power over others.

As I translate this part of my journey into my practice with couples, I suggest that there is a way to be more than a squirrel, claim your gumball, and honor that kingdom within.

Fishing for Control

What explains our distressed reactions when our boat feels tippy, or when the other person has a different sensibility from ours, or it feels as though a truck is hurtling down the road?

Really, we want to feel like everything is under *control*.

Dominick, a man I treated for many years, went fishing every year with in-laws and buddies. These men have many things under control. They can control their behavior at home well enough all year that their wives have no objection to fishing for a week in Vermont. They manage to control where they are going, when they are going, who is paying the rent, how the food is procured, and so on. Importantly, they also control their equipment; how ready it is, how beautiful it is, how well tied the lines are, how flexible the rods are, how new and beautifully made the flies are, and how well they cast the fly and rod. They also are able to choose just the right time of day in the right part of the lake, with everyone staying very quiet as they steer their boats. In all of these ways, they show real mastery.

But can they control whether they catch fish? The fish may not be hungry, they may be busy with something else, dealing with their own family problems, or just not interested. As Dominick has learned to say, "*It's up to the fish!*"

Dominick and his buddies have a choice. They can decide that the fish determine the success of their trip and leave their success up to the fish, or they can decide to measure the success of their trip through things they can control—and *have* controlled—well. The fisherman who gains satisfaction from a beautifully conceived trip to Vermont and a beautifully calculated and performed evening on the lake will have a more rewarding trip than the fisherman who is only ultimately satisfied if he catches enough fish.

Indeed, when we have some things under control, many of us seem to want more. In our intimate partnerships, we often feel this way, as well. If you and your partner can admit how much you both want things to be under control, you will see much more clearly how tension builds between you. You will also begin to notice what you need to talk about as you struggle for control and power. Perhaps it would be useful to talk about how each of you tries to take control and what emotional needs you are trying to take care of.

What Can We Get Under Control?

If you have been involved in addiction treatment or know about Twelve-Step programs, you may be very familiar with the Serenity Prayer. If not, take a look:

> God, grant me the serenity to accept the things I cannot change,
> Courage to change the things I can,
> And wisdom to know the difference.

This reminds us of the value of knowing the difference between what we can control and what we can't control. If you are in a relationship that feels out of control, ask yourself: Over whom am I most likely to be able to exert some control? What is the most productive route to serenity? What choice would lead to the least possible frustration?

One way of speaking about this theoretically is to sense the location of the controlling force, or "locus of control" that you are experiencing. If your locus of control is distant from you (say, held by the fish), then outside factors—including your partner's behavior—will exert more control over your well-being than you do. If it is closer to you, you will experience more self-control and satisfaction.

For instance, when I was asked to perform on camera for a television show I was producing, I suddenly entered a realm in which I had limited control. I intuitively and nervously understood that I couldn't control each viewer's response to me, even though I wanted to. In fact, I realized that there would be thousands of distinct critical responses to my performance. I also knew that when I watched television, I was often brutally judgmental of the presenters or actors—what they were saying, how they said it, how they looked, and so on. What if my viewers were like me?

Before long, I realized that I would go crazy if I tried to control each response to me, so I had to draw my locus of control closer to myself for my own mental health. I didn't know this language back then, but I did realize that I needed to make an adjustment. I shifted to a purposeful focus on the smaller and closer scale of my own behavior: what I was writing, how I presented my thoughts, and the feedback that trusted colleagues gave me about how my performance looked and sounded.

Imagine what would have happened if I'd decided to run around town asking people what they thought of the show instead of focusing on what I could control! I would have been an emotional wreck. I think it would have been like venturing out onto a frozen pond where the ice was getting thinner and thinner. The further my attention wandered from my solid base, the more power I gave the audience, the greater the ultimate emotional cost for me.

So, as we consider self-control, let's admit that "control" is not a dirty word, but a goal that we naturally seek. The art of self-control is found in the way we try to reach that goal, mastering what we can, and letting go of the rest.

CAPTAIN'S LOG

We need self-control and an alarm system that tells us when we are *really* in danger.

6

Size Matters: Feeling Small AND Looking Big

It is normal, and crazy, for *both* of you to feel small and look big at the same time. If you get this distortion under control for yourself, you'll be even more attractive and desirable to your partner.

> The woman in his life was like a mirror with the power of magnifying his figure to twice his size, or shrinking it to the size of an ant, while he kept morphing between the two forms.
>
> - Abraham Verghese
> *The Tennis Partner*

In my practice, I am very persistent in checking in with each person to see what they have learned, or how they are using the experiences they have had with me. This is harder to do with a book, but it is still important.

Take a moment to account for what you think you have heard so far. Here is a list of impressions I hope you have retained:

- Safety matters.
- Talking matters.
- Feeling tense matters.
- Intimacy is challenging.
- We don't listen well enough.
- We want more control than we have.
- Expectations can lead to disappointment.
- You can benefit from seeing things two ways.
- There are different planets and boating sensibilities.
- We need primitive responses, but they happen too fast.
- You can be selfish in ways that tip the boat for your partner.
- You can exaggerate opposites in paradoxical and counterproductive ways.

Now, let's talk about an important concept and another theme of this book: Feeling small AND looking big.

I've been a therapist for twenty-nine years and I am well aware that the key to my livelihood is my ability to listen well and understand what others are yearning to have understood about their lives. I am also acutely aware that it took me about ten years to hear something fundamental about what I was being told. I hadn't truly grasped something that people wanted me to know.

I'd had the privilege of hearing people talk about their most cherished and most intimate relationships, with their soul mates and sexual partners, their parents, their children, or other members of their family. Often, the more important the relationship, the more troubling and upsetting the story was. They all involved the theme of extreme and unfair tension and the need for relief, which was clear. But there was also a very simple and basic dynamic aspect I had missed. It was really about *size*.

Feeling Small AND Looking Big

It finally hit me after ten years that all of these trusting and vulnerable people were hoping I would understand how small they were *feeling* (depressed, anxious, helpless, useless, misunderstood, abused, dismissed, threatened, incompetent, unwanted, judged, undesirable, confused, frustrated, terrified, etc.). They also wanted me to understand how big the other important person in their life *looked* (controlling, scary, powerful, distant, pressuring, silent, hostile, angry, inconsiderate, abusive, uncaring, dismissive, manipulative, addicted, etc.).

Trying to do something about this disparity is daunting. I hadn't addressed this distortion or quite understood it before. I needed my own solution, first. When I understood it was about size, it occurred to me that something crazy and confounding, but perfectly normal, was happening. I was being asked to understand that both people felt small and both people looked big, all at the same time. What if this was simply the truth, that something that sounds crazy was normal? It would explain why people came to me seeking help, and how easy it is to get emotionally stuck in the dynamics of a relationship. How elegant. I didn't need to magically "fix" it because I could simply declare that is was normal, like being on a boat or looking through a kaleidoscope.

I decided to try out my new understanding with couples, asking them to each tell me how big they felt when there was a tippy moment on their boat, and how big the other person looked to them. I started getting my expected confounding answer and pointing out that they both couldn't be small and big at the same time. Or could they? What if it is a *"crazy normal"* distortion?

I began to sense the relief and gratitude felt by couples

when something confusing had been made understandable. I pursued the idea further, holding a pillow, or whatever was handy that had four corners, between the two people and suggesting that there were four distinct things going on as they experienced the quadrangle between them: both people feeling small at the bottom corners of the pillow and both people looking big at the top two corners. There was some resolution in suggesting that this distortion was normal and we could expect it. It didn't need to be fixed or made it disappear—I could build from this understanding, instead.

It might have been adequate to give couples a boost with a dramatic illustration of this crazy normal distortion. Couples clearly left with something different to think about. But, I had also learned in ten years of therapy that people also wanted action, solutions, and direction—not just insight and explanation.

I was very fortunate that the next step did not take ten years, but only a few days. What occurred to me first was that much of our behavior is motivated by a need *to get things more under control* (see Chapter 5). Perhaps we would all benefit from getting this distortion under control and being able to experience that as satisfying, while doing healthy things for our relationships at the same time.

As I was already offering a visual aid and handling the distortion as a square, I took my own cue and wondered how each of the four corners could be more under control.

I also realized the wisdom of the "Serenity Prayer" about the difference between what we can control and what we can't control. More importantly, we need to know *who* we can control in our partnerships—and that the better choice is to control ourselves. Trying to control something about the other person leads to too much frustration and disappointment. Not a good choice. Our odds aren't as good.

What might we control about *ourselves* at each of the four corners of this crazy normal distortion?

My partner is felling small. I can control whether I remember that they are feeling small and that will help me listen to them and not be defensive.
Developing empathy through listening with more attention can lead to a sense of satisfaction and serenity because you have actively focused your awareness on your partner's feelings.

I am feeling small, and it is my responsibility to catch myself, understand my feelings, and claim my needs and wishes. That way, I won't feel so small.
Claiming your own feelings through genuine statements about yourself can lead to more self-esteem because you are taking responsibility for your own mental and emotional process.

My behavior is making me look big to my partner. I am in control of how I sound, what I am saying, and all aspects of the way I am behaving, especially when I feel small.
Modifying your own behavior so that it is less grandiose can lead to a sense of accomplishment because you have controlled your own reactions to feeling small and your impact on your partner.

My partner is looking big but I can't control their behavior. I can control my perception of it, my memories, and what

I am associating with their behavior. I can be mindful and "in the moment" and I won't feel small so fast.

Reducing the associations with your own memories can stall the process of feeling small when your partner looks big because you have interfered with the "transference" to your own past experiences.

Feeling Small AND Looking Big—What to Control?

He's Looking Big.

He **manages** his own big-looking behavior.

She **focuses** on the present event.

She's Looking Big.

She **manages** her own big-looking behavior.

He **focuses** on the present event.

He's Feeling Small.

She **remembers** he is feeling small.

He **claims** his own emotions and needs.

She's Feeling Small.

He **remembers** she is feeling small.

She **claims** her own emotions and needs.

How does this distortion happen?

When there is tension, the other person looks big, and you feel small in comparison. Yes, you are making a comparison. In order to take care of yourself and *keep from feeling any smaller*, you might automatically do something that looks big to the other person. The pattern repeats itself on the other side of the boat.

- What about past injustices?

  They are real and valid and need to be talked about carefully, using skills that reduce tension; or at an appropriate time, perhaps in a therapy session. They are not happening right now. At worst, only *this* injustice is happening right now.

- What if we want to control *more*?

  This is enough. For your own health, you don't want to have all of the control and you don't want to be trying to control something you can't control.

- What if it seems selfish?

  It is, but in a good way that calms both of you.

- How is this satisfying?

  It feels good to control something.

- How is this good for us as a couple?

  Satisfied people who have a sense of self-control appreciate each other more.

- Here are topics for possible conversations with yourself:

When I am at my tipping point and I want the situation to feel like it is more under control, how can I make myself:
1) Remember that they are feeling small; or
2) Be clear and resourceful about claiming that I am feeling small; or
3) Get a grip on my behavior that looks big; or
4) Be more in the moment so they don't look like people and situations I am remembering, and so that I don't feel so small in comparison?

How can I discipline myself and then appreciate that I have controlled something about myself?
Take time to have this kind of conversation with yourself. If you start to find answers to these questions, you'll like yourself more and be an increasingly valued partner.

I had discovered that there were four ways to control the craziness of a normal distortion while picking the right person to control, and doing no harm to the relationship. When I realized that psychotherapy had always emphasized these four things (clinically speaking, 1) *empathy; 2) self-esteem; 3) behavior modification; and 4) transference*) I felt that I had not actually strayed from my training or my professional perspective, but had found another way to frame it.

CAPTAIN'S LOG

It is "crazy normal" for two people to feel small and look big at the same time.

7

First Interlude – Watching and Listening From the Dock

Stepping onto the dock and watching the boats can be very informative. A therapist is a participant and an observer. What have I learned?

> The practice of mindfulness in our relationship to our ordinary, immediate lives can be every bit as rewarding and instructive as taking wild journeys to far-off and exotic places to be with the greatest teachers in the world.
>
> - Joan Halifax
> author of *Shamanic Voices*

Let's slow down for a moment to enjoy the breeze and the adventure. I wonder whether my years of experience working with couples helps to make relational mysteries easier for you to understand, or are these truths kind of obvious? Hopefully, these are helpful observations and suggestions that can help you take care of your precious partnership. You'll need practice and support as we continue the journey, but hopefully we've now got a good start that makes sense to you.

This chapter is written differently. It is my letter to you from the dock as you try to sail your boat. I'll repeat some ideas and offer new ones. Connect the dots for yourself at your own pace and learn what you can.

Tying the Knot
If creating a committed partnership is like building a boat, then it is precious, fragile, and unpredictable. Handle with care.

**

What really matters? Your partnership is intimate, emotional and very personal. It needs awareness and a willingness to step back and catch yourself. Mostly, your partnership needs you to really want to be with the other person. It's hard work with benefits.

**

Stocking up with Provisions
Many of us learned as children that there was a "golden rule." It is easy to internalize the idea that your partner wants to be treated the way you want to be treated. If both of you are doing that, then you may both be treating the other person
a) In a way they did not ask to be treated, and/or
b) In a way that they wouldn't have even thought someone would want to be treated.
It is better to ask than to guess based on what you would like.

**

One day, a mindful husband was pondering powerlessness, feeling small, and needing control when he declared that it feels like your feet are up in the air, like the moment you are born, when they need to feel like they are on the ground. Evidently, we are dealing with this scary emotional problem from the very beginning.

**

Setting a Course

I do try to start my sessions with a question that nobody can fail at. This is important emotionally. I ask for an honest accounting of thoughts, feelings, and behaviors related to being in the therapy process. Every answer is valid, as long as it is thoughtful and honest. It is part of learning that every experience has an impact on us and that we are a composite of perceptions, responses, feelings, and behaviors in a never-ending process.

**

How sure do you need to be that you are right and that things are under control? When a clock stops, it is absolutely right twice a day and is totally useless, unreliable, and unimportant. Do you choose to be a broken clock that can be completely right, or a moving, flowing clock that is close enough?

**

Knowing the Ropes

There are two sayings that I picked up about 40 years ago:

"Chance favors the prepared mind." - Louis Pasteur
"Luck is the residue of design." - Branch Rickey

Through my actions as a therapist, including what I write in this book, I try to model the idea that your thoughts and your imagination can respond to your feelings in a healthy and productive way when life's indignities come your way.
The odds are with you if you are ready to use your mind.

**

Mary Roach writes in *Gulp* that while we take for granted that our very powerful jaw muscles can pulverize our food, they also have the natural reflex to let up at just the moment they have succeeded in mashing the food, when they could crush our teeth, too, in a very destructive and painful tooth-on-tooth collision.

Surely, if our jaws can let up as soon as they have successfully used their power, we can learn to do the same thing and listen well to our partner's response after we have advocated for our needs, instead of creating harm for ourselves. Just imagine that you have to crack the nut, but not break your teeth, nor demolish the nut.

**

Where Are We Heading?
There was once a television show called *thirtysomething*. If you watched the show, you may remember it was kind of puzzling,

but you weren't quite sure why. Actually, the two couples living next door to each other had to talk according to our rules from Chapter 2, presumably to avoid too much conflict.

Imagine a guy going next door to ask his neighbor, "I wonder what you folks are doing today," and the guy next door having to follow the script and say "You're wondering what we are doing today," before he could answer the question.

That's what these tension-reducing conversations sound like. The sad fact is that we don't take the time to talk this way—and it sounds strange when we do.

**

What if neediness, vulnerability, and emotionality create the opposite reaction in our partner, and they respond with logic, thoughts, solutions, and distance? What if they are doing this intuitively to keep things balanced?

**

We Need to Discuss the Voyage Plan

Author John Gottman has shown in his research that our most common mechanisms *for taking care of ourselves when we feel small* are:

contempt,
defensiveness,
criticism, and
stonewalling.

Therapist and couples expert Steve Treat suggests that the ways of responding *but not looking too big* are:
intentionality,

having courage,
making good choices, and
reflection about yourself.

If we are going to respond differently to feeling small, and put aside our dread of feeling even smaller, we need their warnings and advice.

**

Heading into the Wind

One couple concluded that the problem was that they were "playing badminton" and not really coming to grips with how toxic their relationship was. Another determined that they *should* play badminton because they were hurting each other so much and they should play more gently. What's the right answer? They were both right.

Each couple needs to be captains of their own boat with understanding and clarity.

**

Men seem consistently on edge about women's emotions. "If momma's happy, we're all happy" seems to be the guide. Or, "oh, my god, we're going to have chaos." What is there to dread about being deeply emotional? What's so great about logic? Why can't we hold on for a moment and try to find a middle ground, so women don't spin so fast and men use more of themselves, not just the traffic cop part?

**

Getting Our Sea Legs under Us

If we begin to speculate about the other person's subconscious thoughts, feelings, and motivations, and *they* are not conscious of them, we can be sentenced to an endless and senseless debate, where the most concise and honest answer we will get is "I don't know."

**

Some people really like dogs and some don't. Dogs are non-judgmental, oblivious to the details of our circumstances, lead parallel lives, and are innocently friendly and generous. For some people, that is the model for relating well and the most desirable kind of partner. For others, it is annoying and not enough. Which way do you look at partnership?

**

Going Adrift

Your wish for freedom can threaten the other person's need for safety. Your need for safety, reliability, and consistency can threaten the other person's wish for freedom. Being able to direct your own life and having emotional safety are both important factors for both of you.

**

Shame and guilt matter. Try to be aware of these sensations and admit that you have them. Your partner will understand. They have felt them, too.

**

Ebb and Flow

One of the ways family therapist Ivan Bozsormenyi-Nagy implored people to catch themselves and be aware of the whole boat was to encourage *"due consideration"* of others. You are not the only person entitled to caretaking and fairness.

**

What if being angry triggers the rejection we expected from our partner? What if our rejection triggers the anger we expected from our partner? Do we repeat the pattern so that we will be right about their rejection of us—or about their anger?

**

The Wind is Shifting

Emotions can be clear and confusing at the same time. We can experience moments we have been dreading, and suddenly feel relieved or uplifted. Who knew?

The opposite can happen, too. I had a confusing moment sitting in an airplane one time. I was incredibly sad and it didn't make any sense. I had finished my graduate school studies and my thesis, and had rewarded myself with a trip to Hawaii. What could be more uplifting? My sadness could not have been about what I had finally accomplished or about the trip ahead of me. I finally understood that the sadness was about losing something. I had lost the graduate school life and thesis process that I had been trying so hard to lose. It wasn't there anymore. Times were changing and I couldn't go back. I was dealing with loss at a time of great hope and joy for me. It helped to understand what was happening to me. The contradiction actually made a lot of sense.

**

Sometimes your—or your partner's—behavior can seem "prickly."
If your behavior is prickly, try to notice, catch yourself, and see if you can make it less sharp. If your partner's behavior is prickly, imagine being in bed with a very scared porcupine, deciding to take the risk of grasping it very carefully and talking to it gently. Tell them what it feels like to be around a porcupine.

**

Sailing, Sailing, Over the Ocean Blue . . .
Psychotherapy is ministry, but is not the same as church. It is a place to deal with spiritual questions and worries, but it is also a laboratory for making relationships function well.

Therapy is not a spontaneous, intuitive, non-verbal, magical process, even though it can work like one. In the room, it is a verbal, thoughtful, conscious, deliberate, intentional, purposeful, and, thus, spiritual process.

**

I often think that if I ask Eb *and* Flo what their goal is, emotionally, when they act like they are from very different sides of the boat, and I could ask it just the right way, they would both give me this answer:

I am seeking peace, safety and calm. I want things to be predictable and reliable. I want things to feel familiar to me. I want to feel like the situation is under control.

These are surely good intentions: caring about the relationship and about the other person. It is not our intentions that get twisted; it is our way of getting there that wanders.

**

It's Tippy!

There is a lot of evidence that the most creative and innovative people can integrate their attention to detail with their imagination. I had the privilege of watching Canadian Olympic medalist Elvis Stoyko in a private moment when he was sharpening his art. Stoyko was on a deserted, nearly dark, ice rink practicing "figures," the very precise discipline of *copying* the exact pattern you have just laid down on the ice, which was once a required Olympic discipline for skaters. This level of concentration and precision was an intrinsic part of Stoyko's ability to be a flamboyant creative genius on ice.
A couple who can integrate their opposite tendencies will have a more balanced boat.

**

When Venus is spinning and works well, she is more like a gyroscope that is creating a genuine center that is solid and reliable. When Mars is chopping and works well, he is more like the beautiful swing of a baseball bat that is hitting the sweet spot.

**

Stuck in the Doldrums?

It is significant that twelve-step programs for addicts emphasize a *serenity* prayer. To gain serenity, you try to control something about yourself. It is simple and effective to be mindful.

**

Keep It Simple Stupid and *kiss* yourself, give affection to yourself by knowing your own boundaries, your own emotions, your own needs and wants. How could the person in the mirror feel more in control while also being a good companion?

That can be enough.

**

We're usually distorting things. It's what we do. The most important lesson from my first day of graduate school was that I had been naturally and predictably distorting my family history to comfort myself. Each time one of us offered some information about our family, the esteemed professor resolutely and firmly told us it was a distortion. We had our own perceptions of events and relationships, and that was all we really had.

It is evidently quite normal, then, for both people in a couple to have their own distortions about their families and also about their own intimate partnership.

**

Going Aground . . . on a Sandbar

Typically, both Eb and Flo will take genuine positions about what they expect and need from their partner. I like to ask if they could *give* what they are hoping to *receive*. This is a question that requires a clear and honest answer, because we all have our limits, and if we are asking something superhuman of our partner we are doomed to disappointment and frustration. It's important to state what you want, but equally important to be aware of whether or not it is something *you* could give.

**

One way we drive each other crazy is that when our emotional needs are addressed, we want more. Children display this when they are hyperactive or needing attention, addicts display it when they are controlled by their addiction, and disappointed spouses display it when they are not satisfied. It is vexing to try to know when we are entitled to something better and when to leave it alone. Try asking yourself if what you have is enough.

**

I've found that I am not supposed to be a magician, which is lucky, because I don't know any magic. Although couples come to me in real need—and, often, despair—seeking a quick solution, I've found they really want a chance to fix the problem themselves. In fact, if I were to take over and provide an apparently wonderful cure (telling them that I know exactly what is wrong, suggesting a fix, and telling them they need to see me two or three times a week until I manage everything), they would probably decide *not* to come back. I would actually be dismissing their own ability to be knowledgeable and responsible about their lives, and they would react accordingly by being uncomfortable, feeling disrespected and dehumanized enough to skip the next session. My taking over would feel like their loss. Hence, I offer something less magical, which usually feels right, even if it is not the quick answer they had imagined.

**

Distress Call

Men feel slimed and women feel abandoned—*or vice versa.* However the pattern gets started, this is often what couples are hoping that someone will understand. Both are reacting to what they are experiencing and then behaving in the exact way that makes the other person feel even worse. One often responds to attacks, criticism, and corrections by withdrawing or creating barriers in some way. The partner responds to barriers and distance by feeling abandoned and then getting upset and attacking.

It's a cycle.

Slimed? I remember a children's show on Nickelodian, Actors would get green "slime" dumped on them at seemingly random times, for no apparent reason, eliciting the same look of helplessness and bewilderment this dynamic creates for couples.

**

Seeing Landfall—Hope

When couples reach a plateau and feel good about the progress they have made in therapy, I suggest that they imagine that they have been redecorating a room, had some awful rift about the color, size, and cost of a new sofa, and finally found a way to resolve it. I ask them to imagine that they are triumphantly sitting on the sofa, and ask them what happens next? They look around and perhaps notice how tacky the coffee table is, or how old the carpet looks, or how the walls need painting. Reaching a goal is an opportunity to set a new one and find new energy to keep improving your relationship

8

Watch The Weather!
Storms Ahead!

Couples have predictable conflicts over money, sex, in-laws, children, the house, jobs, etc. These are opportunities to try new skills, to say what you want, and to learn about yourself. Isn't that great?

> You don't control the world. You can't control the world. But you are able to respond, and that's a great power, and it's in you.
>
> - Patricia Sun

I remember vividly my daughter's wedding. It was to be on a very hot summer day in a church with no air conditioning. I was watching the weather reports closely, hoping there would be some relief from the heat. I heard a phrase on the Weather Channel I hadn't heard before: "there will be now and then clouds." That phrase didn't help with the weather very much, but it did give me a cue for part of my speech at the reception. As a marriage therapist and father I found myself saying that "now and then clouds" would be a reasonable weather forecast for the happy couple. They need not experience violent storms, but they also did not need to have perfect weather. They could handle now and then clouds.

Predictably, couples enter my office for the first time anxious about being in therapy, wishing they weren't, and at least slightly embarrassed about their issues. When they find their voices, one of them may say "We really have serious issues we aren't getting at." Most of the time I can anticipate what they mean. On a relationship voyage, the bad weather and the rocky seas come in the form of financial worries, concerns about sexual performance or desire, intrusive dynamics with someone's extended family, disagreements about parenting the children, real stress created by their jobs, different priorities about the home they are living in . . . . Need I go on?

We do not spend any day of our life in neutral, without stress, without complications. It is crazy normal for us to be awake, negotiating, compromising, and responding to a complex web of relationships. When we reach our own tipping point, we want to feel like this web of complexity is more under control.

Ways of Gaining Control

Michael Pollan, the author of *The Botany of Desire* and other memorable books about our relationship with the food we eat, suggests that we can be seduced in ways that we find fair and acceptable. To Pollan, we even collude with plants in ways that meet their need to thrive and spread their seeds.

It is more obvious to us, probably, how our pets get us to take care of them. Cats are more direct, demanding their breakfast in the morning, for instance, and fortunately are good at taking care of themselves once they give us enough attention and playfulness to get us to feed and house them. Dogs are a little more complicated, having somehow chosen to be very passive in expressing their needs or at least they presumably were when humans were choosing to domesticate wolves. By rolling around, being playful, or being needy and passive, they do not seem threatening and we comply to their needs by housing and feeding them. At these moments, pets, and perhaps other animals and plants, are manipulating us and shaping our behavior towards them.

Alas, we humans are also capable of being passive and aggressive at the same time (passive-aggressive) in order to meet our own needs. With increased self-awareness, I think we can intuitively recognize this trait in ourselves and use this knowledge when we feel like we are in a bind. Otherwise, we don't really understand what we look like or what impact we are having on others.

One time, I was treating a couple when the woman turned into the expert I needed about passive-aggressive behavior. She explained very clearly that when her husband, or anyone else, acted passively, like a compliant dog, it was easy to deal with. And, when someone was aggressive, like the cat wanting breakfast, it was also easy to deal with. It was the "passive-aggressive" behavior that made her blood boil because of the emotional bind it put her in. When that happened, she would get engulfed in her own emotions and then define her husband's behavior in negative terms, framing it as an attack on her, in order to help her explain the bind she was in.

Remembering the Milk

Soon after that session, I was in a workshop about couples, which was being presented by a very prominent therapist in Philadelphia, Steve Treat. Treat loves to be amusing and illustrate his ideas with stories, like I do. He decided to take his favorite tangent about passive-aggressive behavior, and it went something like this:

A married couple with small kids has split up the responsibilities. He works long impossible hours at the office and she works long impossible hours raising the kids. One day, she calls him at work and asks him to get some milk on the way home.

Now, the wife does wish that the husband was more involved with her and the children at home, while the husband does find the call unnecessary because he is busy making a living, there is a store half a block from home, and—in his view—it should be easy for her to get milk. There is resentment on both sides. This is the unspoken part.

The husband agrees to buy milk, and one of three scenes develops. The *passive* drama unfolds as the husband comes home without milk, completely forgetting because of the stresses of his job. In the short term, that is easy for the wife to deal with. She decides he is unreliable and stops asking him to help. In the long term, however, she learns to do without him and the marriage suffers from both of them being passive.

The *aggressive* drama unfolds as the husband stops at the store but buys bread, thinking but not really thinking. The wife finds this easy to deal with, hitting the guy with the bread and telling herself that he is just oblivious. Again, in the long term, there is little reason to keep the relationship going because there is too much aggression.

The *passive-aggressive* drama unfolds as the husband remembers to get milk and triumphantly brings it home, but it is the *wrong milk*. It is whole milk when the wife and the kids always drink non-fat organic milk in the red carton. This is not easy for the wife or the husband to deal with because it is a mixed message.

The wife feels misunderstood, unimportant, or dismissed. She needs to understand better what is going on and speculates about the motivations behind what the husband did. Eventually, she is sure that he intended to get the wrong milk, not caring that she and the kids are watching their health and weight, perhaps even wanting, subconsciously, to fatten her up, make her boobs bigger, and make her unattractive to other men so she will have to stay married to him. What a mess.

The husband denies any such thoughts, saying he was busy and preoccupied, and says that at least he brought milk home like he was supposed to and saying that he shouldn't be criticized, and that she set him up. She denies her resentments, too, saying she wasn't trying to set him up to fail. They are both being honest (probably) about their conscious thoughts, even though they are also speculating about the other's thoughts and faults.

The moral of the story? Be careful what you think the other person is thinking. It may just be something you were capable of thinking and you could be speculating about something that wasn't a conscious thought, anyway, which will just infuriate your partner.

And, as you work through your own scenario, remember that the phone call itself presents an opportunity to show consideration for your partner. If the husband in the above story had taken a moment to ask, without resentment or hostility, exactly which milk his wife wanted, the drama would most likely have turned out differently. If she had quietly recognized and validated that the husband was wrapped up in his job and then asked him to bring home nonfat organic milk, he would have been more likely to do so.

Controlling the Distortion

When partners are looking and acting "passive-aggressive" it is confusing and frustrating. Both people are feeling small and also looking big. Recall, from Chapter 6, how to gain control of this distortion. You have four options: you can remember that they are feeling small; you can say calmly that you are feeling small; you can make your behavior smaller; or, you can be more in the moment and keep your memories and thoughts from making your partner look so big. These are tough, challenging—and gratifying—things to do.

They feel small

I remember clearly the day my first child came home from the hospital, when she was just three days old. She was lying there in her infant seat, and I was on duty as a father for the first time. She began to cry, and I had a remarkable moment on my hands. How was I going to handle being a father? What did she need and what did I need to do? This really mattered. I felt small, and she looked enormous.

What I recall is that I took a moment to imagine what this scene looked like through her eyes. She had been in a cramped but controlled environment for nine months with nothing too stressful going on, a nice amount of light, nothing too loud or startling, food on hand, and no schedule to keep. For three days, she'd been bombarded with bright lights, hunger, lots of noise, people looking at her, and completely new sensations. Then, a taxi ride through New York City to this place in a seat by the window, with me. Something was bothering her and she had no way of telling me what it was. All she could muster was crying. She needed me, and wasn't going to tell me why. She simply couldn't.

Seeing her side helped me handle the moment. *I calmed down* and tried a few things until she was OK. I couldn't get upset at her, because I understood her predicament. I simply wasn't going to know whether she was hungry, hot, cold, tired, scared, wet, uncomfortable, thirsty, or lonely. I had gained control of the situation by remembering that she was feeling small and dealing with the reality as well as possible.

I feel small

I once had a supervisor who liked to say surprising things to get her point across. I remember her often pointing out that someone would "feel about as powerful as a pee hole in the snow." That stayed with me as a great description of what it is like to feel small. It is about power and it is pretty helpless and insignificant. What is on the surface is tiny, but it probably took a lot of energy (and pee) to create that small hole. Just look at a pee hole in the snow sometime and imagine whether it feels like it will ever be heard or understood.

One way of getting a situation under control is to find a serious and meaningful voice that says that you feel as powerless as a little hole in the snow, and describe what that is like.

It may be that you dread being even smaller than a pee hole in the snow, and that makes you behave in ways that look big.

I look big

One way that boats get tippy in a hurry is that our behavior makes it feel that way to our partner. We have control over our own behavior (you think someone else does?) and are accountable for how we act.

Imagine a security camera in the room where you are, up in the corner, taking in what is going on in the room. What would that camera see when there is tension between the two of you? What signals would your body language be giving off? What would your face look like? What would your posture look like? If you are silent, what does that look like? If the camera also recorded sound, what would your voice sound like? What words would you be using? That is all *your* behavior.

Do you find it attractive? Would you respond calmly to that behavior? Would you be comfortable? Would you feel safe enough to be open with that person? One way to get a situation to feel like it is under control is to get a handle on your own behavior—and give yourself credit for harnessing yourself.

They look big

Your partner's behavior can look or sound enormous and overwhelming, in a passive and/or aggressive way. The perception makes you feel small in comparison. Their behavior probably does need to be smaller, but that part is up to them to get under control. It would be much more satisfying for you if the behavior simply didn't *look* so big to you.

You have memories and associations—connected to the type of behavior you are seeing—that are telling your mind that something emotionally challenging is happening. In reality, however, all this is happening in the moment is the event *of that moment*. The situation would feel like it is much more under control if you could get your own assumptions, memories, and associations off the shoulders of the other person because those are not from the present. No wonder your partner looks big.

You still have valid memories and expectations from your own experiences, but the indignity you are experiencing in the moment is all that is actually happening. How can you learn to be more in the moment and not set yourself up for feeling small?

Learning Mindfulness

It is helpful to practice "mindfulness" by training yourself to be in the moment with yourself. One idea, from a therapist named Terry Fralick, is basically a meditation. To be mindful, respond to an anxious moment by stepping back and *asking yourself what you are doing*. Your answers will usually be obvious things, such as:

• breathing, and/or

- feeling your leg touch the chair, or
- hearing the noise outside the window, or
- looking at that green patch on the sofa, or
- having a *thought* in words, or
- having a thought in pictures, or
- having an emotional moment.

Take the opportunity to do this for a few minutes, asking yourself every few seconds what you are doing. Do not ask yourself questions about why you are doing it, don't attempt to change what you are doing, just observe your own process, noticing yourself. You don't need to elaborate on the information. Doing this kind of exercise will give you a sense of control when you need it.

Always Dynamics, Always . . .

You may be wondering what you can do about the weather on the boat, or how to use these ideas to make the weather better. I think you can apply these ideas whether it is a stormy moment or not.

This time you don't need conflict or unfairness to improve your relationship. You can be flying on a plane, or driving home, or daydreaming, or watching TV, or just doing something mindless, and get to work.

Choose a corner of the crazy normal distortion square, and picture how you are going to get yourself more under control in that quadrant. To make this process even more powerful, your partner could be doing the same thing. For instance:

- If you try to change the way you express yourself when you feel small, and make your behavior smaller, your partner can work on keeping their memories off your shoulders, so you don't look so big the next time you both feel small.

- While you work on staying in the moment and dealing with each incident as it happens, your partner works on behaving the way you need them to so they don't look so big to you.
- If you practice finding the words for how you are feeling or what you are thinking or imagining, they can be working on remembering that you are feeling small and vulnerable, so they can listen more accurately to your statements about yourself.
- If you are working on remembering that they feel like a pee hole in the snow, they can be finding the words for how they feel that way, so it doesn't sound too big.

If both of you control yourselves better, and really notice self-control as something satisfying, you will be more gratified emotionally, have more confidence about uncertain moments, be less tense, relieve your partner of the burden of looking after your emotional vulnerabilities, and be more attractive, desirable, and satisfying for each other.

That's the deal. You get satisfaction from something you are doing to control yourself—and your relationship benefits.

CAPTAIN'S LOG

We can control something about ourselves when we want control.

9

Did You Bring Some Rain Gear?

Who would leap on a boat without some clothing, maybe a paddle, some raingear, or perhaps some food? When the boat feels tippy we may grab for something familiar to take care of feeling scared, insecure, or frustrated. What if we are playing out some kind of script from our family history?

> If the mystery's there, we might as well embrace it rather than run from it. It costs you more to run from a mystery than to enter it. The mystery's going to affect you whether you embrace it or not. You might as well have the joy of participating.
>
> - John Mack, M.D.
> author of *Abduction: Human Encounters with Aliens*

The launching of the boat is so much fun, we forget that the event conceals a very serious decision. In that moment, things seems so deliriously simple and easy: just hop on the boat and sail. Well, we're probably intoxicated, and that helps. Once you realize you are on a boat, it is obvious that you need to be prepared for all kinds of weather. It turns out we are equipped—but in sometimes clumsy or ineffective ways—to handle the uncertainties of sailing.

Actually, it wouldn't make any sense to start sailing a boat without some preparation. Boats are complicated and unpredictable. We are conscious of our own hopes and dreams, which generally include good sex, living a stable and secure life as a couple, having a number of children from zero to ten, being happy, etc. We are *not* very conscious of other ways we are getting prepared, or what expectations we might be carrying onto the boat.

One way of looking at launching the boat is that when we walk down the aisle (or simply begin a committed life together) we have very conscious *Expectations* that are very clear, based on conversations with our partner, popular culture, and talks with our friends. We also have *expectations* stemming from our family and past experiences that are less conscious but are just as powerful. We may expect men and women to behave certain ways, or for communication, emotions, money, children, or sex to be handled in some familiar way.

A wise and beloved family therapist, Carl Whitaker, built his legend around saying risky things, trusting himself, and focusing on the power of relationships. I heard a story once about a classic moment when he was addressing a group of fellow psychiatrists at breakfast, telling them that they were all obviously crazy. After allowing a moment for them all to get uncomfortable and defensive, he noted that everyone is crazy all night, dreaming, and most of us are lucky enough to pull ourselves together in the morning. The point he was making was that our most primitive processes do not necessarily serve us well in the light of day, when we are handling money, sex, in-laws, the kids, and our precious partnerships. We adjust and compensate in order to handle the day—and some of us do it better than others. If Whitaker is right, and we are normally too crazy to handle real experiences, what exactly do we do about it, *naturally?*

Our lives are a mosaic of indignities and small traumas that we are constantly adjusting to. We do *not* need to grow up around chaos or danger to build a system of defenses against trauma. Our brain is built to protect us and to develop strategies for our survival from a very early age.

I was at a workshop once where the presenter described how we are biologically driven to take care of ourselves, and make "clumsy" choices in order to ward off danger. He gave the example of a young boy who loved peanut butter and jelly sandwiches but stopped eating them. His mother couldn't understand why he wouldn't eat something he liked so much. Didn't he know he liked them? Evidently, the boy lived in a very safe household with a dog, a caring dad, and an attentive mother, but one day he had been eating his favorite sandwich when something spilled. The dog barked and jumped, the boy fell sideways, and the mother started screaming. This unusual trauma triggered the boy's brain to protect him from further harm. From then on, he associated the dog barking with tipping over and his mother screaming, so the barking itself upset him. Further, his best solution to the whole problem was to *not* eat peanut butter and jelly because that was the cause of all the chaos *by association*. He acted on his own, as he wasn't even old enough to discuss the problem with anyone.

In our own ways, we are all willing to do anything to avoid the possibility of things spilling, the dog jumping, and mom screaming—even if it is a clumsy choice.

Computers Have All the Luck

Our brains remember an extraordinary amount of information by remembering *associations* with information, like smells or sights or feelings, or other mental handles that help us squeeze information into smaller bits of associated stuff. This is fabulous when we want to create art or music or make love or have dreams. We can't have imagination without this capacity. We can't be creative without it.

On the other hand, computers just sit there and remember, but they can't do what we do with our minds. In a computer mind, everything is blissfully categorized and compartmentalized. The memory stays the same forever. There are no distortions or disruptions or associations with emotions or sensations to alter a computerized memory. The computer puts out what was put in—with no imagination or creativity.

We can't do that. We use connections and associations to help us remember things. This is tricky for relationships, because when there is tension, and we think we notice a truck coming—or the boat tipping—we remember other times when we have felt something similar, and that makes the person we are intimate with look bigger than they are feeling. We put what we are remembering on out partner's shoulders, and they suddenly look big. The problem is that this makes us more likely to feel small, because we are not only dealing with the crap that is happening right now, but something we are associating with it that makes us feel small, too.

No wonder it bothers us. We feel small quickly when we associate the situation with something traumatic, hurtful, shameful, or embarrassing, and this triggers our own well-learned mechanisms for taking care of ourselves.

First Priority: Our Own Defense

Actually, we have several built-in effective defense mechanisms that we use when we need them. These mechanisms also help us build walls and create distance in intimate relationships.

A woman once told me about a terrifying experience she had had, tripping over her child's toy on her doorstep and falling awkwardly onto a railing, breaking a rib. Taking this as an opportunity to learn about her own emotional makeup from the experience, she tried to re-experience the accident. She could still recollect seeing the toy, having her feet slip, falling toward the railing, and falling to the ground. What she could not recall was the actual impact with the railing that broke her rib. This is an example of how she takes care of herself, or perhaps more accurately, how our minds take care of us.

We need *denial* (literally, the ability to not allow ourselves to admit that something painful happened, or to re-experience the trauma) to protect us from too much emotional harm. Her mind did not allow her to revisit that level of pain—and she did not let herself feel it again. There are primitive functional ways that we take care of ourselves, and we often choose to use those methods when we feel tippiness—but there are relational consequences when we do.

The co-founder of Apple Computer, Steve Jobs, was notorious for using his will power to redefine reality, according to his biographer, Walter Isaacson. Evidently, those who knew and worked with Jobs called it his "reality distortion field." Jobs was capable of denying that he was using someone else's idea, that he was telling a lie, that he needed surgery, or that he had a daughter. He presumably needed to do this because of his own needs as an adopted child, his own insecurities and drives, and any other ways he felt tiny. You can imagine how this created tension in his closest relationships.

Another way we are built to take care of ourselves is to simplify our situation by handling something stressful in an expedient way. (We will revisit this idea with "Mr.—or Mrs.—Expedient" in Chapter 16.) We, as humans, need to feel like a situation is under control, and can *rationalize* saying almost anything—or so it seems—to experience at least a momentary satisfying calm.

We are also armed with an ability to rationalize our decisions and behaviors. For instance, Eb and Flo took a lunch break one very hot day from one of my extended "intensive" sessions and ran into a bind of their own. Eb went to the bathroom and Flo concluded that he did not want to go to lunch with her because he hadn't asked her to go to lunch. By the time he had gone to the bathroom, she had made up her mind that she wasn't wanted, and decided to sit in the car (hopefully with the air conditioning on) for the lunch hour. Evidently, a history of not saying much had caught up with Eb, and Flo was more than ready to interpret it as a continued lack of interest in their relationship, or in her.

We can build patterns of behaviors, expectations, and rationalizations that become ingrained in a dance created by partners, and have a toxic effect on our interactions.

Yet another way we take care of ourselves is by *projecting* something familiar about *ourselves* onto our partner. A different Eb and Flo assumed that love was expressed a certain way, and felt they were expressing love. When Eb offered sex, or Flo offered hugs and a cuddle, they both thought they were giving the other something special—but it was consistently interpreted as something disappointing and not as loving as it was intended.

For another couple in a more complex dynamic, a chronically anxious Flo consistently saw Eb's behavior as driven by anxiety, and criticized him for sabotaging situations—when it was just as likely to be her anxiety that had caused a misunderstanding or conflict. It was just more comfortable for her to see it as his anxiety, rather than hers.

How do you account for the wife who says she won't have lunch with her husband because he didn't ask her before going to the bathroom; or the husband who chastises his wife for shaving when she's in the shower because he could get cut by a razor blade when he showers in the dark; or a partner who continues with addictive behavior, when the dependency is harming the partnership?

We are all products of our early experiences. We have watched carefully as important people in our lives have taken care of themselves at highly emotional moments, and developed strategies for handling *our own* tipping points. These solutions are likely to seem "selfish" to your partner—and they really are, in a very natural way. Eb and Flo can both be selfish in their ways: needing to pee before lunch, feeling entitled to shower in the dark, getting intoxicated, needing to feel like they are important to their partner, or needing to relax while shaving and not think about everyone else. We are each our own first priority, especially when we are stressed.

We Need Crutches

Ivan Boszormenyi-Nagy, yet another memorable family therapist, suggested in his writings and teachings that we feel *entitled* to our behavior, even if it is sitting in a hot car, because of our connections to our *family legacy*. He called this the "ethical dimension" and we will explore it more, starting in Chapter 14.

In basic terms, we get on the boat armed with behaviors that we have witnessed, absorbed, learned about, and often tried before, ready to use them when the boat is tippy. We learn our behaviors, mostly, on the boat we grow up on. Our parents are authority figures, whether they are heavy-handed or not, and we study them for ways to handle tippiness. We are always "getting ready." We know we need ways to feel like things are more under control, and we are diligent students of the behavior we are around, looking for our own formula to use when we are in a bind.

So, as we grow, we have a natural—or at least learned—way of using ourselves to take care of upsetting events. Actually, we all need some kind of crutches to lean on some of the time, just not necessarily the ones we inherited or absorbed. They may not be the healthiest crutches. Let's accept and expect this. Hopefully, you'll gain some flexibility and acquire some useful new crutches from reading this book.

Imagine a group of students having a final exam. There's one guy who just broke his leg and really needs crutches just to get to the exam. This feels embarrassing and unfair, but he gets there with a little extra time and planning. Then, there's the woman next to him with a learning disorder. She's spent a lifetime learning how to excel, even though she experiences a different, distracting, and unproductive thought process. Her disability makes her self-conscious; it's not fair, but there she is working toward academic excellence, using techniques she has learned to use when she is taking a test. Next, there's the student who has found learning to be easy, gone out partying a lot, and not taken school seriously until he failed the last exam. He really had to study this time and tell his friends he was getting serious. It's not fair, really, and it's perhaps embarrassing that he had to change his behavior and not party with his friends. He's using a personal and emotional crutch to make himself take the exam seriously. It is awkward, but he is doing the work. All three students need a kind of crutch in order to handle the exam well. They have that much in common, It doesn't seem fair, but there is no need to be ashamed.

One healthy crutch we can learn to use is to look honestly at what associations, memories, and impulses we are carrying around inside us, so they don't surprise us or shame us.

CAPTAIN'S LOG

Things aren't always the way they seem, and crutches may be needed.

10

Whose Garbage Is This?

What kind of "garbage" are you carrying around, anyway? What makes you think the way you think and behave the way you behave? Is there an elegant way to explore yourself and still have dignity and integrity?

> The kingdom of God is within you; you need only to claim it
>
> - Richard D. Waters
> *The Son of Man, 1970*
> (adapted from Luke 17:21)

We've discussed a number of images and ideas so far on this journey. Let's review and visualize a few of them before we move on:

- I'll try to be more than a squirrel.
- When I'm at my tipping point, I need to be careful not to tip the boat more.
- My partner is feeling small, too.
- We are both captains. If our boat is going to float, I need to act like one.

- The soccer ball is coming right at me, but I'm going to get my hands out of the way.
- I'm throwing batting practice to my teammate, who needs to hit real pitches well.
- It's wonderful to have two kaleidoscopic—or planetary perspectives—on any conflict.
- If I listen first, they'll behave better.
- We all need crutches, so maybe they're not so bad.

Do these images work for you? Hold on to the ones that do. Hopefully, by now, you are developing a new way of talking to yourself. Let's keep traveling.

If you've ever felt really enraged, defeated, or confused, and have been floundering around looking for a crutch, maybe it is right in front of you. Cleaned up your room or your house lately?

No, I don't actually want you to go and clean up your house. Stay here.

But, I do want you to think about how you would go about sorting out your personal "stuff"—also sometimes referred to as your "garbage" (or "baggage"), as in "he/she's carrying around a lot of old garbage." Let's talk about how to take advantage of the skills you already use to keep things straight so that you can get some things about yourself in order and you can feel more in control and less confused.

I suspect you are like most people and resist discussing or facing your own issues, but that you don't mind talking about the stuff you have around you in your house (including your family and significant other), your job, the weather, your favorite team, or your community. Have you ever wondered what it would be like to be as comfortable talking about your own emotional stuff as you are talking about your less personal daily concerns? Well, it may not be as hard as it sounds.

Cognitive Metaphors

My experience has been that the visual aides that I use and trust (boats, squirrels, planets, kaleidoscopes, etc.) can calm people, give them hope and steer them away from self-defeating behavior and helpless feelings or negative thoughts about themselves. I've come to trust that a visual image can interrupt a learned or automatic response to an emotional signal. I remember being given a great opportunity to create a metaphorical aid, which I've prescribed ever since.

I was a graduate student learning about family therapy and needed to plunge into clinical practice as soon as possible in order to meet the graduation requirements. I was assigned to an inpatient unit for adolescents at a time when kids would be removed from their families and peers for a month or so for having committed unwanted behavior. Back then, insurance companies didn't ask too many questions. In fact, they seemed really generous—often paying for several therapists, schooling, and a substantial support system for all of the teenagers, for several weeks.

One of the teenage girls at the inpatient center had an addiction problem and a behavior problem, and I was her family therapist. She had barely met me and I had never met her family. It was time for our first family session (which was also one of my first sessions).

She looked depressed. She looked angry and kind of scared. I was anxious, too. "My other therapist says I need to get rid of all my old garbage," she said, as she stomped into the room, and sat down in a snit, apparently angry at the other therapist. This immediately set me to thinking and analyzing the situation. *Hmm. I wonder if therapy can really be that simple. I wonder what that directive sounds like to her. I wonder where her parents are.*

We sat uncomfortably until enough time had gone by to

make it pretty clear that this teenager was not only involved in drinking and/or drugs, hospitalized for an endless time and trying to deal with a therapist telling her to change herself 100%, but her parents were not going to arrive, abandoning her with no explanation. *Gulp.* I hadn't been preparing to offer individual therapy. I felt small.

I didn't have much choice but to push on. We acknowledged that her parents didn't seem to be coming. Restlessly reviewing my own resources, I knew I'd worked in theater and broadcasting, and I had gathered that therapy is about listening, so I picked up the cue that she had offered.

"So, lets look at some garbage, then," I said, picking up the wastebasket. *Why not?* "What was in the wastebasket?" you might ask. I was lucky. I found what I needed that time.

There were three items in the wastebasket. There was a chewed piece of chewing gum. Not pleasant. There was the paper wrapper it came in, and the empty metallic container that once held five pieces of fresh new chewing gum. Items everybody can relate to. *Good. Now what?*

We talked about garbage. Not the way the other therapist did. We talked about cleaning up her bedroom and making decisions. Her parents would probably have been astonished. We talked about the options she would have if she were doing the cleaning. What if she was to handle her personal garbage the way she already knew how to clean up the house? What choices would she make? How would she know what to do?

Messy Toxic Stuff

Once we had a visual metaphor in hand, she was more attentive. I started saying that I thought I knew what the other therapist meant by garbage. We agreed that she had lots of "garbage" that consisted of emotions, deep feelings, behaviors, and thoughts that were all connected, but were swirling around in an unhelpful way.

I suggested that we accumulate stuff as we grow up and develop, and the stuff we accumulate is the *filter between the things we experience and our reactions*. Our garbage determines how we are going to think, feel, and behave in any given situation. Her other therapist was saying that if she was going to keep hurting herself in some way, then she needed to throw out the garbage that was making her do that. Otherwise, that garbage would keep pushing her in toxic directions that would be destructive for her.

I said I wanted to suggest something quite different about this problem. I wanted to make it easy to do and desirable— not punitive and impossible. I suggested that we imagine she was cleaning up her own private space, being purposeful and making choices, because her well-being mattered.

Could she identify parts of her that really were like chewed-up chewing gum, kind of messy, maybe even smelly, like stuff in her bedroom that was clearly toxic (dead squirrel in the corner; old sandwich under the pillow; half-eaten can of food or moldy glass of milk on the table)? Were there things that she would definitely throw away without any hesitation? Sure. Like banana peels or leftover chicken that's over the edge. That's the stuff the other therapist had been talking about. Unfortunately, all of us have some smelly garbage we are in denial about or try to avoid or don't want to talk about or feel ashamed about. We'd know what to do with it, too, if it was as simple as cleaning up a room.

This is certainly hard to do. Perhaps she pictured having a hangover, her indifference to danger, her fascination with being popular, or the joy she got out of being high. All of them were related to self-defeating behaviors that carried with them a cost to her well-being and a lot of tension in her family.

Anyway, we really threw out the piece of chewing gum.

Emphatically. Never looked back. It was icky, toxic, smelly, gross. Just gumming things up inside. Who would want to keep that?

Parts of Me Are Wonderful!

What next? She was still upset about the other therapist, I suggested, because he had said *everything* in her was awful, toxic, icky, and needed to be thrown out. I pointed out that if you start looking at yourself really carefully, you're going to find things you really like and don't want to throw away. There are ideas and feelings and beliefs and actions that help us know who we are, and we stand by them.

Perhaps she pictured her generosity, her loyalty to her family, or her skills at taking care of a smaller sibling.

We all know that we stash stuff in closets and attics, put things back in the cupboards. That stuff doesn't stink. We hold on to it. We could throw it out, but we make a different choice. One reason she was upset was that she believed some of her garbage was special, precious, valuable, and sacred. Sometimes things aren't even stashed in the closet, but we cherish them and display them on the mantelpiece, or on our walls.

I have all kinds of things in my office that are special to me, and which I wouldn't consider throwing away. They range from a useless little red stapler and a golden slinky, to paintings, old lamps, and model cars. Don't we all have those kinds of things in our rooms? Don't we make those kinds of choices all the time? What are we saying by keeping them and displaying them?

Working with my young client, we made the choice to claim the gum wrapper and keep it. Why? For one thing, it said "CAREFREE" on it. Now, this was something this teenager really needed in her situation. "Carefree" was something she needed to express and feel. In fact, we agreed that she should pin it on her shirt.

I suggested that there is a catch when you decide that something about you is worth holding on to. The problem is that it often doesn't match other people's expectations and standards. There can be a mysterious and confusing cost. I asked that she wear the gum wrapper so that she could take a stand about the things she valued about herself when people wondered why she was wearing it. This was a challenge that required self-confidence in order to build more self-confidence.

Imagine how much courage it took for her to return to the inpatient adolescent crowd wearing a gum wrapper, even if it did say something important. It's that hard to express our belief in ourselves sometimes. Not only that, she was there to change her behavior, not cling to it. Was she going to stand up to a therapist or her parents and say that she was going to be "carefree" about her addiction? Hopefully not, but she might have been able to say that she believed in herself and was capable of taking care of herself, liking herself, and making good choices in a carefree, relaxed, and confident way.

What do your pieces of garbage look, smell, and feel like? Do they stink? Are they a destructive part of you? Are they causing harm? Or, are they pieces of marvelous "stuff" that aren't causing harm and that you will stand by and own about yourself? Are they a part of your identity that you will continue to explain and defend? Choosing what to keep and what to throw away may not be easy choices, but they are important to talk about.

Recycle!

There was more. My newly carefree client and I started talking about recycling. What do we recycle? What kinds of things? The answers were very interesting. We recycle old news. We recycle empty cans and bottles.

How do we make that choice? What *qualities* do those items have? The stuff isn't useful to us any more, even though it was precious once. It doesn't stink. We don't need to keep it. It's empty, or it's just old news, but it was vital and full of meaning when it was *today's news* or when it was full of flavor or fizz and nourishment.

Don't we have responses and thoughts and behaviors that were well learned in our families or culture—or somewhere in our past experience—that are old news, or a lot like an empty can of peas or an empty Coke bottle? Can't we do something with them? If we're really exploring our garbage, can't we tell what's old news?

The metallic container for the gum also said "Carefree" on it, but it was definitely empty and of no further use as a gum container. It wasn't toxic, just empty. She definitely did not need another carefree gum-thing pinned to her. What to do?

We decided to recycle the gum container as a finger puppet.

We filled the empty recyclable "garbage" with something new. Kind of like getting today's newspaper or a new can of peas or a new bottle of Coke, and putting them in the empty place we have just created by choosing to see that something else was no longer useful to us.

All of our learned responses and behaviors can be replaced with careful therapeutic recycling, right? Isn't that the point of seeking guidance and trying to change?

The garbage metaphor is a metaphor that works for many people. I've used it a lot. We can see and feel the process. It's familiar. We can make *choices* that are healthy about "stuff" that isn't. Often, it turns out that much of what we perceive as pathological "garbage" isn't so awful after all. It can be managed, if you give yourself *permission* to manage it.

What happened in the case of the carefree client of our

story? I was a student and was only in the hospital part-time, and wasn't always told a lot. The young woman was discharged pretty quickly, even before I came back the next week. Maybe she felt much better and she could talk about it and her behavior changed. I don't actually know. I'd like to think she finally realized that she had permission to make choices about the source of her feelings, thoughts, and behaviors.

I do know that telling her story gives me a powerful and useful shorthand I can use. When I'm working with a couple, we can refer to "needing to recycle that" or say "What are you going to choose to do about that garbage?" or "Where did you pick up that piece?" When you're trying to work with others—even co-captains—it helps to have a shared language and something to visualize. When someone comes back and tells their own story of pausing to re-evaluate their behavior or their impulses, I know we have injected something between a squirrel-in-the-road moment and their behavior.

By reading this book, you are engaging in a reassessment of your own behavior, as related to your emotions, feelings, and thoughts. It is a process. Someone in enough pain to seek help is often seeking a way to slow down the jump from impulse to behavior. It is my role in this process to provide some guidance, give you ways to filter and slow your processes, and offer some kind of map. Granting yourself permission to explore the garbage and make choices can create just such a map.

Who else has this kind of reassessment helped?

Phil was a depressed young man with a history of losing jobs, getting angry at his child, and withdrawing from his wife. He'd been in therapy before, seemed hopeless, and had just been prescribed an anti-depressant. This time, he felt the need to face his own "garbage."

Whenever Phil feels a loss of control due to an impulse that may have been destructive, or feels more depressed, we discuss the feelings and thoughts and behaviors that come from his "garbage," take a close look, sniff around, and make choices. He now attends our infrequent sessions in a brighter mood, has a minimal dose of medication, feels positive about his new job, and has rebuilt his relationship with his wife and child. We have a common language, and he has applied it well to his own life. He seems to like himself more, and he treats himself better. He has actually named the garbage that he has discovered and made choices that make him healthier.

Melanie realized she was carrying around her father's negative perceptions of her as part of her garbage. That realization gave her the courage to imagine sending those perceptions to the dry cleaner, and put the clothes she'd been wearing in the closet, where she could check in with dad when she felt she needed to. She was free to think differently about herself and support her husband in ways she hadn't been able to before.

Tricia named the trait she found toxic, wrote it on a piece of paper, burned the paper, and put the ashes where she could see them as a reminder to catch herself and avoid costly choices. The process of handling her garbage helped her find a voice to use with her husband when she needed him to consider her needs and the impact of his behavior.

With a simple metaphor as a tool, you can pick up your own cues from emotions that warn you that you are about to repeat a pattern or harm a relationship. It can be used when needed to avoid failure or to relieve pain. Or, like Tricia, you can even use a visual crutch that interrupts an automatic rush to feelings, thoughts, and behaviors that you are trying to change.

We've already described your emotional tipping point in a few memorable ways (the boat is tipping, you're a squirrel in the road, you are feeling small, you are from different planets). Maybe it will help if we equate it to seeing a cockroach. Stay tuned.

CAPTAIN'S LOG

You have permission to make choices that clean up your thoughts, feelings, and actions.

11

Cockroaches!

Even when we feel like the boat is running smoothly, something can be so overwhelming that we have the same old response. What's going on?

> There is power when individuals discover that no one is coming to rescue them—that if they don't do something different, nothing in their life is going to get better.
> When that thought connects, it's electrifying. A lot of people turn their lives around in quite marvelous and exciting ways, simply because they decided to stop waiting for help.
>
> > - Nathaniel Branden
> > author of *The Psychology of Self-Esteem*

Let's just say for the moment that the seas feel a little calmer, the storms aren't as frequent, and maybe you're even creeping a little closer to each other from your outposts on each side of the boat. Maybe you are getting the hang of this idea that you are both captains and it takes work to communicate well, but you've always wanted to do the right thing for the boat. The reality is that there are plenty of issues that could make the boat tippy again, stemming from the familiar list of money, sex, in-laws, the kids, the house, the job—and compounded by your own "garbage" and the way it directs your responses. It's still a boat and it is not under your complete control.

It is not always easy to catch yourself at your tipping point and modify your behavior. Sometimes you "just do it," but it is really obvious that you shouldn't. Consider the ad on TV for a local hospital that featured "friends" of a fellow with a painful knee injury. A helpful friend twists his own knee and asks "Does it hurt if you do this?" and after the poor victim presumably groans, he helpfully chirps, "Well, *I wouldn't do that*, then!" Perhaps it hurts as much as a knee injury to behave the way you are behaving, when you really think about it, and that might be much more obvious to a friend or partner of yours. It might also be kind of obvious that you shouldn't be behaving the way you are, because your behavior hurts *you*.

Once it had hit me so hard that it is crazy normal for *both* people to feel small and look big at the same time, it became a mission of mine to keep identifying situations that were intuitively obvious "feeling small" moments. The search was on for ways to connect familiar experiences to the idea that the sensation of feeling small is predictable, reliable, and possible to handle. I looked high and low and found a true story about my own family that illustrated exactly what I was talking about.

That Overwhelming Moment

My mother was not a drama queen, and that seemed like a good thing because it created a sense of safety and stability. I took her even-keeled nature for granted until I needed to look more closely at my family in order to work effectively with couples and families. I began to wonder how it was that she remained calm when unexpected or difficult things happened to her. Eventually, I connected the dots between my mother's stoic calm and a story about her and cockroaches. When I started thinking about this story, it occurred to me just what it is like, emotionally, to experience what I call *a cockroach moment,* and what we all struggle with—even if we are calm most of the time.

According to my theory, one explanation for my mother's serenity must be that she grew up in a home without cockroaches. She was fortunate enough to miss that whole traumatic experience of finding an unexpected cockroach in the kitchen, and thus got used to the world being a manageable and predictable place. When she had upsetting moments, she could calm herself by asserting her belief that there was nothing impossibly alarming. Not everyone has this luxury, however, and we might conclude that our experiences with or without cockroaches determine our destiny.

Certainly, everyone has moments when they feel small, or when the boat is tipping, or when there is a truck coming down the road. But, if we are not conditioned to jump at those cockroach moments, maybe we are less likely to jump at other moments, as well. It seemed plausible to me and gave me another way to illustrate an emotional challenge.

Bigger and Bigger Cockroaches

Well, it so happens that every boat is different from the children's perspective. When I was growing up, from our perspective as children, it was important to be sure that my mother would be emotionally solid under dire circumstances, so we knew that we would be safe and secure. My older brother took the lead in challenging my mother's ability to stay cool—for her sake, of course.

When he was done with college, married, and the father of a baby, my brother moved to New York City and lived in an apartment. Naturally, my mother was invited down to New York, but this was actually a challenge because she really was going to come face to face with New York cockroaches. She had a choice to make between avoiding possible trauma, or being a mom and grandma, so of course, down to New York she went. In New York, the cockroaches are an inch or two long and don't like it when the lights are on. I presume my mother had a serious learning experience about cockroaches.

New York roaches do scurry back to darker places when the lights are on, however, and this was apparently good enough for my mother. When we both visited my brother and his family, I recall that she slept with the lights on, presumably so she wouldn't be overrun at night, and she covered her eyes and flicked the kitchen lights on in the morning before venturing in to make her coffee. As far as I know, she didn't lose her traditional cool and passed the New York test.

I Missed!

Of course, children are relentless about their parents' emotional health, and just staying civil around New York cockroaches was not enough proof for us that she could always handle trauma. After my brother's second child, the family moved to an apartment in the oldest part of San Juan, Puerto Rico, where the cockroaches were enormous and they didn't care if the lights were on. The roaches had been living there forever, and the humans were the real intruders. Grandma was once again invited to visit, and she had a choice of whether to rest on her laurels or try to handle Puerto Rican cockroaches. She made the obvious choice and headed for San Juan. This time, however, she did not hold herself together. According to family legend, this is the scene that unfolded:

In the kitchen on a sunny day, the two grandchildren were with their mother and grandmother—and the usual cockroaches—when all of a sudden grandma had reached her limit. She took her shoe off and swung wildly at a cockroach on the floor, but missed. "Damn it—I missed!" she yelled.

Anyone who had known her for very long would have realized that this was an exceptional moment, and those in the room were startled and silenced—all except for her youngest grandson.

Immediately attentive to his upset grandmother, the little boy tried to take care of the situation while everyone else was startled. Not knowing how rare it was for her to be upset, he immediately comforted her by saying "Poor Grandma," and then he tried to counsel her by saying, "Don't worry, Grandma, there will be another one. You'll get the next one. There are plenty of them."

There Will Be Another One

How does this story tie in to what we've been talking about? Well, now that you are getting used to being on a boat, you need to realize that there are going to be many startling moments when it doesn't feel like things are under control. Whatever guide you use, whether it is an inspirational book, a more clinical book, individual therapy, or the direct experience of marriage counseling, you will be starting with the little cockroaches and working your way up. There is no other way to do it. It is a learning process, and you will build a different foundation in your garbage that you will be able to use as bigger cockroaches come along. When you do have a cockroach moment at your tipping point, it is an opportunity to learn how you are doing, what size your various cockroaches are, and what issues still cause trauma for your relationship.

The other reason this story is important is that my mother said something very important when she screamed and lost her cool.

Let's say that you are taking this process seriously and identifying your tipping point and your vulnerabilities regarding your partnership. Let's say you are beginning to identify your own cockroach moments—the triggers that make the boat feel tippy to you. If one of those moments comes along and you lose your balance, but you can say "Damn it—I missed (my cockroach)," then you are owning your own difficulty with holding yourself together under those circumstances. Simply owning that vulnerability—and that failure—can make a special difference in your relationship.

Consider how my nephew, age four, would have responded to his grandma if she'd finally just let everyone have it by screaming about how dirty all of their homes have been, how they always had cockroaches and didn't seem to care, how it was their fault, etc. What would he have said? The answer is: he probably would have run from the room and hidden somewhere. Instead, because grandma owned the problem— even as she was melting and screaming—he could hang in there, find a voice, comfort her, and offer counseling. That is exactly what you want your partner to be able to do.

Hence, if you are the person falling to pieces because you are reaching some kind of limit, then owning the moment—and the behavior—creates an opportunity for you and your partner to seek comfort, inject some perspective and humor, recognize how hard the person is trying to overcome their cockroaches, and build partnership.

I know that it is hard to see these moments as opportunities, but they really are. In fact, why not imagine that you are in the fog at these moments, out on that boat. You are sailing the boat as co-captains, you built the boat and invested in the boat, and now you are in the fog. We will return to this idea in Chapter 26, but for now let's consider a definition of "FOG" for both of you. What could FOG stand for?

FOG is a F---ing Opportunity for Growth

This kind of unsettling moment is decidedly a mixed blessing, and it feels like it. It may not be a moment you enjoy—it's probably a moment you'd like to avoid—but it is full of potential for your personal maturation, development, and growth.

A cockroach moment gives both people an opportunity. When you are upset, it is your opportunity to catch yourself, limit the damage, and own your vulnerabilities. If your partner is the one who is upset, it is your opportunity to let them be emotional by being non-judgmental, while offering encouragement and support. At a tipping point—or a cockroach moment—you can define yourselves *and* your relationship. Both of you are challenged to grow as these opportunities come your way.

Can this happen? Can two people handle situations eye to eye (I to I), both be powerful and distinct, and create something greater than the sum of their parts? That is the next stage of our journey.

CAPTAIN'S LOG

When you're trying to change your reaction to tension, there are lots of opportunities.

12

Eye (I to I) Level Connection

Couples can catch themselves and become calmer, more equal partners. Looking into each other's eyes and souls can make the journey feel safer and more meaningful, even if it is still unpredictable.

> What I'm describing is called *mutuality . . .* as a perspective, a mind-set, it offers a solution to the central struggle of any long-term relationship: going forward with your own self-development while being concerned with your partner's happiness and well-being.
>
> - David Schnarch
> *Passionate Marriage*

Maybe this mindful and unconditional intimacy seems like a stretch to you right now. Maybe you didn't expect this commitment to feel so much like a boat in rough waters. Maybe you really weren't prepared for the disappointment or the tippiness. Maybe you simply need some reassurance that what you are experiencing is normal.

What Kind of Boat Are You? What Kind of Boat Have You Built?

I've been assuming that you built a sailboat, but there are many variations of craft that fit that general description. Different sailboats are different sizes and speeds and are chosen for different purposes. You weren't necessarily discussing the boat while you built it, and (as we discussed earlier) you may not have even known you were building a boat. What do you suppose your intentions were?

Maybe you really don't like boats. Maybe the whole idea of being on a boat makes you seasick. Maybe that's why one or both of you dragged your feet about this commitment.

Maybe you really are both sailboat people, but have a different idea of your kind of sailboat. Is it more like a dingy, or a surfboard with a sail, something more lake-appropriate or ocean ready, or is it a very comfortable yacht?

Maybe you aren't really a sailboat kind of person at all. A battleship or speedboat or, at the very least, a boat with a motor is more your style. Maybe you picture yourself on a canal boat, easing your way up and down rivers, or a boat that carries passengers across a lake, or a compact, fun motorboat that gets to that breathtaking remote island quickly with some great sunbathing on the way.

Is that the same kind of boat your partner has built?

What do you suppose you built together? Is it some kind of hybrid of your two kinds of boats? Is it some kind of compromise, and you are still working out the details? Can you take a moment to appreciate your handiwork? Is there a way to make the whole boat even more seaworthy than just combining the sum of its original parts?

I don't even know you, but I suspect you can be a content couple if you get used to the idea that it is *your boat* and you are both captains, needing to be ready to make decisions, recognizing that there are risks involved, and working together to get wherever you are going, while relying on yourselves to handle the unknown and the unexpected. Those are the qualities of a good sailor—and a good partner.

Real Couples Handle the Boat

In other parts of our lives, I think we all experience the difference between *building* a boat and *sailing* a boat. For instance, in most jobs (including childcare) there is a planning aspect and a doing aspect. When we are planning, dreaming, designing, or creating something, we might also be selling, buying, proposing, imagining, or enjoying high expectations. We may find this part of the process attractive and fascinating, perhaps because something is mysterious and unknown, perhaps because of the thrill, or that competitive, exhilarating, hopeful "I'm special" feeling that can turn us on.

When we are in the "doing mode," by contrast, we are experiencing responsibility, a budget, a timetable, productivity, comparisons, pressure, the risk of disappointment, perhaps a lack of control, and possible defeat. There may be depressing, boring, complicated anxious feelings of "I'm not special; I want to know the answer; where are we going, and what's going to happen next?"

One of the ways we set ourselves up to be upset is that we forget that we are on a boat—or that building a boat is different from being on one. When we are making that sale to a new customer, starting a new relationship, teaching a child, designing a new project, or changing things around, we are in boat-building mode; when we are reviewing the budget, dealing with sexual issues, money, or our kids, keeping to a schedule, holding a meeting, meeting a deadline, or keeping a customer happy, we are on the boat and co-captaining. The planning aspect usually feels more exciting, creative, competitive, and fascinating. The maintenance aspect is more responsible, complicated, and risky—in a less-positive way. One aspect makes you feel you are doing something new and special, while the other may make you feel ordinary, and perhaps stuck—or even worthless. If this is what you are experiencing, you're not crazy.

I am very grateful that I chose to go into the field of couples therapy. The work I do is a privilege and it keeps me very alive. Sometimes the dividends are fascinating, as they were one spring day that seemed like any other day until a few of my visitors provided the gift of serendipity and synergy that led to this chapter, simply by using their hands.

First, an always-interesting Eb and Flo came in, who were learning to navigate their two-captain boat, remember the other side of the kaleidoscope, and be more than squirrels. Eb had done a lot of personal work to listen better to Flo, collaborate with her more, and not just handle things his way. Flo was very appreciative, and began to describe the changes she had been making. Flo had learned, with the help of her own therapist, to slow down her reactions to Eb's behavior, and to let him experience the impact of his own actions by being less protective of him. She had needed to do this for her own integrity and mental health. Then she began to talk the language of our sessions together.

Flo had realized that she was "also a captain" of the boat, and was responsible for pulling herself up to a level of equality with her husband, speaking to him in a direct way, owning her own side of the boat and acting like an important person. She *used her hands* to show how she had been smaller than her perception of Eb and raised her self up to an equal middle level with Eb by making him look smaller and her self feel bigger through dialogue, listening and interacting in a healthy way. She held her hands in midair at an equal level as she described the satisfaction and serenity that came with this kind of relationship. To me, the key thing she was saying was that claiming her half of the boat in a responsible way led to a satisfying, hands-level, eye-to-eye relationship that was somehow elevated and animated in midair.

This talk of connecting on an intimate, and balanced, level made me recall another couple that used my language to develop their own. They talked about the danger of "taking an elevator" (looking big too quickly after feeling small) and realized that what they wanted to have was "gumball to gumball" conversations, where both people could tolerate and admit to feeling small by sharing their insecurities and vulnerabilities.

Responsibility

Another couple you've met came in that day. They were just beginning their journey, not quite aware yet that they were both captains or ready to concede that it was a boat. They presented quite a dilemma. This Eb apparently showers in the dark, but Flo doesn't treat his shower as a priority. Flo shaves in the shower and leaves her razor blades dangling when she is done. Eb is terrified that he will be cut in the dark and tells Flo sternly that she needs to pick up after herself when she showers. However, Flo shaves first, and then lets her creative writer's mind wander, forgetting about her razor blade by the end of her shower, despite Eb's demands.

Taking a cue from my earlier visitors, I asked how they were going to reach an eye-to-eye level connection, illustrating with my hands. Eb saw Flo as absent-minded and uncaring about his needs. Flo saw Eb as demanding and detail-oriented. There was a complete lack of communication about Eb's real fear of being cut in the dark, Flo's need to chill out, or their shared responsibility regarding the shower. Really, either captain who was ready to change and not hold a grudge could have taken responsibility and moved the small *and* large dynamic to something more even and balanced.

Gradually and grudgingly, Eb offered to check for Flo's razor blades before turning the lights out, recognizing that Flo was taking a break from baby care, being creative, and not thinking about details, as he put them out of harm's way. Equally, Flo eventually offered to really notice the shower and picture Eb in the dark giving himself a moment of escape and contentment, and to make sure it was safe for him, without resentment. When these thoughts and cares were seen as considering the other's need for a restorative balance—and not as caving in to the other—either one of them could take the initiative without losing dignity, and defuse the situation.

I to I Contact

My next session was with a man who intuitively trusts the clinical process of personal growth as an anchor throughout the intense drama of his life. While we were talking that day, Alan proudly coined the concept of "I to I contact," positing that it was both more compelling and important than "eye-to-eye contact," while clearly being related.

Alan had played with words in a way that connected him to Eb and Flo. He was using his hands the same way to illustrate a fascination with balanced intimacy as a dynamic between two people at the same level, looking at each other and being themselves with each other in a way that was special for both. We went on to discuss the benefits and challenges of relating at "I-level." We discussed how challenging it is to have a strong voice as a captain, or to share control of the boat, or to experience open-ended foreplay without quite knowing how it will turn out. I again noticed that when this type of relating is illustrated with hands, that the hands are suspended in air, creating an active, trusting fluid dynamic, forged by the two hands being at the same level.

I to I in Action

David Schnarch, who also writes books for couples, but focuses more on sexual dynamics, has actually titled one chapter of his book *Passionate Marriage* "Eyes Open Orgasm." He is using the idea of a moment of fully aware and shared orgasm to create a compelling image of what he means by "differentiation"—a point when a couple can *both* share intimacy *and* see each other clearly as distinct, separate individuals. Imagine sharing an intimate moment when you are also fully aware of your partner and how they are distinct, unusual, and definitely different from you, in an exciting way. That is exactly the kind of "I to I," "gumball-to-gumball" moment that my clients were discussing that day. All of them were recognizing the special energy that comes through trust and shared responsibility, when both people are feeling the same size, accepting and appreciating each other, and enjoying the moment

For one couple I've worked with, this I to I approach meant a balanced response to intrusive in-laws, while to another it meant finding a consistent way to parent their blended family so that his kids and her kids can turn to both parents and know what they are likely to hear. For still another couple, this meant sleeping separately, even after having sex, because they kept each other awake at night and needed the sleep.

It may not all sound very orgasmic, but I encourage eyeball-to-eyeball give and take when couples communicate boldly in my office and at home.

Strategies for Intimacy

It occurs to me that we are trying to redefine intimacy in a profound way. While it is clear that couples crave intimacy, it is not clear that we know what we are measuring—or how to know if we are getting what we want. There are some helpful examples of ways that you can redefine what you are measuring, so that you can actually begin to get the satisfaction that you seek.

For instance, on a local radio show about relationships, a couple shared that they take the time each evening to listen to each other's narrative of the day. They don't interrupt each other and they don't have to make comments. They share their stories, listen well, and then get on with the evening. They feel this relationship has been more meaningful than any other they have experienced. Their daily "I to I" ritual is not measured in orgasms or flowers or gifts—or even hugs—but has given them something special.

I recall Felipe, who kept gravitating to the problems he had with his wife's behavior. I eventually asked him to measure *his own* behavior, instead. I helped him to understand that it was simply pointless to keep using someone else's behavior as a reference, unless the goal was to be frustrated and entitled. If Felipe really wanted peace of mind and a sense of mastery, he needed to notice his own responses and actions, and to measure how he was handling himself. I kept telling him he would be even more attractive to his wife in an intimate way if he could take charge of his own insecurities in a more self-reliant way. Eventually, this change of focus helped him to be more of a captain and less like a dependent crew member, freeing both Felipe and his wife of *his dependency on her reactions*, and helping them appreciate each other with more clarity.

Whether we are in creativity mode or responsibility mode, an intimate balance is the goal of our work. I hear testimony every working day from people about feeling something deeper and more satisfying when they are able to strive for balanced and collaborative "I to I" reactions to tension, take the responsibility of being a captain, or use a strategy that increases intimacy in all of its potential forms.

We, as humans, are quite capable of developing, negotiating, and executing strategies that are good for us—and for our relationships. Those of us who will really thrive and raise solid, healthy children will be flexible about our strategies, listen well, make our needs known, keep our balance, and take the risk of intimate and complicated connection.

CAPTAIN'S LOG

Intimacy can mean a balanced response to each other, I to I.

13

Second Interlude – Calmer Waters

Sitting on the dock and watching the boats again. What might the neutral observer notice that could be helpful the next time your boat feels tippy?

> The message of the crazy wisdom master is, "You're not so important, and reality is much, much bigger than you." It's a message that allows us to step back and be lighter, and that's exactly what we need to do.
>
> - Wes Nisker
> author of *Crazy Wisdom*

Again, this chapter is full of reflections and open-ended ideas. Read it in a way that is comfortable and see what it makes you think about.

All Aboard!

Perhaps we carry around a map that says women like to be

pleased and men like to be *impressed*. We can apply this formula to our parents and partners, to our expectations of our children, or to ourselves as we define ourselves and see if it is valid in a useful way.

**

Recently, I was asked where in my body my voice was coming from. What a wonderful question. If our voice is coming from a place high in our body, it has less force. If we are using all of our body and we can feel it starting in our legs and working through all of us, it is a much more meaningful voice, and our partner will notice. We are told the same thing when we go to dog-training school, which, of course, is really people-training school.

The lower and deeper our voice, the more likely our dog is to hear us and respond to what we want. Perhaps we should apply the same principle to our partnerships when we have something important to say.

**

Batten Down the Hatches

"Diplomacy is the *art* of letting the other person have it your way," said my sage supervisor. Everybody wins when we take the time to be diplomatic and considerate, and put aside the idea that we need to *win* to be fulfilled.

**

If you have a baby who is just learning to stand up and walk, what do you do? Do you always protect them from harm and constantly try to catch them? Do you let them fall so they learn about getting hurt? Do you pad the floor and hope they feel safe *and* competent when there are risks? The safety of someone important to you can be a constant dilemma and requires a balanced approach.

**

Aye, Aye, Captain

I've learned to expect you to have these characteristics:
You're likely to feel small at tense moments, and not want to feel any smaller.
You're often measuring something about yourself, in comparison to other people.
Your normal mental process is helping you to create your current distortion of your situation.
You are taking care of yourself in order to grow.
And, you desire a calm, safe sense that things are under control.

**

Your responses don't need to be elegant, as long as they are yours. You may be familiar with the beloved TV detective, Columbo. He got at the truth in a clumsy, amusing, disarming, reassuring, and surprising way. He admitted that he was smaller and more confused than the other characters, and he always solved the case.

**

Hold On!

Sometimes an image is hard to forget: A cartoon drawing

depicting a conference of "Adult Children of Normal Parents" (by Jennifer Berman—go ahead, google it) is actually an almost empty auditorium with two odd looking people attending. Please be aware that other people are not from perfect families, either.

**

Finding it hard to handle two other people (your partner and their mother, your child and their parent, your sister and her husband)?

Imagine the three of you as points on a triangle.

It is important to understand that relationships form triangles. We have multiple tangled triangles in our families and that is normal.

In each and every triangle, there are two direct personal relationships for you to guide and one other line that you can't really reach because the two solid lines that involve you directly hold you in place.

Concentrate on your own relationships and remember that you can't control the third side. This works both ways. If someone seems to be intruding on your relationship with someone else, they can't *really* manipulate your relationships. Those are up to you.

I call this the rule of the triangles.

**

Navigating By The Stars

If we think of adolescence *positively* as a remarkable opportunity to claim what is distinct about ourselves and find out what we are passionate about, then we can look forward to the same exciting crossroads when our children are adolescent, and maybe even when our grandchildren are adolescent. It is merely an opportunity to challenge ourselves, ask big questions, make adjustments, and grow.

**

Checking The Compass

On my own personal journey, I've been exposed to the idea that "categorical thinking" is a liability.

To discriminate, categorize, or simplify our perception of someone else costs us, as we lose perspective on the worth and dignity of that person, and jeopardize our chances of building a meaningful connection with them.

This is not only a warning about sexism or racism with strangers, but a reminder that we can be oversimplifying our assumptions about our partner due to some "garbage" of our own.

**

Do you know when you look big to your partner (or anyone else)? When you use a voice that you feel is reasonable and the *reaction* you get makes you sit up straight and feel like an arrow just went over your head, you are looking big. Your behavior has made them feel small.

**

Changing Tack

Is it that surprising that our intimate partnerships change when we have made a commitment to each other and made it more permanent? We are often very different as job seekers than we are as employees. Ask any employer who has hired someone whose performance is far short of expectations.

Surprised employers are constantly seeking a more reliable way to know how we are going to perform, as are disappointed partners. We change when we are hired, just as we change when we enter a serious partnership, or get on a boat.

**

If we naturally *distort* our perceptions in order to have them match with our most comfortable understandings, then perhaps the most authentic dialogue would sound something like this: "This is my distortion. What's yours?"

**

The fortune cookie reads, "The hammer forgets but the board always knows" as they experience abusive behavior. We are much more aware of our own feelings and our impressions and memories of others than we are of the impact of our behavior on others. It need not be surprising that a hammer looks different from the board's point of view—not to mention the nail's.

**

Squalls Ahead

Men do get the message that emotions are messy and avoidable, and as boys they learn to leave them to girls and women, who learn that emotions are more like the ocean, ebbing and flowing, or the boat bobbing and tipping, but always there.

These are very different experiences.

Men can learn that their emotional life flows in a continuous way, and there aren't clean answers, in spite of the male cultural messages that they bring into their relationships. Women can learn that there can be valuable times of structure and relief from emotional churning. Both can step back and take a break from what seems to come naturally.

**

Making Headway—Set the Spinnaker

A couple I know was once helped by a doctor in a way that may help other couples.

My understanding is that when she was diagnosed with lupus, her doctor met with both of them, said that the condition was chronic, and told them they would need to make adjustments. She would only have a certain amount of energy and they would need to make decisions about what they wanted to use that energy for (a job, sex, cleaning the house, travel, and raising children strike me as obvious possibilities). The part I know is that they decided not to put energy into cleaning the house and that she would work part time. They lived with the limitations, stood by their decisions, openly acknowledged their house was messy, and handled her chronic illness while raising two children.

Accepting both of your limitations, discussing what they are, and applying your energies to what you both want can be a successful strategy for a couple.

**

After the Boston Marathon bombing, the mother of the Chinese graduate student who had died apparently spoke of children as

"Buddhas" who exist to help parents grow. What a wonderful perspective, to see children (or our partners) as a blessing during the endless process of our own personal growth, even at a time of loss and change.

**

Rocky Ride

Caretakers, co-dependents, rescuers, and empathizers beware, there are times when the person being taken care of can experience your attention as arrogant, infantilizing, and dismissive. As a professional caretaker and co-dependent, this has been a harsh lesson.

**

I witnessed honest outrage firsthand when an organization suddenly decided to start downsizing by releasing a part-time employee. The staff, myself included, were seemingly unanimous in wanting to address the injustice by earnestly holding meetings, seeking solutions, discerning the real needs and wants of the organization, and so forth. We were moved by our emotions to take constructive action about a place we had trusted. Our actions felt good, but no policies were changed. The next time someone lost their job there wasn't as much outrage, and it gradually slipped into being a place that people chose to leave as it became more toxic. It is important to grasp the moment when our relationships are at a tipping point, address the issues, risk some discomfort, really seek lasting solutions, and make changes before we lose our sense of injustice or outrage and just accept a situation that just gets worse.

**

We're At Loggerheads

Is one of you more organized or more spontaneous than the other? What are the benefits for both of you?

Be careful if you don't want the other person to "be so controlling," because their ability to organize things *or* to be intuitive may come from their desire to have things feel like they are under control, and it may work. Be careful what you *don't* wish for.

**

One husband discovered that he had "tunnel-vision." I suspect this is true of many men—thinking in a linear and logical way, being expedient, simplifying when they can, and avoiding emotions because they're messy. A dose of this may be just what their partners need when they start spinning.

Many women say they just want to be heard. If the spinning is actually going to slow down, it is important for *him* to listen first and offer a small dose of tunnel vision.

One wife discovered that she was "an emotional sponge." I suspect this is true of many women—thinking in a global way, being extremely aware of feelings and emotions, and elaborating on their inner experience when they can. A dose of this may be just what their partners need when they are stuck.

Many men say they just want to be understood. If the "stuckness" is going to loosen up, it is important for *her* to listen first and offer a small dose of the emotional sponge.

**

No Wind . . . We're Becalmed

Expectations are fascinating. Maybe we have a set of expectations about our partner as soon we have sex with them, based on how foreplay unfolds and how we have sex.

Perhaps a man expects that once it happens, he will be wanted and desired by this person and she will always be available to him.

Maybe a woman expects that she will be protected and loved by this person and that he will always express himself openly, exclusively, and gently with her.

It is jarring when lovemaking is not a permanent statement of something safe, reliable, and fun, but rather a door to more complicated intimacy, instead.

**

I use a pillow to illustrate to a couple that both people are feeling small and both are looking big.

	[PILLOW]	
person	[PILLOW]	person
	[PILLOW]	

The vertical side of the pillow facing each person represents the escalation that transforms a moment of feeling small into a behavior that looks big. The bottom edge of the pillow represents the connection they can have when they are both confiding that they feel small, while the top edge represents conflict between two people who both look big. Both people can do something about their side and aim to *reach out along the bottom* rather than staging conflict across the top. We can also develop strategies to address all four corners of the pillow in order to feel like this crazy normal distortion is more under control.

**

Bermuda Triangle

The husband confided, "My parents were so disappointing that I decided not to be disappointing. When I am being criticized or judged, or talked about behind my back, I fly into a rage."
Have you defined yourself in comparison to your parents and set yourself up for anger at yourself?
What does anger at yourself look like to the other captain?
When your parents' behavior is still powerful, what happens on your boat?

**

Shipwreck

It is normal to compare yourself to other people and have feelings about fairness. Perhaps you are involved in sports and have a visceral reaction when the umpire or referee judges against you or your team. If you slowed down your reaction you would realize that you are biased toward yourself and most of the time the referee's neutral objective view is accurate.
What would instant replay tell you?

**

Sometimes when someone is telling me about their partner's faults, I'll interrupt and ask them to imagine they are talking into a mirror. How often are we talking accurately about our partner and how often are we *actually* talking *accurately* about *ourselves*, based on what we know, or don't want to know, about ourselves?

**

Sailing is Not a Picnic

In a game like football or golf, *unknowns* within the structure of the game are exciting but not threatening like personal change can be. The excitement from contained uncertainty does lead to a fascination with drama, conflict, and tension, but at least not knowing what is going to happen isn't deeply threatening. It is actually more challenging to succeed when the unknowns are less well contained and something is at stake emotionally, like they are when we are seeking personal harmony and intimacy.

**

I have this theory that came to me during the excruciating drama after the 2000 presidential election between George W. Bush and Al Gore. Our Western democracies generally divide pretty equally between liberal and conservative, and I wondered if maybe there is a discernable psychological divide based in our families of origin.

My theory is that each of us, within our families, fall into one of four camps:
Some want to please our fathers.
Some want to oppose our fathers.
Some want to please our mothers.
Some want to oppose our mothers.
And, in my theory, the father-opposers and mother-pleasers are liberals, while the father-pleasers and mother-opposers

are conservatives. One of the four camps could be the most important place for us to be. This could actually be what splits us in half when we vote, or respond viscerally to the events of November 2000.

The premise is that liberal ideologies emphasize the feminine virtues of collaboration, peace, fairness, etc., while conservative ideologies emphasize the more masculine virtues of structure, being punitive, being superior, being independent, etc. Perhaps we simply pick which response to our parents is most important to us for our own well-being and vote accordingly.

14

Who's in Charge Here?

Is anyone steering the boat? It's easier to know whether you feel like a captain than it is to know whether the co-captain feels the same way. How do you find out how well you are doing at navigating this boat?

> You can't sail straight into the wind, and if you only know how to sail the boat with the wind at your back, you will only go where the wind blows you.
>
> But if you know how to use the wind's energy and are patient, you can sometimes get where you want to go. You can still be in control. . . . Good sailors learn to read (the weather) carefully and respect its power, . . . they know when to take down the sails, . . . drop anchor, and ride things out, controlling what is controllable and letting go of the rest.
>
> - Jon Kabat-Zinn
> *Full Catastrophe Living*

At some point on this voyage, you are going to look in the mirror and wonder if you are a good enough captain of the boat. It is natural and important to try to judge your own performance, but that does not mean that it is an easy matter. The dynamics of an intimate relationship get complex, and it can seem like things are happening too quickly and getting out of control. It is when having control matters to us that our behavior can be negative or hurtful.

Imagine a family with a young child, about age six, who has been so difficult to parent that a mental health professional has suggested that the child be hospitalized because of their escalating attitude and behavior. If you were the parents, you would feel pretty helpless and overpowered. You could also be very willing to try family therapy at the hospital to try to defuse the destructive dynamics that are leading your child to take risks that are potentially very costly for them, and making you feel like you've failed.

I worked at a hospital, and was assigned to work with the families of young children who had entered the inpatient unit. I knew that each family would be attentive to my efforts, but I also felt the urgent need to try something inventive that would make a difference in a short time. Everyone in the family wanted peace and safety. The question was how to illustrate that everyone was responding the same way to a lack of control.

Escalation, Furniture, and How Big You Feel

At the hospital, I was using a very small office with a very clean desk, small chairs for the children, and bigger chairs for the parents. It became a laboratory for illustrating how people respond when they feel small.

I would start by treating everyone equally and not blaming

the young child for the family drama. By simply asking *how* tension typically built up in the family, I would kick off a discussion of dynamics, and it would usually create enough tension in the room for the hospitalized child to stand up. That was my cue to point out that the child was responding to tension and pressure about dynamics that were troubling to everyone, by making himself bigger. I framed this moment as the child raising the alarm that something was troubling or uncomfortable. I would ask for an example of a way the child's behavior seemed big at home—perhaps it was his or her refusal to eat a simple meal or not come to the table.

I would then ask how the parents responded to this initial behavior, while noticing that they were physically sinking, defeated, perhaps ashamed, into their chairs as the child stood up and disrupted our conversation. Often, the mother would say she was the one at home, and she would scold or try to discipline the child. To illustrate the dynamics of power, I would have that parent stand up, too, making the child relatively small again. Asking what would happen next, they would describe an escalated behavior by the child—for instance throwing food or yelling at the parent. I'd have the child stand on a small chair, making the mother small again. What would the mother do, then? Perhaps she would call the father for reinforcement, and he would come home and threaten the child with some sanction. I would ask him to stand up, too, making the child feel small again.

The drama would escalate from their narrative. Each time the child's behavior escalated, I would have the child stand on a taller piece of furniture, and each time a parent reacted, I would also elevate them to a higher level in the office. Eventually, the child was standing on the desk, with the parents on chairs. Perhaps, by that point of the narrative, the parents had sent them to their room and taken away the television, while the child had kept shouting, perhaps breaking something or wrecking the bedroom door and acting out in ways that could be dangerous to all involved, especially the child. We had recreated the behavior that had alarmed the family (and/or a therapist) enough to make hospitalization necessary. That is when I would stop the drama and have *everyone but the child* return to their original seats. The child would be towering over the family from the desk, and I would ask everyone what they were experiencing.

Invariably, the parents would say the child was getting what he or she wanted, finally having power and control over the family from above. They had consistently been trying to keep the child from having control and had been defeated. What was the child's perception?

Every child who experienced this surprised their family. They all said they wanted *to get down*. They expressed that it felt "wrong," or "upside-down." They wanted to be in their little chair, smaller than their parents. They did not like having power. The parents were speechless.

This crucial moment in family meetings gave me an opportunity to work with the parents, talking about the pattern, their responsibility as the adults, the way they were responding when they felt small and their child looked big, and the fact that the result "felt wrong" to their child. I only held the child responsible for responding to tension to begin with, as a family barometer. I needed the parents to change their responses, to handle the challenge differently. I hope these were helpful, empowering, and meaningful learning experiences.

Instead of shrinking into their seats and then bursting into behavior that made the child small, the parents finally realized they needed to be more ready for their own discomfort, and have more tools to use that wouldn't make them look so big.

This is also true in your relationship with your partner. Just imagine one of your conflicts resulting in one of you wishing you weren't alone on top of the desk, and see if you can use some of the tools in this book to keep it from happening.

It is our behavior that makes us looks big to the other person. It is normal within our crazy normal distortion for our own behavior to seem smaller to us than it does to our partner. If you are viscerally and intuitively noticing their response flying over your head, it is because you are looking bigger than you are feeling. You can not control their response, but you can control your voice, your actions, the words you are choosing, the tone of voice you are using, whether you interrupt them, how you are sitting, whether you are using eye contact, your attitude, etc. They can't control your behavior. It's all on you—and it makes a difference. If you want your dynamics to feel better, for there to be less tension (and more intimacy), you have the power to change your reaction to feeling small and behave differently. If you know, through listening, what makes your partner feel small, you can adjust your behavior accordingly. After all, why do something that makes them feel small if they are just going to compensate by doing something big?

How much do you know about behaviors that make your partner feel small? Do they feel slighted if you walk past them and don't have any eye contact? Do they feel unimportant if you interrupt them? Do they feel attacked when you react impulsively to something? Do they feel unwanted when you turn on the TV and grab a beer or grab the phone and connect with friends or family? Does it frustrate your partner when you contradict yourself? What is going on at their end of the kaleidoscope?

Feeling Like a Captain

You want to be the best possible captain of your boat. The problem is that you can't measure what we would normally measure in judging the captain of a boat. Boat captains (or military officers or airline pilots) are excellent leaders, according to certain standards. Were there any accidents? Did everyone follow orders? Did everything happen on time and as planned? Is everyone safe? Were things done the way they were supposed to be done?

Being measured against these standards is fine if the platoon is at war or the boat is at sea or the plane is in the air and there is real danger. The crew needs to follow guidelines and authority is important. The problem is that in your family you are not always in danger—and success is not always a simple matter of people doing what they are supposed to do. In your intimate partnership, it is flexibility and balance that matter, so what are you going to measure when you wonder if you are doing a good job? I think what you can strive to measure is whether *the other captain* feels like a captain. Ask the other captain. If they feel like a captain, you're doing a good job.

If this was easy, it would simply be a matter of asking and getting an honest answer, but it is a hard question to handle for both people. The person who brings up the topic needs to be authentically curious about the condition of the boat and whether teamwork is fortifying the other captain. The person being asked needs to be in touch with whether they feel fortified by the sharing of responsibilities. Nonetheless, if your co-captain does feel like the boat is under control, and they have some empowering role in that, then you are being a good captain of the boat. And this is important if you want to maintain an intimate partnership, with "benefits."

Captains and Sex

It is usually true that the person with the least sexual desire has the most control over whether a couple has sex. This is especially true because of the very clear social constraints we all understand about forcing our partner to have intercourse. It is ultimately up to the person who wants it least, and this creates a position of power that actually does not feel very powerful—in the same way the child in my office felt "wrong" towering above the rest of the family. In this situation, neither person feels like a captain. The dilemma for you, as a couple, is figuring out how to balance power better, so that the person with more desire is not powerless, and the person with less desire does not acquire so much power that the power itself feels confusing and uncomfortable. This trap can suck the energy out of a couple.

As awkward as it can be to talk about sex—and as much as we might assume that it takes away spontaneity to talk about it—it is important to face a desire imbalance. It may well be that your partner is confused about this dynamic and is finding it very hard to enjoy their sexuality. Discussing intimacy in a way that shows you want your partner to feel more like a captain can be part of being a good captain. Either of you can start by saying that there is less energy, or that you are obviously stuck, and maybe it has to do with power, control, and the mystery of having too much power.

Here are some pointers for tippiness about intimacy and desire:

- People who look powerful do not necessarily feel powerful.
- To be an effective captain, the other captain also has to feel like a captain, and vice versa.
- *Ask* the other captain of your boat what the weather is like, how big they feel, or whether they feel like a captain.

• Balance the use of control by claiming responsibility for your own reactions and behaviors and asking your partner to be responsible for theirs.

Sustainable Relationships

In couples, good captains share leadership and control in ways that improve the journey. You are stewards of the vessel you have built, and responsible for safe passage for both of you, and often, children. This is not easy to do automatically. It takes awareness and purpose. How challenging is this?

In a very global example of how challenging this is, Thomas Friedman suggests, in *Hot, Flat and Crowded*, that we can improve our relationship to our planet through "sustainability," and collaboration. He feels that our country can take leadership in this mission by "out-behaving" other countries. He says we can outperform others in the same way that doctors who apologize for their mistakes are sued less often. Perhaps you can out-behave others by holding yourself accountable for your behavior. If we work to sustain our relationships, have clarity about our accountability for our actions, communicate clearly, and collaborate with others, we can take the lead in our private lives, too.

For example, one Eb and Flo worked hard to clarify that they were having less sex because Flo would be tired due to taking care of their three children and not have much desire for sex. Eb would then feel inadequate and feel entitled to the kind of affection he had experienced when he was growing up—or when they were building the boat. This would upset him and he would retreat in a way that looked and felt like he was abandoning Flo.

When I suggested that Flo had too much power and Eb had relinquished his responsibilities, they made an adjustment. I encouraged them to discuss their responses in terms of desire and control. (Remember: to "encourage" someone means you are giving them "courage.") What were their real intentions and feelings? What were their perceptions, interpretations and responses? How might they work together to change the dynamic?

Through having the courage to discuss this difficult topic and being open to trying new forms of foreplay, Eb understood that Flo's lack of sexual desire was simply that, and he could share his desires without upsetting her. When Flo expressed her disinterest and could see that it didn't upset Eb, she experienced more desire (not right away, but later) and was relieved of the responsibility of controlling whether they had sex. Both of them felt a more balanced and sexual connection, and liked themselves better. They were sharing control, and it was paying dividends.

Two captains on a boat can share control of the boat, manage themselves well, and feel more connected with each other. In author Jon Kabat-Zinn's words: ". . . if you know how to use the wind's energy and are patient, you can sometimes get where you want to go. You can still be in control."

CAPTAIN'S LOG

Having too much control is confusing, and can be just as disabling as having too little.

15

It Just Doesn't Feel Safe

What if we have just brought too much anxiety and fear on board with us and it isn't helping that we are on a boat?

> An unexamined life is not worth living.
>
> - Plato

If you are to take the lead and feel like a captain, you may need to repair some unwelcome personal cargo. Before we explore that "garbage" again, let's consider what the key messages have been from the first fourteen chapters:
- You didn't expect to be on a boat. It is complicated and disappointing.
- As captains, you are both entitled to say your side *and* have your side heard.
- If you listen well, the other person will behave better.
- We respond to increased tension in predictable ways that *increase* tension.
- We need an alarm system that tells us when we are *really* in danger.
- It is "crazy normal" for two people to feel small and look

big at the same time.
- We can control something about ourselves when we want control.
- Things aren't always the way they seem, and crutches may be needed.
- You have permission to make choices that clean up your thoughts, feelings, and actions.
- When you're trying to change your reaction to tension, there are lots of opportunities.
- Intimacy can mean a balanced response to each other, I to I.
- Having too much control is confusing, and can be just as disabling as having too little.

You will find that this growth process involves getting complex and then simplifying—and then getting complex, again. So, here we go (again):

When you use the built-in sensibility from your planetary (or other) origins, what is your emotional goal? What is the end game? How are you hoping to feel? Is it about changing your partner's behavior, or ending up in a better place for yourself, emotionally?

I believe the answer everyone would eventually come up with is that the problem is more about feeling small than it is about the other person looking big. When how we feel is the issue, the goal for our response—and our behavior—is to feel safe, secure, calmer, more relaxed, less tense, less anxious, less small, or like we have things more under control. That could be what drives our responses from wherever we come from. Whether we use a straight-line approach or a circular one, we have the same needs and intentions for our own peace of mind. It so happens we are also driven to build boats and start lives with partners who are from different places and families, which creates complexity, tension, and normal, predictable, reliable *tippiness*.

The Voice on the Radio

I have had the good fortune to know a prominent therapist from our area named Dan Gottlieb, who hosts a weekly show on public radio called *Voices in the Family*. I have not had a chance to discuss with Dan *how* he manages to know what to say to his listeners, but I have an idea. Callers to his show are typically people having problems with their relationships who are looking for support and help. All Dan has to work with is their voices. What does he do in order to keep the situation under control for himself? How does he manage all of the possibilities? I imagine he has a checklist:

Does this person sound
    __*Mad?*
    __*Sad?*
    __*Scared?*

Our behavior, including the tone of our voice, signals to someone else something about our emotional state, and the caller's tone of voice is what Dan pays attention to when he is listening. If the voice is angry, he relentlessly explores the thought process and emotions that brought on the anger. He asks the speaker to look back *before* the anger and account for their emotional reactions that led up to their current state. Often, he can steer a caller to identify themselves as sad or scared.

If the voice is clearly sad, Dan accepts that, and asks about any personal loss, defeat, or recent changes that have deflated the person, validating the sadness and trying to understand it. If the voice is clearly agitated, stressed, or anxious, he accepts that and asks what the person is afraid of, seeking an understanding of what puts the person on edge, or—in my language—he asks what makes them feel small or squirrelly. He is not afraid to identify dread or fear or anticipation of danger as a normal emotion in a relational situation.

Feel the Fear

If feeling afraid of danger or expecting defeat or pain is so normal, how do we deal with it? One way is offered in a book called *Feel the Fear . . . and Do It Anyway,* by Susan Jeffers. The importance of this book is that it simplifies a fundamental part of the learning process you can go through so that you can have a stronger relationship with your partner. You don't need to read the book (although you might), but I am going to summarize it so that you have a way of tolerating tippiness and feeling small, and then becoming a stronger, more attractive captain.

Essentially, Jeffers's book asks you to identify an action or behavior you are avoiding. This may be a difficult decision, a conversation about money, sex, your in-laws, the children, etc., or it could be some new way of behaving that takes courage and could trigger a dreaded response in your partner. The book asks that you recognize your avoidance and resistance as based in fear, anxiety, stress, and/or tension, and to feel it honestly as a vulnerability of yours. Once you have explored this vulnerability, understand its roots, get used to it, and accept it about yourself, the next stage of her book unfolds.

Jeffers asks that you use your imagination to visualize what would happen if you risked doing the behavior that raises your anxiety. What are all of the possible outcomes, from wonderful to dreadful? Will your partner be grateful and relieved and thrilled? Will your partner be angry and punitive and judgmental? Something in-between? Lots of possibilities in between? Imagine them all. Then, once you've imagined all of the outcomes, you are ready for the real lesson of her book.

Imagine how *you* will feel in each of these scenarios. Are you ready for your own feelings and thoughts and impulses? Be clear with yourself what might happen inside you emotionally, based on all of the imagined outcomes. Jeffers's short, helpful book suddenly ends, stating that you are now ready to try the behavior. You will *not* be surprised by *your own* emotions, because you've imagined them, and that is about as ready as you are going to get.

But It's Really Scary

What if you and your partner are so stuck in a pattern of behavior that it is really overwhelming to imagine changing your dance?

I was treating a young woman and, one day, she was describing her repetitive situation: working all week, coming home to her apartment on Friday with no energy or willpower, and then spending the weekend drinking too much, pursuing worthless activities, getting no lasting pleasure out of her time off, and eventually resolving to change her life—at the end of every weekend. Monday, she would start the pattern all over again.

I told her it sounded like she was in a swamp. I pictured her coming home on Friday and barely treading water. Suddenly, she would feel like she was about to drown and respond to the fear of drowning by setting up some worthless activity, fleeing the swamp by running up the same hill she had run up the week before. The path would be slippery because she had used it before, but she would scramble up the path anyway, pulling off branches or pulling up plants to help her get to the top, away from the swamp. She might make it to the top during the weekend, but she would start to slide back down into the swamp eventually, making the path more slippery and muddier as she slid through the unsatisfying weekend. Back in the familiar swamp, on Monday she would head for work with a sense that she ought to change the pattern. When she got home on Friday, her *fear of drowning* would amplify and simplify the situation, and she would scramble back up the same path, and keep re-experiencing dissatisfaction, dependency, and decline.

I suggested a really challenging solution that even surprised me. I told her that she had choices she could make when drowning scared her, but it was not some kind of practical formula like calling a different friend or trying a different activity. I prescribed that she choose to *drown* instead of escaping up the hill. I was basically asking her to feel her feelings (the fear of drowning), account for her actions, and take a big risk with an unpredictable outcome. I wondered what she would do and was relieved when she returned the next week.

She had taken my advice, faced her fears—hated me for it—and stayed home on Friday night, feeling like she was drowning. She told me that to her amazement, she found her footing in the swamp, stood up and looked around, and could describe seeing the well-worn path up the hill from a new vantage point, still having all of her family and friends around, but with her feet firmly on the ground. The world had slowed down, and it was safe after all. She had not actually drowned or fallen through the middle of the earth. She had overcome her fears by facing them, had taken care of herself, and had found some ground to stand on. "Drowning" is taking the opportunity to feel the fear, take a risk and knowingly choose a different challenging direction while not giving up or tuning out.

Another woman told me a true story about a rogue wave that carried her so far out into the ocean that she knew she couldn't swim back safely. The two men who had also been caught by the wave told her that the only thing they could all do was wait for the ocean to carry them back to shore. They conserved their energy, waited a long time, and landed on a beach a couple of miles from where they had started, safe, and sound. This is a profound example of *letting go* of fear, risking drowning, but not tuning out. There is a difference.

Working Together Because We Feel Small

What if we become couples in order to have company when we are vulnerable, and our partnership is the safest place to admit we feel small? What if the swamp is an available shared place, but it seems too intimidating right now? If, instead, it seems that we have built an overwhelming, disappointing, and scary place and are afraid of drowning, how do we reverse that? If that safe feeling has disappeared, how do we rebuild it? The answer is both simple and complex: We rebuild it gradually, and with care.

As we've noted (in Chapter 9), your memory is not as clean and safe as a computer's. It is messy, and so is your partner's. It is our memory that makes it so obvious that the other person is big and dangerous. We have absorbed associations with that person's behavior that tell us we are really experiencing—in the present—a past injustice, injury, or indignity. We are wired to warn ourselves that something is on the way that we need to be cautious and careful about, or even that we are in real danger. Unfortunately, seeing the other person as large makes us feel small in comparison.

It is really striking how essential, how absolutely crucial, it is to keep from feeling any smaller when things feel like they are not under control. We can not (and do not) risk disappearing or simply melting away. What can you control at this crucial moment when you risk feeling even smaller? Not your partner's behavior. We've already determined that the other person has to control their behavior because you can't.

One thing you can control is how big they look to you.

What's making you feel small so fast? You need to understand what your memories are of your family, your childhood, a previous intimate relationship, or some previous important dynamics, and keep them in their place. They belong in a deep conversation about yourself with your partner, your therapist, or with yourself, where you see how these memories are affecting you. In the moment, you want to *only* experience the crappy moment of unfair tension with your partner, and *only* what is going on right now. You want to be in the present, in a mindful place, for your own sake—yes, selfishly—so you won't feel small so fast. This is the essence of *mindfulness*, a gift you can give yourself.

But, it can take more than your mindfulness to transform your relationship. Imagine how powerful it can be if both of you take charge of all four quadrants of the crazy normal "feeling small *and* looking big" distortion. It takes courage to let yourself drown in your relationship by working together.

Each corner of our familiar distortion offers an opportunity for teamwork, for collaboration, for foreplay, by giving both of you something you can always work on. Each quarter of the distortion has two halves, one for you, and one for your partner. For instance, when you are working on owning and expressing your feelings, your teammate/co-captain/partner is working on listening and being emotionally available by remembering that you feel about as powerful as a pee hole in the snow. While you are working on harnessing your behavior that looks so big to them, they are working on being mindful and present, so their remembered associations don't make your behavior look too big. When you are trying to stay in the moment, they are trying to curb the behavior that irritates you. When you are remembering that they feel small, they are clarifying their feelings so you can better understand what is bothering them.

A reminder of the formula for both of you to help you both feel more like captains—and get the benefits of "drowning":

- Remember that they feel small,
- Own your own feelings,
- Manage your behavior well, and
- Stay in this mindful moment.

When both captains follow these guidelines and collaborate this way, that crazy normal distortion feels like it is more under control and you both benefit from feeling less tension.

The degree of partnership and shared emotional responsibility we've been considering can help both of you overcome the fears and insecurities you brought on the boat with you. Choosing to "drown" in your shared emotional swamp so that you have your feet under you can bring more stability to your joint enterprise.

"Drowning" could be good, you might say, but is it fair?

CAPTAIN'S LOG

Feeling and facing your fears can bring you the security you crave.

16

It Ain't Fair (or Familiar)!

How is it that women so often feel abandoned and men so often feel attacked (or slimed)? What makes us react to sliming by retreating and react to abandonment by sliming? Does fairness matter more to us than our dignity and our ability to work together? Perhaps a better understanding of injustice and power can help.

> Once we recognize that we are interdependent, it only makes sense to work together. It does not make sense to try to beat out the other guy, because there is no such thing, in the ultimate calculus, as "I win, you lose." I can only win when we all win.
>
> - Willis Harman
> author of *An Incomplete Guide to the Future*

When you walked down the aisle, or moved in with your partner for life, or exposed your vulnerabilities to your partner the first time, let's assume you had some very clear expectations—but you also had some you were less aware of.

Not everyone is your classic generic Eb and Flo. Sometimes couples have a distinct story that you can learn from. Bill and Diane had the usual expectations; that they would live happily together, have children, be faithful, etc., but it turned out that they expected other things, too. Bill was from a large family that argued all the time and had one captain. Diane was from a small, quiet family with little sense of direction but plenty of love. What would feel familiar to each of them, as if they were safely at home?

Lots of pregnancies and conflict, with a rigid sense of order, would feel right to Bill. A small, quiet family with shared values and responsibilities would feel right to Diane. Bill would expect dad to be in charge and Diane wouldn't. Bill would expect rigid rules and punishments and Diane would not. Bill would expect a lot of noise and conflict and Diane would not. Both of them would want the home to feel familiar. What was likely to happen?

Bill and Diane would feel small whenever they experienced something unfamiliar that alarmed them. Just like any squirrel or boat captain, or anyone seeing a cockroach or feeling misunderstood, they would get tense, refuse to feel any smaller, and compensate for their discomfort. It wasn't pretty. The conflict was chronic, constant, and harsh. Nobody was listening and both people were suffering. Neither person felt like the situation was under control. Nothing felt fair. Sometimes I feel like the most effective thing I could do for couples would be to stop every therapy session every ten minutes and let both people shout, "*It ain't fair!*"

Injustice

It's important to understand that fairness is emotional, and it drives our behavior. If we think about the boat feeling tippy because of an injustice (or indignity or imbalance), then perhaps it makes sense that it feels like an injury and we feel entitled to *justify* our response to the injury. We are simply taking care of ourselves and trying not to get hurt.

I was fortunate to be mentored by family therapist Ivan Boszormenyi-Nagy in graduate school. As students, we were immersed in his particular framework for understanding relationships, which he called "Contextual Family Therapy." He believed, for good reason, that fairness and justice matter to people and drive behavior. Like all of us, he came by his beliefs and understandings naturally—in his case, as a victim of the Nazi occupation of his homeland. His family had to leave the country. He had experienced injustice firsthand, and was able to translate that into a better understanding of what moves us. The cornerstone of his theory was that we all care about our partners (or family members), have a multi-generational sense of injustice, and can either behave *constructively* or *destructively* when we feel entitled to balance the unfairness. The sense of injustice and entitlement may be inevitable, but reacting constructively or destructively is a choice, according to Boszormenyi-Nagy.

I Must Be Right!

One clear way to justify your own constructive or destructive way of handling things when you feel small is to make sure that you are right. It feels good to be proven right.

Paul and Judy had developed a destructive dance that was satisfying this need to be proven right. Paul would get angry whenever he felt that Judy retreated from him, contradicted herself, or didn't listen to him. He justified his actions by saying that she was frustrating him. Judy closed down and just said whatever she felt like saying whenever Paul got angry. She justified her actions by saying that he had "an anger problem."

It was easy for both of them to be right. Almost any

conflict (over money, sex, in-laws, and lots of other possibilities) provided a trigger for the behavior that would induce each person to validate their partner's expectation. If Judy would handle a situation in an uncertain, vague, unclear way, Paul would get angry—and Judy would be right. If Paul would handle a situation by getting frustrated and getting upset, Judy would retreat—and Paul would be right. It was a mess, but both of them were getting what they expected and feeling right about their expectations. But at least they could each say they were right.

Another variation of this need to be right that boomerangs on couples happens in bed. There are a lot of ways to perform badly, sexually. Sex can be pretty complicated, emotionally, and *performance* matters a lot. And if, for instance, there is no orgasm, or there is premature ejaculation, or someone has been too slow or too fast for the other, or has not understood what pleases the other, then performance begins to be a more conscious and powerful factor. As soon as either of you is conscious of your performance being "poor," it is natural to be anxious about your next performance. When you have your next opportunity to perform, that anxiety gets into bed with you.

There is no way of really measuring this, but research shows—and it makes sense—that enough of that anxiety will affect your performance, creating the boomerang. Doing it right matters, and anxiety about doing it right makes it less likely that you'll do it right, which is a loop that is hard to get out of—just like Paul and Judy's loop. Both loops are built on an *expectation* of getting it right, or getting it wrong, but still an expectation. The results eventually become *familiar* and keep reproducing themselves, which becomes both a comfort and a problem at the same time.

Mr. (or Mrs.) Expedient

Faced with all of this unfairness and feeling small, we seek simple solutions. That's what can attract us all to books like this. Even without a book, it is normal to be trying to reduce tension, find peace and harmony, and stop feeling so small.

I've made up a story about a man I call "Mr. Expedient." He did actually call me twice, and I've made up the rest to illustrate what lengths one or both of you could go to when the world seems too complex or confusing—or unfair. He could be either of you.

Mr. Expedient called me one day in a big hurry. He said, "My wife's leaving me. I need an appointment." I could barely squeeze his name and phone number out of him because he was in such a hurry. I told him I would see him and his wife at ten o'clock that Thursday morning. Later, I imagined the background of his story.

I imagined his wife really did want to divorce him—and surprised him by saying so. He was likely one of those husbands who thought everything was OK. Handling the moment expertly, he agreed to call a therapist, and got an appointment. Perhaps she was thrilled at his sudden understanding and responsiveness, as well as how seriously he took the threat, and rewarded him with a lovely evening, benefits and all. Maybe the next morning they woke up and she asked when the appointment was. Having forgotten all about it, he fumbled around and found that they were to see me at ten on Thursday, triggering an almighty explosion from her about how he never had any idea of her schedule, she had "always worked on Thursdays; (he) doesn't care about (her)," and so on. He immediately responded to the crisis and called me to cancel the appointment—which is what he really did.

He left me a message, saying that they needed to cancel. When I called back, *I* was the sudden *source of tension and pressure*, so he needed an expedient answer for me. Not very able to think beyond the crisis—or to be authentic with me about his confusion and frustration—he dispatched me with a well-learned strategy: he made a pronouncement and a promise that turned out eventually to be a lie.

Mr. Expedient told me that they *would* be there on Thursday, after all. I hung up, and the pressure was off *him*. He had gotten me to go away, which is what he needed in that moment. But, then I was the victim of his expedient way of dealing with pressure. I realized it felt like a lie, and would turn into one, but I couldn't confront him in case it wasn't. And, anyway, it wouldn't have been appropriate or professional to tell a complete stranger I thought he was a liar. I went to the office Thursday morning and they did not appear. I made my standard, pleasant call, encouraging them to call to reschedule, and left it at that. What do you suppose happened next? Back to the imaginary part:

My imagination says that his wife still wanted a divorce, and said so again. This time, he needed to account for their not seeing me. As Mr. Expedient, knowing he could play loosely with the truth, it would have been easy for him to lie about me and say that I didn't call back after he cancelled. He might even have gotten a lot of sympathy as a victim with good intentions, until his lying or his expediency helped nurture another crisis full of pressure that he handled in his familiar, expedient way. Whatever happened, they didn't contact me again.

Nonetheless, it is often important for each of us to handle pressure immediately and feel like you are right and—if you are not careful—you can learn a *destructive* way to do that.

How Do You Exert Control?

If you feel pressured enough, it is likely that you want to regain control. There are many ways to do this. Driving home one afternoon from the office, on a major highway, I had a distinct, unusual, and memorable ride. As I was getting on the highway, a driver was driving dangerously fast in the right-hand lane as I was trying to enter. His speed caught me by surprise and made me—and the other drivers around him—pay attention to him and drive differently. His need for control, expressed by driving fast, taking risks, being grandiose, and imposing on us, made us feel like we were not in control. A little later, when I was almost at my exit, a driver was in the middle lane driving fifty-five miles per hour, and everyone needed to pay more attention and drive differently to adapt to the way he was driving. His need for control (a fear of going too fast or getting lost? a fear of getting arrested for going fifty-six?) made me and the other drivers drive differently. He had control of the situation. These are two very different ways of having control, but they both have the *same effect on others*. The rest of us had to defer to the way those drivers were taking control.

Both the fast driver and the slow driver were being compelled by insecurities, indignities, injustices, and/or unfamiliarity, and both were being grandiose in that their behavior spilled over into the experience of the other drivers. This, in turn, could have felt unfair to another driver and trigger anything from a distraction to road rage. At home, situations can escalate just as quickly as on the road—especially when everyone feels justified.

Good Intentions Are Controlling

Both you and your co-captain want to achieve fairness, tranquility, serenity, and peace. Both of you try to get tense, unfair moments under control. At rocky moments, it would work better for you to interpret each indignity or injustice as your partner trying to help calm things down by getting them under control.

One of you may view these challenging moments as opportunities to be powerful, expedient, or grandiose, expressing a need for safety and justice. One of you may view these moments as opportunities to insist that feelings matter the most, expressing a need for safety and justice. "Get out of the way and let me fix this" meets the tyranny of emotional purity. This clash creates a toxic climate for both people.

In this toxic climate, "I'm protecting her" looks like "he's deceiving me," or "he's not connecting with me." In fact, sometimes "I care" feels and looks like "they're controlling (or attacking) me" in a thoughtless and draining way. One of the confounding mysteries about how quickly we feel small is how the other person's best intentions can lead to those feelings. As a partner, you need to be careful about how you are expressing care. If your caring is received in a way that seems arrogant, or diminishes the other captain, that will not be good for the boat.

The art of being a healthy caring partner includes genuine caring, an understood boundary, not stifling the other person, and allowing for give and take. This balanced approach to being a caretaker is also a healthy approach to being a couple, even though it is hard work. Remember, *diplomacy is the art of letting someone else have it your way*. One way of consistently creating justice is for both sides to feel like they are succeeding. When you really want both of you to be satisfied—rather than engaging with your partner in a dance that primarily meets your emotional needs *through* them—you can be an effective diplomat and attractive partner.

CAPTAIN'S LOG

How we gain control when things feel unfair matters.

17

I Want to Feel Wanted

Sometimes we lose track of what we actually want. It doesn't do any harm to ask each other a simple question.

> Our discontent is actually a gift of spirit. It is the backside of the dream, the part of us that is held back at this moment. It shows itself as a feeling of "I'm not happy. I'm feeling a longing, and I don't quite know what that is." The early stage of dream-building is to honor your discontent, which is the greater part of you yearning to be discovered and expressed. Honoring the discontent is the doorway to the next dimension of life.
>
> - Mary Manin Morrissey
> author of *Building Your Field
> of Dreams*

I visited an experimental preschool one day many years ago and was immersed in a very different culture for one day of school. Remarkably, the founder of the school,

Margaret Skutch, had been able to enforce a rule that *every* conversation would be structured a certain way: *Three positive statements and then the question, criticism or negative aspect of the conversation.*

Conversations with the children started with the positive, but so did the children's encounters with parents or staff, or between parents and staff, or between visitors. The theory was that this was the most nurturing climate for a preschool child, and what mattered the most was the way everyone was spoken to. This reminds me of a couple of things. First, how much the way we talk matters; and, second, how vulnerable we can be to negative statements. Skutch was teaching that we don't listen well or accept another perspective until we have been calmed by some positive feedback. She was also acknowledging that we have serious, risky things to say to each other that may trigger defensive reactions.

Perhaps you were not handled so carefully as a child, or have not been in your adult relationships. Perhaps you don't feel listened to or important or very visible. Perhaps you can identify the moment when a partner has not shown an interest in you, sexually or in some other way. It can be very powerful to feel unwanted or undesirable, and it is very difficult at those moments to have perspective on your partnership.

As we noted in Chapter 14, the person having less (sexual) desire acquires tremendous power, and one way the power is transferred is through the inner workings of the person being ignored or unappreciated, who desperately wants to recover the love, attention, or intimacy that had been expected. Our neediness empowers the other person, but only from *our* perspective. On their side, they don't necessarily feel powerful or big. You can put the other person in charge of your needs when you need them to appreciate you even more, but although you are feeling entitled and justified, you could simply trigger your partner's helplessness—not their support. In times like this, it is important to ask what you both really want and need.

It is helpful in those moments to remember that there is different weather on each side of the boat, and that you are both captains with the ability to discuss your perceptions, thoughts, and feelings.

Family Climate

What is the weather like on your boat? What kind of emotional climate are you and the rest of the household experiencing? Stormy or calm? Lots of sunlight or not so much? Lots of positives or more negatives?

Whether you are raising children, or you are simply the captains of your private boat, you are establishing a family culture regarding communication style, ways of connecting with each other, and ways of handling tippy moments. If you are a parent, you are establishing your family's climate while your behavior is demonstrating and modeling what appear to be the best practices for young people eager to learn how to cope when they feel small and the weather is stormy. Your parents had that responsibility, as well, and your children will create their family climate for the next generation.

Hopefully, calling this the "climate" or atmosphere on your boat gives you some ideas about how to manage it. I have found this to be useful when I visit leaders of organizations and they need a solid handle on how to take leadership. They grasp that they are responsible for the climate and begin to see ways to have an effect on it.

Your boat is a personal and emotional place, and each perception of that place is valid. Many times, when working with a family, I have taken the time to pass a normal (non-wedding) kaleidoscope around the room, asking each person what they really see when they look at the rest of the family.

You can imagine the youngest child seeing everyone as impossibly old, the father seeing himself outnumbered by women, or the oldest child seeing authority figures *and* younger siblings who need caretaking. These are very different perceptions and experiences, yet they can all happen in the same family.

One family I would be curious about are the adorable turtles named Slowsky who inhabit the advertisements for our cable TV and Internet service. They see the Internet as too fast for themselves, and instead gaze lovingly at each other and listen carefully to each other as they react slowly to the changes around them, including having children. What would the climate be like in a family like that? Would there be more consideration and conversation? Would children and adults feel listened to? Would feelings be understood and validated? Would people feel like they mattered? The only obvious value they have enforced is that they operate slowly in tandem, not like captains moving in opposite directions or drivers moving at wildly different speeds. This gives tremendous dignity to their interactions and could be a very healthy value to enforce.

The String Quartet

If you develop a healthy shared climate in your partnership, what needs to happen when the ship still seems to be tipping? One way to slow things down is to simplify what you talk about, perhaps recalling the "rules" about describing your own perspective and having intense curiosity about your partner's.

One year, at the annual conference I love to attend, the keynote speaker for thousands of therapists was, of all people, an orchestra conductor named Benjamin Zander. It was an interesting combination. What would he know of "our world," and how would he handle talking to all of us? He thoughtfully was provided with an excellent string quartet, which we presumed was so that he could have them play something beautiful if he lost his nerve or forgot his train of thought.

Indeed, the speech was so inspirational and insightful that many of us couldn't wait to hear more of his ideas, and decided not to attend the workshops we had signed up for. Instead we found ourselves moving to an overcrowded ballroom for more of Zander and the string quartet. During his next presentation, Zander stated that he could illustrate an effective family therapy session for us—which at first seemed a little presumptuous, considering that he wasn't a therapist. As it turned out, he knew exactly what he was doing.

What he did was have the string quartet play a beautiful piece of music, and then ask each member, one at a time, to say *what they wanted* as they experienced the piece of music. Each musician had his or her own private point of view about the well-rehearsed and beautifully presented masterpiece. Each of them saw the music through their own precious kaleidoscope. Each person had something they wanted, perhaps wanting to play their part differently, or wanting someone else's part to be more prominent, for the good of the group. They knew the music intimately and welcomed a chance to openly express their feelings about how to make it even better. The leader of the group shared his own wishes, including his observation that it was hard to have to be the leader, to be so decisive, and to have so much responsibility. Zander then simply had them play the music again.

It was abundantly clear to all of us that the music was played even better after the intervention. We were collectively stunned. He had not worked with this "family" before, but he knew that they were experts on their own dynamics and wanted something beautiful to be even better. All he asked was for them to say what they wanted, and the results were measurable and obvious, even to an audience of outsiders.

From Brain-dead to Authentic

One way you can make a relationship more complex is to measure how much you are giving and how much you are getting in return. An intimate partnership is an invitation to create a complicated contract, and then start measuring who owes whom—kind of like keeping a bank account or a ledger.

Consider the situation of Marty and Sue, who decided to get married and then spent more than a year in suspended animation. Marty, by his own admission, was "brain-dead" and had developed "tunnel vision," while Sue waited for action that would indicate Marty was ready to move forward and get married. They had homes they needed to sell, legal papers to locate, and promises to keep, but none of it seemed to be happening. Sue felt she had been promised that they would live together and blend their lives together, but Marty had delayed so much that Sue began to charge "interest" on her investment, wanting better and better evidence that Marty was serious. Marty was behind on his payments, so to speak, the bank was raising the interest rates, and he sounded just as exasperated as a customer at a bank who couldn't see their way out of debt.

Marty still wanted to marry Sue, but the relationship had become very conditional and he couldn't improve his behavior enough to make up for his earlier failures. Each slip made Sue more certain that Marty didn't really want to follow through. Eventually, after both of them had clarified their positions with me, Marty decided he had nothing to lose, and chose to name his real needs and wishes. He calmly declared that he wanted to be considered and accepted—faults and all—as someone trying to be better and still wanting to be married to Sue. He had found a solid, authentic truth and could claim it and repeat it, regardless of Sue's reactions.

Over the next month or two, Marty began to believe in himself, realize that people depended on him (especially his children, whom he had custody of), sound more authentic, and sleep much better. He became much clearer about his feelings and needs, and was able to relax and privately laugh at himself about how he had been brain-dead and had clearly been frustrating Sue for over a year.

As an intimate relationship involves growth, constant transactions, and rebalancing of the ledger, the relationship also, then, became different for Sue, who needed to adjust to this new way of getting what she had been hoping for and somehow drop the interest charges. This was difficult, as we all know that being the bank is a powerful and secure place to be. The eventual result was an ongoing conversation about themselves, with less focus on the balance of the account. When his children graduated from high school, the couple was able to bring their lives together in an authentic, collaborative way.

In contrast, we can consider the fate of James and Becky, who came to me for a lengthy intensive session, walked in the door saying that they didn't expect the session to help, proceeded to tell me their complaints, and then eventually relax, take their shoes off, face each other on the sofa and share a very genuine eye-to-eye quiet discussion about their issues for several hours.

At the end of the day, they put their shoes on, told me the session hadn't changed anything, and walked out the door—presumably still more comfortable with their standard way of not communicating, not taking risks every day with their relationship, and feeling justified in thinking that nothing could really change. To my mind, they had the vast potential to change their lives, but found it more comforting to continue the reliable, yet unfulfilling, dance they were already doing, maintaining the patterns that didn't challenge them or demand awareness of their changing relationship with each other. They had presumably benefited from a few hours of responding slowly to each other and exploring positive ways to communicate, but were not ready to embrace it with their everyday shoes back on.

Being Real

If it helps so much to be mostly positive, to slow down, and to say what we want in a sincere way, let's consider some useful ways to consistently approach a relationship:

- Can you give what you are expecting your partner to give? Could you change the way you are playing your tune as much as you want them to change the way they are playing theirs? Can you think of three positive things to say before being critical if that is what you want your partner to do? Can you slow yourself down and be available the way you want your partner to be?
- Are you being the person you want to have dinner with tonight and then spend the night with? Are you the kind of person you like to sleep with? Do you realize you are going to spend dinner and the night with yourself, whether you like it or not?
- Are you prepared for climate change? If you are responsible for what the climate is like, how are your actions affecting your journey and your vessel? Are there adjustments you can make that will have an impact on the climate?
- Are you a good listener and a considerate, slow partner? Have you learned your part of the music in a way that you could speak passionately about how to make it even better? Do you know what your partner wants? Are you prepared to ask each other what both of you want?
- Are you hedging your bets and seeking love insurance?

Lobsters apparently do have another partner in mind in case a partnership doesn't work out well. Is that how you operate? What impact does that have on your relationship? Have you considered making sure you're there to love your partner *and yourself* when you need support? Are you lovable and available in a slow, positive, and thoughtful way?

It is hard work to develop the awareness and the courage to communicate and share in an authentic way. Perhaps you can keep the conversation positive, or get a grip on the climate, or be like the Slowskys, or maintain authenticity even with your shoes on. It will help to ask yourself and your partner what you really want. Encourage yourself as you take on this journey and try to enjoy the ride.

CAPTAIN'S LOG
Slow down and say what you want for climate control.

18

Infidelity: Where Are You?

What about really damaging things that happen? Sometimes we look around and our partner doesn't seem to be on the boat anymore. What about infidelity?

> When we are bringing in the new and the different, in the beginning it looks like, "My God, we are in terrible chaos. Everything is falling apart!" What's going on is that the system is trying to break those old bonds and make room for the new and different to come in. This is really a wonderful opportunity. The only thing that is really risky is not to take risks.
>
> - George Land
> co-author of *Breakpoint and Beyond: Mastering the Future Today*

"Every time I hear the word 'Washington,' I lose it," Joan whispered bitterly as she worked her way through my box of tissues. "I didn't know what I was doing," Jonathan blurted out, helplessly. Their baby slept blissfully in his portable car seat. Joan and Jonathan had built a boat, but their dreamy bubble had burst.

I wonder if it is possible to build a boat without some awareness that it may capsize. If anything, that knowledge can put us on edge, make us want to get the job finished, and make us hyper-vigilant about tippiness. We might even use defenses that are available from our garbage that actually make the boat *tippier* for our partner. There is no doubt that the most sudden sinking feeling that couples experience is triggered by infidelity.

Indeed, the most common reason for seeking help with an intimate relationship is emotional or physical betrayal. In fact, it is usually enough for one partner to *believe* they are losing the other for suspicions, doubts, and feelings of abandonment to creep into a couple's dynamics. The intentional act of reaching out to your current partner for love and connection carries with it the potential for loss and disappointment. The relationship that offers intimacy, support, and security is also fragile and vulnerable enough to be fertile ground for insecurity, tension, and pain. Trust and faith are the glue that help us build the boat, and they can be the first victims when the boat is unexpectedly tippy. Pat Love, whose name is perfect for an expert on intimacy, suggests that *kindness and consideration* matter, because when you are not expressing them, you are sending the first signal that the boat is in trouble, and it may be the first hint of betrayal inside the bubble.

Betrayal and infidelity take many forms, including a retreat into pornography or addiction, a budding friendship with someone new, simply tuning your partner out, or a seemingly innocent encounter. Ultimately, whatever you are doing is a violation if it simply violates the understanding the two of you have. For some people, it could be disruptive enough to simply look at someone else, while for others it could be acceptable to have multiple sex partners, but for most people it is something in between. You have something to say about what the rules are. You are the captains of your boat.

The Washington Story

Joan and Jonathan were young and carefree. They happily fell in love, got married, and had their first child, effortlessly jumping through the financial, professional, and personal hoops that they encountered. One lovely, innocent day their life changed dramatically.

Jonathan flew to Washington for a business meeting, and met a woman on the plane. He had dinner with her, but didn't tell Joan until the next day. Jonathan's unexpected interest in another woman, and his secrecy about the encounter, were enough to burst their bubble.

Joan's worst fears were suddenly inescapable. A presidential campaign was big news and the word "Washington" worked its way into every news broadcast, making it possible that every time Joan wanted to catch up on the news, one word could rock her world. She would be flooded with emotion by association, again experiencing that sinking feeling.

The fact that Jonathan withheld the information for a few hours was also enough to make this a case of betrayal in Joan's eyes. Most of the time, the lack of appreciation and kindness that turns into a distraction, then confiding with a new person, and then into something more intimate, is not shared openly with a partner. We avoid saying things that we know will trigger our partner's anger. There is guilt involved, and possibly shame, but there is also the wish to protect your partner from the information that would upset them. Whatever the reason, ultimately it is often the silent and secretive breaking of trust that hurts more than the amount of intimacy which is shared with the new person. I ask whether the secrecy or the infidelity is more troubling when a couple dealing with betrayal comes to my office. Most of the time, it is the secrecy that really hurts the most.

Jonathan could not be contrite enough about his behavior, and Joan could not get past the injury. Regardless of how fleeting and temporary the action seemed, this was a violation that required the same attention as a long-term affair that had been uncovered. It did not matter how sexual the encounter had been (or had not been), or how the secret was kept. What mattered was that the bubble had burst.

Handling the Fallout

Infidelity is a violation of, and an assault on, a relationship. The violator has not taken into account, for whatever reason, the impact of their behavior on their partner. Having said that, both partners must look closely at themselves when repairs are needed.

Anyone thrust into this abyss can sense that what has been lost is a sense of trust, and it is bewildering for both people. There are two distinct tasks when the bubble has burst. One is trying to handle the instant crash that can happen as soon as the word "Washington" is heard (or whatever the cue is for the injured partner). The other is to explore the dance that created fertile ground for distractions, loss of kindness, and/or confiding in a new person.

Generally, when the boat is sinking, couples do not want to talk about how well it is maintained or things they are neglecting. It is easier to just believe the boat will be fine—and many times that faith is justified. But, often, it turns out that you had not really finished building the boat when you launched it, and some cracks had been left unpatched.

Maintenance through dialogue is needed.

When a violation has been discovered, every day there is a potential crisis—because there may be new evidence or because there may be a new reminder. The alarmed victim is likely to be angry, impossible to comfort, and constantly suspicious. They can be acting like a detective and be very reactive to any indignity. The wandering party is often contrite, but that is usually not enough, and they can expect to be asked an infinite number of times to explain their thoughts, feelings, and actions that they don't completely understand—when they feel like they've already revealed everything and explained it as well as they can. As much as they feel they have expressed remorse and regret—and want to move on—they can't move on until their partner is ready.

These dynamics are exhausting and frustrating for both people, but also lead couples into conversations that are very long and intimate about who they are, what they really want, and what has been happening to them. This is actually an opportunity to have those discussions, even if they cost you sleep or serenity or money. Taking the risk to be authentic with each other under these circumstances is going to be your best chance to maintain the relationship you have invested the most in. Don't be surprised if the cycle of suspicion, defensiveness, giving up, and exhaustion keeps repeating itself. You are trying to clarify your relationship, and it is not an automatic, "one size fits all" process.

The Toxic Dance

The equally difficult task is to share an exploration of how your dance developed the way it did. How is it that one of you thought nothing of being distracted, being less attentive, and perhaps confiding in someone else about your private voyage? If you crossed the line into sexual behavior, how is it that you

163

could think that it wouldn't be harmful, or that it could be kept secret? What were both of you experiencing as the boat got leaky and the weather got stormy? How did both of you try to raise the alarm or fix the problem? What went wrong?

We all have deep emotional needs, and we each try to get them met in our own way. One way to take care of those needs efficiently is to tune out the needs of someone else. (When we feel small, one way to compensate is to do something that makes us feel bigger.) Our behavior may be uncaring and grandiose, but it can meet our deepest needs and insecurities. It is easier to be impulsive or expedient than it is to explore the complexity of meeting someone else's needs. It is easy to lose track of your consideration for your partner or to let go of the kindnesses that had become routine, familiar, and expected in your relationship. It is easy to imagine that when a boat feels tippy, both captains can get caught up in this simpler, more expedient dance. This is, unfortunately, what love insurance is for. As I mentioned, even lobsters know this. We end up seeking some available form of security to ward off our fears and anxieties about intimacy.

If either partner is sufficiently disappointed in the relationship, or perhaps feels entitled to absolute attention and consideration from the other—because of their expectations about being a couple—there is the potential for a further step into the abyss, if the opportunity arises. If it just seems more comfortable (or less stressful) to spend time with someone else, because they make you feel desirable and attractive, or they are available emotionally to listen to you, it is enticing.

If your interactions with that person become enjoyable and meet your emotional needs, you can begin to justify overriding the promises you have made to your current partner. As you become distracted, your partner will probably notice, but you may believe that you can juggle the complexity and you can confide in the new person, which makes it even more comforting and helps you justify the risks you are taking. It may even seem risky and exciting in some way to keep the information from you partner. Remember, this does not need to include sexual activity for it to be toxic for your partnership, because of your shared expectations of exclusive privacy when you built your boat. Once you are hiding the truth, it is natural to grow closer to the person you are being authentic and open with, and more distant from the person you are deceiving.

If you are also vulnerable to taking these kinds of risks because of vulnerabilities you developed while you were on the boat you grew up on—such as witnessing infidelity or a lack of consideration, poor communication, or emotional cutoffs— then you can again feel that it is not wrong to be escaping, expanding your horizons, or sharing your confidences. You may even feel entitled to do so.

Most of the time, when secrets and infidelity are involved, the bubble bursts, the emails are found, the suspicions become evidence, the secrets are revealed, and there is a tragedy at home. For some reason, it almost always catches everyone by surprise.

Reconciliation

Whichever one of you went down this dark alley, it will take some teamwork to get back out. One of you has personally injured the other. You may require a mediator, which is why there are marriage and family therapists, psychologists, social workers, clergy, and others who can be a neutral party. You will find out a lot about yourselves and how important your partnership is to each of you. We'll revisit Jonathan and Joan to illustrate how reconciliation can work.

The bubble had burst, but I had to tell them that *I don't build bubbles* full of dreamy expectations. They were experiencing the full blast of infidelity, and I told them I would treat it just that way. They were totally dedicated to their child's well-being and to sustaining their partnership, and attended sessions regularly for several months. They worked through all of the ideas in this book, from boats and cockroaches to gumballs and kaleidoscopes. They remembered that both of them looked big but both of them felt small. They talked constantly with each other about how they had drifted apart, how the level of consideration had changed, what their emotional needs were, and how they each tended to get them met. There were ups and downs, and the constant reminder provided by the news broadcasts throughout the presidential campaign.

One day, Joan made the pronouncement that made the biggest difference in their voyage. She had resolved that she didn't like being the spy and the suspicious person she had become, and decided to put her energy into being mindful and present with Jonathan. This was a solution that Jonathan could have proposed as well, by saying that he was ready to face his needs and responsibilities in a consistently present and mindful way. Either one of them could have provided this elegant, heartfelt breakthrough and asked the other to go along. I use their solution as an example for other couples, but it is more meaningful and more effective when a couple gets there through the hard work they are doing to fight for their relationship.

Jonathan and Joan resolved to be aware enough of themselves to tell the other when they were at *their own* tipping point emotionally, even though it would upset their partner. This meant that Jonathan would admit that he wasn't being attentive or focused on their relationship, and that he was distracted or frustrated or disappointed. It also meant that Joan would say when she was fearful of abandonment, suspicious about Jonathan, remembering Washington, or feeling unwanted.

The other half of the resolution was that they would both pay *immediate* and *direct* attention to their relationship when they heard this information from their partner, even though it was upsetting to hear. They would try to interpret the news as a cry for help and attention. Both of them resolved to be authentic with the other, to respond with immediate and genuine caring, and to be emotionally available—even when they might have had the opposite reaction. This was a very special deal for both of them. Jonathan no longer had to somehow dig himself out of the hole he had dug for himself, and Joan no longer had to be a detective or a punitive person. They could both relax again. It was not going to be easy, but it was going to be better than holding a grudge—or owing for injury.

Joan and Jonathan decided to take the risk of telling each other the last thing the other one wanted to hear, and they both agreed to relax, be present, listen, and talk when they heard the last thing they wanted to hear. This goal of agreeing to speak the hard truths—and listen to them—is the goal I lay out for couples when they need me to help with infidelity. This path out of the jungle of betrayal is utterly simple and elegant, extremely challenging, and the best solution I have seen or heard.

Lessons Learned

There are a variety of lessons to learn from both betrayal and healing:

- One confounding dynamic that we get caught up in is that we often deceive our partners in order to protect them from pain, not *just* to protect ourselves from their anger.
- Keep in mind that both of you are vulnerable to feelings of loss and betrayal. I've noted that men tend to feel

slimed and women tend to feel abandoned *or vice versa.* One leads to the other. Your partner could feel frustrated and lonely, too.

- We all have a visceral reaction to the unexpected, and we need to get things back under control. This usually is reflected in our impulsive responses that are likely to happen when we are dealing with a sudden feeling that the boat is sinking. It is important to recognize that your own feelings and responses are not actually surprising.

- President Eisenhower is famously quoted as saying, "In preparing for battle, I have found that planning is essential, but plans are useless." You can not have a precise plan for handling a sinking boat, but you can plan your journey well, know yourselves, and take precautions.

- It is important to understand that people develop boundaries between each other, right in the middle of their relationships. To me, a healthy but challenging boundary is like a window with a latch and a Venetian blind on *both sides.* Both of you have some control over how open the window is from your side, but the actual boundary keeps changing depending on the combination of your actions. At any one time, one side can be closed while the other is open, or one can be a little open while the other is closing, and so on. To conduct a healthy partnership, these dynamics need to be accepted, and not surprising.

- When there has been a violation of trust, the violator is truly worthy of blame, especially when there has been sexual infidelity. The art of recovery is for the consequences to be clear, but not destructive to the relationship. The victim must make it clear that a limit has been reached but not do more damage to the couple's connection.

- Have you been abandoning your partner? If you have, what has that been like for them?
- If your boat is sinking or the bubble has burst, that is your situation. You are not on someone else's boat. You built this one. It's yours to sink or sail.

CAPTAIN'S LOG

You have cheated if your partner feels cheated. Face the music together.

19

Who Do I Owe for This Trip?

What is that eerie feeling that this voyage might be costing too much? Could it have more to do with the boat you grew up on than with the way your partner is behaving? You might ask yourself: Who am I taking care of?

> If you ever expect to be loved, you must reveal who you are.
>
> - Leo Buscaglia
> author of *Living, Loving, and Learning*

Being in an intimate relationship may be harder than you expected—or wanted—it to be. It can begin to feel like a voyage to nowhere. It may not be meeting your expectation that you could improve on the climate you grew up in. You might be adding up the costs and wondering about the benefits.

Expectations are quite powerful. I've noticed, for example, that certain days of the year tend to trigger complicated therapy sessions for couples. Thanksgiving, Mother's Day, birthdays, and Valentine's Day come to mind. One year, I tried using fairness and expectations as themes to help couples deal with Valentine's Day.

Dawn and Rob were walking on eggshells because they had nearly split up the year before on Valentine's Day. This year, Rob remembered the holiday, bought gifts for Dawn, came home on time, and was especially attentive. But Dawn felt that his gestures weren't authentic because Rob was just trying to do better than the last year, and Rob felt that Dawn wasn't appreciative of his consideration and attention. They were confused and frustrated when they visited my office on the day after the holiday.

I offered the idea that they had opened a bank account on Valentine's Day and had made deposits and withdrawals all day, measuring the balance in the account, and treating their transactions accordingly. I suggested that they also had a long-term account that mattered much more to their relationship than the account they created on any designated day that made them artificially vigilant. This observation helped them shift their focus away from the content of the day before and onto the process of being a couple.

It may well be that you see your relationship as a contract, and see it as obvious that you would keep track of who owes whom. Actually, this may be something you can discuss and adjust—not something set in stone. On Valentine's Day, I found myself exploring with couples the ways that they had treated their account with each other. Think about your relationship for a moment.

- Do either of you act as if you are owed? Did that begin as generosity, or a way of gaining power?
- Have you started to charge interest on your loans to your partner? Do you act like a power broker and maybe raise the interest rate when they get close to paying you back?
- Are you the one who is always in debt and can't quite

get out of that hole? Did that begin as an entitlement or expectation that your partner would take care of you?
- What are your expectations and your transactions? What is the currency?
- Do you look at your relationship like keeping a ledger, but with an emotional balance?

In Chapter 16 we talked about fairness and the ideas of Ivan Boszormenyi-Nagy. He would suggest that once we begin to establish an account based on fairness or justice, we are entering what he called an "ethical dimension" of relating. At this stage, our sense of balance and *entitlement* begins to direct our behavior. As we noted earlier, we can be either constructive or destructive as we operate in this dimension. It is easy to take care of our need for justice by keeping a ledger in our minds about how much is owed, who is ahead, who is behind, and on and on.

It can feel as though this intimate journey, which seemed so dreamy and effortless when we were building the boat, is now constantly costing something and not coming out even. This can lead to resentments and frustrations that are very powerful.

How Families Are Like Slot Machines

In our relationships, we may feel entitled to fairness and comfort that we rarely achieve in any meaningful way. But, we can be counted on to invest in the possibility that we will achieve a fair result or a sense of safety.

Designers of slot machines understand that our families are disappointing and that we will, nonetheless, keep trying to get our needs met. In 2004, Gary Rivlin wrote an important article for *The New York Times Magazine* in which he quoted psychologist Nancy Petry from the University of Connecticut:

> The slot machine is brilliantly designed from a behavioral psychology perspective. The people who are making these machines are using all the behavioral techniques to increase the probability that the behavior of gambling will reoccur.

What the article is getting at is that we are all prone to keep trying for a reward if we are only rewarded *some* of the time, or we find the surroundings stimulating in a *familiar* way. As Rivlin observes:

> The machine's ability to hook so deeply into a player's cerebral cortex derives from one of the more powerful human feedback mechanisms . . . *intermittent reward.* Children whose parents consistently shower them with love and attention tend to take that devotion for granted. Those who know they'll never be rewarded by their parents stop trying after a while. But those who are awarded intermittently—in the fashion of the slot machine—will often pursue positive outcomes with a persistent tenacity.

Most families match this description of "intermittent reward."

Apparently, slot machines don't hook us into helplessly inserting more quarters if they pay out steadily *or* if they never pay out. It's when they behave more like our intimate or family relationships that we can't stop gambling. Something unexpected and less conscious is at work here. Instead of simply wanting rewards, we are comforted by familiarity and hooked by the possibility of increasing positive feedback when it is intermittently given. Something matters enough about our relationships that makes us willing to keep investing in the possibility of change, even though the change we seek often eludes us.

Just notice how often you check your e-mail, perhaps gambling that there will be a memorable or satisfying message, even though you get spam and ordinary messages most of the time. You are responding to intermittent rewards.

Interestingly, Boszormenyi-Nagy tied this powerful dynamic that operates in our family history (and in our intimate relationships) to our "loyalty" to the emotional needs of members of our families. He is implying that the familiar intermittent rewards hook us to the emotional needs of those closest to us through accounts that open when we are very young.

Is it possible that we operate in our current relationships according to some sort of emotional account that we continue to maintain with our family of origin? Do we seek an emotional gain for ourselves by being tied to the needs of others? Can this get in the way of authentic and productive relating in our partnerships? Is there a way to neutralize the power of our loyalty to our first families?

Very Busy Baby

I've found that families often find it helpful to consider the connection between a parent's emotional well-being and their child's current behavior. Sometimes I speculate that a teenager is really obnoxious because of how much they care about their parents, or I will point out ways that the adults are still caring about *their* parents. Once you see the dynamics through this lens, there are plenty of opportunities to speculate that someone is motivated by loyalty to the emotional needs of their parents.

Several years ago at a training seminar, I watched a

videotape of an experiment that featured a mother and her very young child. The experiment was intended to show how important it is for a child to bond with one of his or her parents, and the videotape powerfully illustrated this need. Of course, it is important to remember that we have all been innocent and vulnerable children needing to connect with someone who protects and cherishes us. But, I chose to watch this videotape through the lens of family loyalty, curious about the dynamics between the infant and his mother.

Sure enough, the mother and infant were bonding with each other by smiling back and forth, each reinforcing the other's smile. As I watched for signs of loyalty at play, the little boy, perhaps six months old, would occasionally turn away from the mother and toward the camera, clearly taking a deep breath and rolling his eyes, as if to say "Phew, this is hard work, but I owe her and it's worth it!" Through this particular lens, the little boy owed his mother for giving birth to him, needed her to be well enough to take care of him, and was working hard to keep her well.

Then, the experiment got even more interesting. The mother was directed to stop smiling at her son. As you might guess, the little boy kept trying to smile at her, and then began to wail. This behavior—as analyzed for the presentation— clearly showed that he needed to bond with her and was upset when he couldn't.

Actually, it looked even more traumatic than that to me. It looked to me as though the boy was trying to keep boosting the mom, and when she kept a straight face, he changed alarmingly quickly to an emotional collapse. Through the lens of owing, having an account, and expressing loyalty, this baby boy felt like he was in deep trouble because he needed to count on his mother's caretaking and was helpless without her clear-headed and emotionally stable support. His response was totally and understandably self-centered: not able to ensure his mom's stability and connecting smile, he began to feel very unsafe, and then became desperately lost. To me, this interaction illustrated the intense power of our loyalty to our parents' emotional well-being.

Getting Locked In

It is not only infants who get locked into the emotional needs of their parents. It is my experience that this accounting lasts for a very long time, and needs to be specifically addressed if it is to be stopped. In fact, it is very rare for a parent and child to cut that umbilical cord and actually talk about balancing and resolving their account. We simply do not have enough of these conversations. Instead, parent and child are often locked in a prolonged loyalty pattern that lasts well into the child's adulthood.

For example, I remember a visitor named Julius, whose father, unfortunately, had just died. Julius, who was in his late 30s, loved his father and did not expect him to die just as Julius settled into his young adulthood, establishing his career and forming a family. This early loss of his father came as a shock, and he sought comfort in my office.

As his insurance benefits dictated that he could visit me only briefly, I tried to simplify his treatment by suggesting that an old chair of mine was his father, and that he could say things to the chair that he had meant to say to his dad. Through experience, I knew this approach to be helpful and direct for someone mired in loss. Julius began to talk to his imagined father, clearly grateful to his dad and grieving the loss of him.

After a short time, I felt that Julius was transforming his father into a magically powerful and perfect person, distorting who his dad probably was, and certainly feeling smaller than his vision of his dad. I suddenly grabbed the chair, opened the door, and flung the chair out into the hall. As I returned to my chair, I realized that I had probably deeply upset this mourning son. I momentarily wondered why I'd reacted the way I had—and whether it was the best course for my client.

But Julius was sitting calmly, ready to talk. "That's exactly what my father would have wanted you to do," he said. "I was putting him on a pedestal. He was a real person and I wasn't relating to him in a real way. I was still his adoring [and owing] little boy."

Julius was telling me that he had been so loyal to his father's needs that he couldn't have a truly personal relationship with him. He was also suddenly realizing that his father didn't really want it that way, that he hadn't needed to be put on a pedestal and would have preferred to be a real person in his son's life. Somehow, by tossing the chair, I had communicated all of this to Julius. He was relieved and felt that he now knew his father better. Until that moment, he and his dad had not gotten past the "initial accounting," and reconnected as authentic adults. Even though he had lost his father, he had gained a better understanding of the man and more clarity about their relationship.

Build a Better Boundary

Take this opportunity to concentrate on what you can learn from your own behavior. Just imagine for a moment that you start connecting the dots between injustices or injuries that happened in your family and your behavior in your current partnership. For instance, you might be quite surprised to find that you sound just like one of your parents, even though you were determined to behave differently from them.

Perhaps you are imitating them not only because they set an example for you, but also because you're trying to help them deal with their insecurities by *being more like them*. Let's face it: any parent is proud when their child copies them. If you haven't fully understood the power of that parent-child connection, you might end up regretting your behavior with your partner when you could have prevented it by being more aware of these dynamics. Or, there may be a more concrete way you still owe your parents.

Before I met with Jose individually, his wife, Maria, tipped me off that he had admitted to her once that he "owed" his mother for leaving home when he was a teenager, and causing her so much distress. Maria felt that this loyalty dynamic between Jose and his mother interfered with their marriage because Jose was consistently blind to the inappropriate way his mother was treating others in the family, including Maria—and refused to confront his mother.

Fortunately, over several sessions, Jose was very open to the possibility that he was like both the baby in the video and the man who saw me toss the chair, and he learned to talk openly with me, and his wife, about his blind loyalty to his mother. The couple was able, through more open conversation, to bridge a gap that had grown quite wide—with Jose standing up to his mother when he needed to. Having spoken with many mothers of adult children, I suspect that Jose's mother handled the change quite well, and maybe even wanted him to stop his unconditional responses to her. Mother and son have a more authentic relationship now, and she is more aware of the consequences of her actions. Meanwhile, Jose and Maria feel much safer and more connected as a couple.

If you are going to be co-captains of a boat and be able to talk about feeling small *and* looking big, each of you needs to be aware of the loyalties you've brought onto the boat from the vessel you grew up on. If you still "owe" your parents for their hard work, and are so sharply attuned to their emotional needs that the connection subtracts from the depth of your intimate partnership, it is time to address these issues with a direct and honest accounting. Speak frankly about your emotional needs and your family history. Perhaps you can balance the account with your parents. Take a good look at the assets you have with you on the boat, become aware of the costs and benefits of the transactions you're making, and hold yourselves accountable. Knowing who you "owe"—and acknowledging how you try to pay them—will help your current account because you'll be more conscious and aware of your side of the ledger, and the boat. It might even help your next Valentine's Day go more smoothly.

CAPTAIN'S LOG

Intuitive family investments can cause more debt in your current account.

20

Third Interlude - Sex!

What about sex? It's been mentioned a lot and it's always important. What's useful to know about having sex on a boat?

> Living with uncertainty has a kind of vitality. It keeps the world open to wonder; it keeps us prepared for surprise; it keeps our relationships alive.
>
> - James Carse
> author of *The Silence of God*

We'll take a different kind of intermission, with a hotter title, this time. Although many of these ideas show up elsewhere in the book, it is time to recognize that sex is never far from our minds, and plays a major role in how we feel about our intimate relationships. Having sex with your co-captain and keeping it invigorating, enjoyable, and meaningful can be a challenge. So, we'll take a break and talk about taking a conjugal interlude from the routine of running the boat.

Your passion for each other helped you build the boat. The way you experience that passion can change once you are sailing the boat. When you are doing something serious, the fun part can be different from what you expect.

**

My impression is that the *expectations* about sex are the source of trouble for couples. If you expect sex to be hot, frequent, and spontaneous, you could be setting yourself up for disappointment—and plenty of tension.

**

There is a precious non-verbal aspect to our sexuality; spontaneity is great, but there are too many distortions if sex is not discussed. Opportunities for understanding and for exhilaration are actually lost when we think it will detract from something special if we talk about it.

**

Having an orgasm thrills and relaxes you. That may be what you find so important about sex. Try to also be aware of your partner. David Schnarch calls it having orgasms with your eyes open—actually appreciating the other person while your own needs are being met.

**

It is likely that the two of you will experience different levels of sexual desire. You need to be careful when that happens, because the person with less desire has more power and control, and really determines whether you have sex or not.
The person with more desire, holding back out of consideration, ends up experiencing less power or control. The person with less desire does not feel powerful, but has power. These are

issues to address and be creative about. How are you going to adjust your sexuality so that both people are more comfortable with the way power is distributed?

**

When sexual performance is an issue, be careful how you pressure the person who is having a performance issue. The more they are conscious of trying to perform better, the more anxiety they will feel in bed, and the less likely they will be to perform well, touching off a vicious cycle. It usually takes two to have a performance issue (whether related to erections, orgasms, or ejaculation), and both people need to make adjustments when they happen. Explore it together and think of original solutions. It's your boat. There aren't absolute rules about how to enjoy your sexuality.

**

You may decide *as a couple* that you are going to have sex on Sunday mornings but sleep apart, that you want to explore your fantasies, that penetration is not for you, that you like the idea of masturbating together, or that you will be on the lookout for a ménage à trois. Your decisions are private—and part of the privilege of being a committed couple.

**

Just think; if you are really intentional about it, foreplay can be as exciting as a really hot conversation following the guidelines in Chapter Two. Imagine that one of you takes the lead and describes where and how you want to be touched. Your partner listens really well and does what you ask. They ask for what turns them on and you listen well. Your reward for listening is asking for and getting more pleasure for you, and so on.

If you pay attention to each other and let things develop, sex can be as wonderful as a special conversation.

**

Our sexuality is an expression of our spiritual, emotional, and physical self. We attach tremendous meaning to it and it is too easy to equate our performance (or the frequency of our sex) with our identity. It is too easy to decide that we are not desirable or competent or significant when sex is not satisfying or not happening. Catch yourself and ask how you happen to be making this assumption. It may be just as confusing and personal for your partner—and it may be very meaningful to talk about it.

**

I find out quite a bit about the people I work with, including how frequently they have sex. Frankly, I don't think it correlates as directly as you would think with anything else. When I think about nearly thirty years of work, I really don't see that having *less* sex makes people less happy, more anxious, less rich, less likely to stay married, or less healthy. Frequency is thought about a lot, but it just doesn't seem to match up consistently with anything else that is important. What having sex *means* to you may matter more than *how often* you have it.

**

It is worth remembering that sex is not simply a way of having pleasure, but it is also the way we declare that we want to reproduce ourselves by making a child. There is a life-changing aspect that is easy to forget when you are taking precautions, but our minds and emotions don't always know the difference between something casual and something special.

**

On an ad for a TV show, the young boy who walks in on two adults having sex says, "I don't know what they were doing, but it seemed like dad was winning." Sex can satisfy our fascination with being powerful, or taking a risk, or having something challenging and edgy happen. The flip side is that it can be uncomfortable, threatening, or degrading at the same time, like any power struggle.

**

If you grew up in a family culture that treated sex as messy, dirty, shameful, and embarrassing, does that mean that you also feel that anyone who indulges in it is somehow weak or undignified or unreliable?
Don't treat your cherished, passionate partner as if something is wrong with them just because that was the message you got as a child.

**

Making love is more intentional than having sex. It is a more mindful, shared experience with the expectation that both of you will have a special time in whatever way turns you on. It is usually gradual, entered into without foreknowledge of how long it will take or how good it will be, and depends on both of you to interact as a team for your mutual pleasure.

**

You are entitled to treat your bed as a sacred place where you can be naked with each other, vulnerable, and authentic. Sex is just one opportunity for being that way.

**

It may be brilliant that we tend to expect sex at night. It may be just what we need to literally shake us out of whatever we've been dwelling on and head for a relaxing sleep.
It turns out it's a great way to start the day, too.
You and your partner can develop you own rhythm and practice.
Do it with empathy, curiosity, and creativity.

**

Having a masculine way of approaching sex or having a feminine way of approaching sex may be familiar or especially satisfying, but it is the blending of the two sensibilities that can be the most exciting.

**

When the glow of sex with someone new wears off, you may be left with a much deeper response to sexuality. Your formative experiences can complicate the way you respond in a sexual situation. You can have expectations and feelings that you associate with sex that make it uncomfortable to enter that territory with sustained comfort.

When the novelty has both been wonderful and worn off, or you have been successful at procreating, you are still who you are and have your own associations with intimacy or sexuality that you have absorbed over your lifetime. This is worth understanding and discussing.

**

Like it or not, it is assumed that a commitment to live with someone or get married is also a statement that you can curb your sexual urges enough to be faithful to one partner and not have those urges become more important than your contract with your partner.

That is a reasonable expectation, and you *can* be self-disciplined enough to respect the promise you are making. That is usually your partner's expectation.

**

It can be exciting to secretly be sexual with someone you confide in outside of your primary relationship. After all, it is not unusual to seek love insurance. But, nobody can be that special forever. It's simply asking too much. It is simply less exciting to be with the same person when you are not taking risks and constructing special, clandestine moments. You might want to think about that when you consider cashing in your insurance and betraying your partner.

**

You don't want to use your head too much when you are handling a topic that may seem like a minefield, especially if you grew up hearing that it is an extremely embarrassing and private topic. You need to be relaxed enough about sexuality to talk openly about it, but not overanalyze your behaviors or your responses. Seek a middle ground between "total spontaneity" and "a research project."

**

Enjoy your differences and your sexual growth. See if you can keep that creative, exploring, risk-taking spirit alive that drew you sexually to your partner to begin with.

21

Where Are We Going?

What if you can gaze into each other's eyes, feel heard, and feel calmer together, but still have big problems that don't seem to go away? How do you talk to each other then? Maybe you just need to be hungry for something to change.

> You can't have conflict resolution without conflict. Both on the international level and in my own bedroom, I have found that if you either fix it too fast or try to avoid it, you will never reach resolution. You have to learn to dance with conflict and to transform it. When you do that, you can really have resolution.
>
> - Danaan Parry
> author of *Warriors of the Heart*

Let's just say that you and your partner have both been reading this book, discussing the ideas, each applying them to your side of the boat, and trying to put them into action. You find that you are calmer, your reactions to each other are slower, and you are remembering some images just when you need to. For instance, you might be remembering that you are looking big and they are feeling small. You might be picturing a kaleidoscope or a boat or a cockroach or a gumball. You might really have mastered authentic statements and active listening, finding that they reduce tension, and that the climate is improving.

We're Stuck!

Even if the climate is improving, one or both of you may still be insisting that the "issues" that tarnished your relationship are not resolved, and could rock the boat again at any moment. It could seem that it is not enough to be able to communicate better and feel more whole at any given moment. It may feel like you haven't really reached closure about things that matter to you. The journey may be going better, but you may still be wondering where you are headed.

Even people who listen actively to each other and speak authentically about themselves and their feelings experience moments when they are at a loss or feel stuck. Listening and talking are great, but there are also times when the captains need to make decisions or deal with issues that they consistently disagree about. A difficult, uncomfortable discussion may be what is needed, with both captains advocating for their own side, using good techniques for reducing tension, and finding a creative way to solve problems as a couple.

If that is what you are experiencing, and it is disappointing, please be assured that it is normal. It can still feel like there is an itch to scratch even though things have been healing. It is still a shared journey on a boat with two captains who are two different people. What you may need is an addendum to that comfortable, validating discussion (Chapter 2) between two people remembering to play soccer and risk intimacy with each other.

The Waves Keep Coming

Let's say that you and your partner are Eb and Flo. Imagine that Eb moves to his side of the boat, advocating for a sense of direction, saying that problems need to be solved. Flo goes to the opposite side, to keep the boat from tipping over, and takes a firm position that you don't need to fix everything and—if you relax a little—things will work out. Flo doesn't really want the boat to go around in circles any more than Eb does.

It is just too scary to imagine both of you passionately pushing for *your* solutions and forgetting the importance of the emotional climate of the boat. Too much conflict will make the boat too tippy, and may affect the passengers. Too little conflict will keep things unresolved and keep the boat from going anywhere. Neither captain is mustering the courage or strength to take the lead, because neither can really trust that it will be safe to face important issues.

The important issues are not a mystery. As mentioned before, it is not surprising when money, sex, the in-laws, the kids, the jobs, or the house cause tension in your relationship. That much is reliable and predictable.

Let's say that the two of you realize that the same huge wave keeps hitting the boat, or that you keep running aground on the same sandbar. It truly seems like your problem is a force of nature, seemingly inevitable, and constantly disrupting your dreams for a peaceful and safe ride. Your boat isn't that different from your neighbor's boat, or your parents', or anyone else's. Sure, your story is unique—you have your own distinct experiences of that story—but the issues are predictable. Perhaps one of these times, when that wave or sandbar crops up again, one of you captains will see it as an opportunity and take the lead. You are a team, there is no shame in handling a storm or perhaps changing your course, and if you keep avoiding finding solutions you'll just have to grit your teeth and go through the ordeal of handling the same challenge the next time, too.

All it takes is one captain, summoning the courage to say that the boat is facing a familiar problem and that the captains need to solve it. All the other captain needs to do is listen, see that the problem is not going away, and realize that there is nothing to lose if the two of you face the issue. Doesn't that sound easy?

Get Hungry!

Under these circumstances, I recommend that you brace yourself in these two ways:

1) Realize that thoughtful listening and authentic telling do calm things down, but may not help you *enough* when you need to be decisive; and

2) Get yourself into a frame of mind where you are *hungry* for a solution to the constant nagging problem with money, sex, in-laws, the kids, or whatever is stormy.

Let's at least imagine this is going to be fun and mentally head out to find a restaurant where you can finally solve this riddle that has been vexing your relationship and making things toxic. You'll need to remember you are *hungry*, because this is going to be rough going.

First, I want each of you to imagine the restaurant you would like to go to. Perhaps one of you would solve a problem really comfortably with a fast burger and fries or a pizza, or maybe a beer or two. This person wants to just figure it out and be done with it—no frills, no music, quick and dirty does the trick. Perhaps the other would be comfortable in just the opposite way. For this second person, a problem is not really given its due consideration unless you spend the whole evening discussing it; study the menu, enjoy the candlelight, eat a complex gourmet meal, dance to the music, drink wine slowly, and look into each other's eyes.

When I ask couples where they would go to get this conversation accomplished, it is rare that they name the same type of restaurant.

That is fine with me, because my request is that you can *not* go to either of the restaurants you would be comfortable at. I want you to act as if you are walking through town *together*, taking time as a couple, get hungry, and end up at a place you haven't tried before. Perhaps the menu will be in Greek, you won't know how long the meal will take, you won't know the staff, the price will be a surprise, and you won't quite know what the food will be like. This unknown restaurant is ideal for your needs.

Once you are at this unfamiliar place (and hungry), it is time to order your meal. I suggest that you take the risk of advocating for your own needs, wants, and desires about the issue you are discussing. Don't expect to agree. If the level of tension rises, have a good listening interlude where you use active listening and authentic I statements (as were discussed in Chapter 2). When you have calmed down, keep *advocating for your needs*. Your real emotional needs and your statements about who you are and what you desire may not match up well with your partner's. Don't be surprised. You have done your best to choose the food that you really want to eat.

When you have revealed everything you need to reveal, and it is all on the table, it is time to eat the meal by having your discussion. Don't forget that you are feeling hungry for the boat to sail more smoothly, not run into sandbars, and not get swamped by huge waves. Now is your chance to really be co-captains, offer leadership, have ideas, and answer your needs with a sense of purpose and good intentions.

- The *quality* of the conversation you seek is genuine,

plausible, believable, and authentic. Use your listening and non-defending skills.
- Be problem-solvers, not just expedient damage-fixers.
- Try thinking outside the box. What could you try next, considering all of the information on the table?
- Discuss ways to measure whether an idea is working. Set yourselves up to succeed by planning a follow-up discussion. Be prepared to try something else next time.
- Consider all of the needs, wants, and desires that have been expressed.
- It is *your* boat. You built it. It is not someone else's boat. You are the captains.
- Remember you are hungry!

Hopefully, making yourselves talk about personal issues that rock the boat can give you a new way of experiencing each other as serious, flexible, and intentional adults who want the boat to run better. You need to handle the insecurity of approaching things in a new way and be prepared to keep revisiting the material that you have shared, as you try solutions and measure their impact on your journey.

This is a difficult assignment, but I have seen it work. Gut-wrenching decisions about whether to move across the country, whether to try again to get pregnant, how to co-parent the children, when to retire, and whether to stay married have been explored at this imaginary restaurant. I can't say that couples have enjoyed it, but they have survived and benefited from the experience. I think this is because both people accept their discomfort, advocate for their needs, listen well to each other, and collaborate for the boat because they are hungry.

Eating the Meal

So, right now, you may be asking: Imagining a conversation at a restaurant and remembering to be hungry can reduce tension on the boat? Blending logic and emotion is healthy and safe? You can come up with solutions this way? Here's some support for this idea:

Focusing on negative emotions is not productive, but balancing emotions with logic can be a gold mine. It may be time for you as a couple to find this balance, rather than continuing to tip the boat when your partner goes too far in the other direction. According to clinical psychologist and researcher Susan Johnson, a developer of Emotionally Focused Therapy (EFT), and a prominent advocate for focusing on emotions: "We're now at the point where emotion . . . has been identified as an inherently organizing force, essential to survival and the foundation of key elements of civilized society, such as moral judgment and empathy. Emotion shapes and organizes our experience and our connection to others . . . . It is the great motivator." It is important to note that, in the same journal article, Johnson notes that "(*only*) venting strong, *negative* emotion . . . is nearly always a dead end" for relationships. Although her compelling research has shown that our emotions are central to our mental health, strictly venting pure emotion is not as productive as balancing an awareness of your emotions with a practical sense of:

1) How you both are behaving;
2) What your goals are;
3) How you each respond emotionally to what is important to you; and
4) How to communicate effectively.

When you have the courage to put all of your insecurities and needs on the table, it is your opportunity as a couple to be creative problem solvers. You need to be co-captains of your boat, or think of yourselves as having a business meeting where you are trying to solve a problem that keeps reoccurring. It's time for a shared executive decision. It is time to really eat the meal. It may be useful, at the same time, to consider the state of the art regarding creativity and innovation in organizations.

To start, you can try an idea that has developed since the 1940s as a useful way to get ideas flowing. Alex Osborn is credited with popularizing the process of "brainstorming" in order to get a group process moving. He defined brainstorming as "using the brain to storm a creative problem and to do so in commando fashion, each 'stormer' audaciously attacking the same objective." In brainstorming's purest form, ideas are not evaluated or discussed until everyone has run out of ideas, which could be very difficult for you as a couple, because it takes time. What is important is that every idea is considered legitimate, even if it is far-fetched. Every idea should be given respect. The idea is that an abundance of ideas about any given issue taps our brain's capacity for lateral thinking and free association, so that we can use our most creative capacities.

Research into brainstorming, which has taken place since the 1940s, indicates that it is not enough to simply pour out your best ideas. You still need to come up with a plan of action that will be effective. In fact, simply brainstorming has proven to be a good beginning (kind of "getting you in the mood") that needs to be followed with purposeful negotiation. You are at an uncomfortable meal, intentionally disagreeing, but you are hungry for a plan, and it turns out that you will need to handle negative emotions and reactions to achieve a good solution.

One researcher, Charlan Nemeth from the University of California at Berkeley, put together groups of people and gave them different methods of solving a problem. The key difference was between the 'brainstormers,' who were instructed to keep everything positive, and the debaters/

dissenters, who were given permission to criticize the ideas that were offered. Her conclusion was that "properly managed dissent" worked better than remaining unconditionally positive in helping people be innovative and productive in coming to a workable conclusion. Certainly, it will not be hard for the two of you to include debate and dissent in your discussion. What is frequently difficult is knowing how to "properly manage" the debate.

Jonah Lehrer, who writes about psychology and neuroscience in his book, *Imagine: How Creativity Works*, suggests that Nemeth's research shows us that we "need to think about someone else's thoughts, embrace unfamiliar possibilities" and handle criticism in order to come up with a creative solution to a problem. For example, he shows that, at Pixar Animation Studios, the consistent and unblemished success of their animated movies has been a result of a process they call "plussing."

Evidently, every day during a production at Pixar, there is an open-ended meeting where successes are noted, but flaws are explored without apology. The rule is that the criticism of a flaw is offered *with a suggestion for improving on it*. In this theory, adding on is an essential part of the process, as is the criticism. "Plussing" is the way that they "properly manage" the creative process.

Imagine what it is like to really take your time eating a meal, as you eat it slowly, really taste the food, and experience the nourishment that comes from deliberately seeking value in the meal itself. Don't be afraid to taste the food, appreciate the different tastes and textures, and really chew on the complexity of it. If you discuss an important issue this way, you will be helping each other handle your emotional conflicts by using what you know about the other person's emotions, needs and desires as you suggest solutions.

Finally, leave the restaurant with a plan that you will review, knowing you are measuring its success by reviewing the emotional costs and benefits that were shared when you were ordering the meal and both of you stated your needs and wants. Expect to revisit the conversation and see how your new solution is working. Judge your solutions with awareness of what is important to each of you.

It's Your Boat

So, the research and guidelines say you need to be hungry, uncomfortable, creative, and critical. You need to negotiate with empathy, manage dissent, and add value. To do all of those things, you need to act on your desire to improve your relationship, know your needs and desires, have the courage to be intimate, and strive for both of you to be healthy and whole. That is the journey you are on.

You will need to make your own joint decisions based on your needs, vulnerabilities, expectations, and garbage. You are both who you are, have built the boat together, and are responsible for sailing it. As aggravating as storms, sandbars, and tippiness are, this book can't give you specific answers to your issues. That would make me overly intrusive, claiming to know more than you do about who you really are, and ultimately it would not be helpful because they would not be *your* answers. The dirty little secret is that, in spite of the complications and indignities you are experiencing, it is *your boat*. As much as you want answers, they need to be yours.

Overwhelming? Inspiring? Confusing? Enlightening? Let's keep this challenging meal in mind, review where we have been, and try to simplify the process again so you can reach your goals.

CAPTAIN'S LOG

When a problem makes you hungry enough, you can fix it.

22

Maybe It's Not a Boat!

This is hard work. Can we go over that crazy big & small distortion again? How do we know when it is happening and what do we do about it? How do we get better at it?

> The very quality I find so repellent and irritating in another person is actually an unrecognized trait in me. I can tell it's my problem because of the emotion it arouses in me. And if I find qualities that I really admire in someone, it's because I am seeing my own unconscious potentials in the other.
>
> - Vic Mansfield
> author of *Synchronicity,*
> *Science, and Soul-Making*

If you feel like you are drowning after that last chapter, let's take stock for a moment. When you began this book it may have felt to you like you had built a boat full of hopes and dreams, hopped on, and found it disappointing. It may have made sense that the more each of you tried to keep it from tipping over, the tippier you were making it. Perhaps you've come to realize that what really matter to you are *safety* and *control*. Getting your own emotions and behavior more clearly under control can lead to more intimate moments, more confidence about your relationship, slower reactions to cockroaches, more dialogue, and more peace of mind. Perhaps you have become more conscious of the whole boat, and the importance of the weather on the other half of the boat.

Maybe it is not really a boat, after all, even though it can feel like one. Have you considered the possibility that your relationship is not as dangerous as a boat—that you can manage your situation as two captains and it won't capsize—that the waves are just waves? Consider the possibility that you've actually built something with substance and that it is *not* about to be blown away in the wind. Your mind might be so tuned in to danger and disaster that you may not have noticed that the two of you manage the storms as well as you do. Maybe it is the tuning of your mind that can rescue you from disappointment or the temptation to give up. It really is safer than you may think, and it really is possible to co-captain a relationship based on affection, love, consideration, and good intentions. Trusting your own reactions—and liking who you are—will give you faith that two navigators can make this trip.

S-l-o-w Review

Let's review the journey we've been taking together. We'll take some time and change the pace. I'd like you to read the following paragraphs one at a time and s-l-o-w-l-y. Take your time. Pause and think about each idea before you move on to the next one.

•• Squirrels actually *need* the stress and anxiety that warns them that there is a truck coming down the road, the same way we need to feel tension when we need to be attentive. Squirrels do not have our capacity to talk to the truck driver, to learn from a bad experience, or to really know whether it is a truck, or something less dangerous, that is alarming them. We can be more than squirrels.

•• In many ways, the journey a couple makes is like building a boat and sailing a boat. When it feels like it is tipping away from you, you need to be careful that your response does not make it tippier for your partner. You are both captains and need to pay attention to the weather on the whole boat.

•• If you really listen, your partner will behave better. This is more important than "fixing" the problem they are talking about.

•• Whether you are looking through the kaleidoscope, or reporting the weather on your side of the boat, mean what you are saying. If your partner is taking their turn, remember that they mean what they are saying. If it doesn't seem authentic, ask them to try again. If your partner asks you to be more authentic, try to describe what you are seeing, feeling, and thinking so you can mean what you are saying.

•• You may have different intuitive styles for handling tension. But, on the most basic level, both people want safety, control, and serenity.

•• It is predictable and reliable to feel alarmed and for this to be a signal that both of you are feeling small *and* both of you are looking big. It is easy to see when you feel small and your partner looks big, and harder to notice when they feel small and you look big.

•• When your partner looks big in comparison to the way you feel, you feel small. You may have an automatic *default* response that keeps you from feeling any smaller because that would be even worse. It is that automatic response—which can happen quickly—that probably makes you look big to your partner.

•• You are taking care of yourself when you avoid shrinking, and so is your partner. This may seem selfish, but it is perfectly natural. It is *how* you take care of yourself that will matter on your voyage.

•• If you can catch yourself when this crazy normal distortion is happening, you can experience serenity by gaining control of something about yourself.

•• The other person is feeling small, try to remember that they are feeling about as powerful as a pee-hole in the snow. You can't fix how another person feels, but you can offer emotional support by listening and being present.

•• You are feeling small. You can own your feelings and say "ouch." Communicate your vulnerabilities and hold your ground. You mean what you are saying.

•• You are looking big. Your behavior is pushing buttons on your partner that can make them shrink. Your behavior is up to you. You can adjust it according to what makes your partner feel less vulnerable.

•• Your partner is looking big to you, but they are not feeling big. Their behavior may have temporarily helped them feel less small. They are taking care of themselves. Meanwhile, you are associating their behavior with something you have experienced before. You can be more in the present moment, trying to keep yourself from re-experiencing threatening moments that make this moment look bigger than it really is.

•• If you are trying to handle your own tipping point effectively, and you miss, just admit that you goofed. There will be another opportunity.

•• Your own life story has prepared you to behave, think, and feel the way you do. You have permission to review your own processing and make choices about what is toxic, what is precious, and what needs recycling as you edit your responses.

•• You may be tied emotionally to the needs of someone in your past with whom you have an account. Be careful not to bring that account onto this boat. In your current account, you could be claiming some entitlement, charging interest, or giving away too much power in ways that are costly to both of you.

•• Know the difference between your fire alarm that goes off when you are actually in danger and your wake-up alarm that goes off when something is upsetting, unexpected, or not under control. Respond differently— and appropriately—to the two kinds of alarms.

•• You can control numerous details, but not all of them, and you can not control your partner's feelings or behaviors. Remember: "It's up to the fish!"

•• Communicate your needs and your values. Listen well and negotiate well. Take the risk of being different from each other and enjoy the intimacy of being distinct *and* connected.

•• Consider what you have experienced while reading this book. What impact has that had on you? What stands out in your memory?

These are healthy, "mindful," self-controlling strategies. You will be more coherent and clear-headed if you take control of yourself in these ways. Whether it is an innocent misunderstanding, an important conflict, or a dangerous moment, you will be more able to respond effectively, and will become a more attractive partner in the bargain.

What was it like to walk slowly through those ideas? When you slow down your own processing, you are giving yourself a treat by activating more of your mind in ways that are good for you. No hurry.

Embracing the Obvious

There are many ways you have been encouraged to use your awareness of tension, or your "tipping point" in the previous chapters of this book. Your tipping point is the signal that tells you to take care of yourself. The natural tension you feel makes you want to get things under control, and you have choices to make.

Perhaps it has occurred to you that it is really easy to notice when you are feeling small and your own alarm system is going off. Now what you need to do is learn to reverse your automatic defensive reaction to the alarm, embrace the signal as a trusted way you take care of yourself, and apply a new tool from this toolkit to the situation that is setting off the alarm.

Imagine standing by a mountain stream and trying to decide how far out to venture into it. Your feet are wet and the weather is hot. That feeling is familiar, but you've never been in this particular stream before. You want relief, but you don't really know what is under the water. You control how much risk you are taking and how fast the water will be moving by deciding where to stand in the stream. You are balancing a need for safety ("I'll just stay hot") against a fascination with movement and risk ("I just need to cool off, whatever happens"). This personal decision requires awareness and self-control.

Embrace the moment. Don't just stand there. Move toward the faster water carefully and find your new comfort level.

Feeling Small and Looking Big Again

Let's assume that as soon as you feel tippiness, you can count on four things that are happening: Your partner is feeling small, you are feeling small, you are looking big, and they are looking big. You would feel better if this distortion was under control and if you don't want to get frustrated it is a better bet to try to *control yourself* and get satisfaction from that.

When your partner is feeling small, try to remember my baby daughter in her baby seat. There was no way she could tell me what she was crying about and there were multiple new experiences that could have been bothering her. I calmed myself by picturing those experiences from her perspective. Another way you can control yourself, which we have discussed, is by picturing your partner as feeling about as powerful as a pee-hole in the snow.

When *you* are feeling small, try to remember the burly football player who found satisfaction in being able to say "ouch." Or, determine whether there is a threat to your gumball—or the equivalent of a truck coming down the road—and muster a voice that describes both accurately and effectively the emotional trouble you are having.

When you are looking big, remember the television audience that couldn't be controlled and the option of writing and telling the story as well as possible, while choosing clothes and grooming to the best of the announcer's ability. Or, imagine that you are climbing out on a limb with a saw and for some reason beginning to saw on the part of the limb *below* you, making it very likely that your behavior will cause *you* great harm.

If your partner is looking big, remember that your memory works by helping you associate something happening in the present with emotional moments you have experienced before. Those moments are *not* happening right now, despite the power of the memories and clarity of your emotional reaction. If you had a computer's memory, you would know the difference, but you don't. You *can* be mindful, however, and keep those associations off the other person's shoulders.

One of the people you may put on the other person's shoulders is *yourself*—and all of your own fears or flaws. It is natural to project something irritating about yourself onto your partner and then see them as big, giving you a chance to be upset about it. Be aware that this really makes for a crazy normal distortion and can be very confusing. Perhaps *you* are the person you are getting angry at.

It may help to realize that this distortion is part of a natural process that you both use to take care of yourselves. If you fly very much, you know that you are constantly reminded to put on your own oxygen mask, first, regardless of whom you are with, so you will be well enough to have a relationship with that person. When either of you grabs the oxygen mask, it is a necessary first step. Be careful not to think of that as "selfish."

Here is another version of a chart we used before. The four familiar quadrants remain:

Feeling Small AND Looking Big—What to Control?

I Look Big.

I'm out on a limb and sawing hard.

How am I behaving right now?

They Look Big.

My memory is not like a computer's.

What is happening right now?

I Feel Small.

The football player could say "ouch."

I'm having a gumball moment.

They Feel Small.

They feel like a pee-hole in the snow.

The baby can't say what is wrong.

How Does this Help?

The intention of all the advice in this book has been to help both of you find healthy ways to relate to each other as whole individuals. Try this list, but at a normal pace this time:

- Troubling feelings are actually healthy. Managing them is what is hard.
- Crazy distortions are normal, too. Getting them under

control is what we need. If you *each* do the things that are under your control, you will be a great team.

- When you feel small, especially about money, sex, in-laws, the kids, the house, or the job, it may be very helpful to remember a visual cue from this book instead of reacting to your insecurity in a learned, automatic way. You can interfere with your usual responses with the help of these crutches.

- When feeling critical, harsh, and contrary—especially about something that repeatedly rocks the boat—there may be a constant obstacle or a storm that you can't seem to avoid, and it may be time for an executive session. Be *hungry* and try to solve the problem. At the restaurant, practice properly managed dissent and *plussing*. Add value to your relationship when things make you testy or vulnerable, and manage your precious partnership with care.

Hopefully, you are accepting that this ride is complex, that it drifts, and that you have a unique vessel that you have built together, which requires the fondness and devotion you give to something that is yours. It is *your* boat, not someone else's, and you are in charge of the journey you are taking together.

If you are getting comfortable with these possibilities, then it is worth paying attention to the times when it *doesn't* feel as tense or tippy as a boat anymore. Monitor yourself, and appreciate the changes you are making.

CAPTAIN'S LOG
It's a distortion. Both of you are feeling small AND looking big.

23

Children: How Are
The Passengers?

When children join us on the boat, they add another dimension
and new challenges. What happens to us, and the children, on
this voyage? What is going on with those teenagers, anyway?

> The person who upsets you the most is your
> best teacher, because they bring you face to
> face with who you really are.
>
> > - Lynn Andrews
> > author of *Medicine Woman*

When the boat takes on a new passenger, it changes the boat's
dynamics. The most profound way this happens is when you
have a baby, but it could also include a short-term visitor,
retired in-laws staying with you, or grown children moving
back in. Of course, with a new baby, the change is permanent
and dramatic.

There are plenty of times—other than upon their first
arrival—when children have an effect on the boat, especially

if either of you is becoming a step-parent in a blended family, or if a child is experiencing a new stage in their lives, such as becoming an adolescent or a young adult. It also affects the boat when all of the children have swum away and you and your partner are left on the boat alone.

Parenting is an art. Each child is unique, and each circumstance is an opportunity to try your hand at creating a good result. Most of the decisions you make will be based on emotional information, so you may need some guidelines. As with anything else in life, a better understanding of the art will help you trust what you are doing.

You need to be aware of whether you are imposing your emotional needs on your kids. When there is a storm on board and it involves a child, it is worth asking yourself whose needs you have been trying to meet. Even in the simplest of situations (for instance, when your infant doesn't want to eat or sleep, and you insist that they need to), you are actually addressing both your needs *and* theirs. They do need food and rest, but you also need a break and you need to feel like you are good at nourishing or nurturing your child. It is not always clear whose needs are more important, or what difference it makes in the development of your child. Handling both sets of needs is a balancing act and a complicated journey.

Attention: Surplus and Deficit

The baby who needed to bond with his mother in the filmed experiment (described in Chapter 17) was expressing something we can all relate to. Simply put, we are constantly aware of awareness. We constantly shift the focus of our attention, and so does anyone who is important to us. We know we are paying attention to what gets our attention, and we know when we are not getting someone else's attention because their awareness works the same way. Whom we pay attention to, and the attention we get, are going to matter emotionally to us—and to our child.

Evidently, pushing and pulling for attention will always happen, and we tend to equate it with affection. Yet we need to understand that, when a parent withdraws attention, it does not mean they are withdrawing affection.

It is easy to see how quickly a young child responds to attention, and how much they want. A child's need for attention seems to be endless, and it is an early test for us as parents to see if we dare limit the amount of attention and/or affection we are giving. The decision to cut off our indulgence in our child's needs is a complex calculation based on our own experience as children, our expectation of ourselves as parents, and other more immediate factors like whether it is time to cook dinner, or go out to a restaurant as a couple, or leave them at school for the first time.

Once a child starts school, another kind of attention issue becomes apparent. If your child pays attention in an unproductive way, they can be labeled as having Attention Deficit Disorder. Actually, we all fall somewhere on the "attention deficit" continuum. For instance, you or your child may be:

1) Unaware of some things that are important to others; or
2) May have a limited number of details that you, or they, can handle at once; or,
3) May get so focused on something that you, or they, can't change gears.

All of these blind spots make relationships and group situations challenging. We all have some capacity for handling details, and we all have varying emotional responses when our capacities are reached. Let's not be surprised if you pass your characteristics on to your children, or if their particular capacity doesn't fit the optimum level needed at school, and you need to support them. Try to understand how paying attention works in relationships and what is helpful when productivity or performance matters, and then be your child's teammate as they handle that jungle of expectations.

- If your child is overwhelmed or unfocused, try to understand that they feel small.
- If you're feeling small about your child's flaws, try to provide helpful structure or guidance to your child as an expression about your frustrations and keep your insecurities to yourself.
- If your behavior is keeping your child from focusing on their activities successfully, you need to look carefully at how big your behavior looks.
- If your child's inattention or poor performance looks big to you, stay in the moment and try to see their problem as a step in their growth that requires your attention.

Limit Stretching and a Slinky

The preschooler who refused to eat his peanut butter and jelly sandwich (in Chapter 9) was clearly preoccupied with his own *safety* and the fragility of his world, especially if his mother and the dog got too upset all at once. Generally, parents are even more aware of the fragility of their children, and think through all kinds of strategies to keep them from getting hurt—from buying a stable baby carriage, to yelling when the child gets anywhere near the stove, to screaming at the teenager who is having trouble learning to drive. Safety is an issue that will always be on the minds of both parent and child.

Children seem wired to discover what the safety limits are for their behavior. They need to know what we consider the limits to be, so they can avoid our wrath and feel protected by our good judgment. However, when your child is carefully searching for these limits it constantly seems like a battle. It is hard to know whether you are being too harsh or too soft. Many parents have raised the white flag of surrender, feeling like their child will never learn how to behave, and certain that the child is out to make their lives miserable. I'm not surprised to meet these families in therapy.

I have found it helpful to talk with children about their own feelings in situations they are likely to be attentive to. For instance, children understand that they do believe in limits and safety issues when they are in a car and the driver is staying to the right side of the middle line in the road, or stopping at a stop sign. Even the most oppositional child will usually advocate for following the rules when confronted with the driver's options at those moments, and will clearly recognize that the rules are there for protection and safety. The art of working together is creating a dialogue around that kind of intuitive understanding.

Finding it challenging to help families who felt overpowered by their children—while raising two young children of my own—I found a helpful idea in an unexpected place. One day, I noticed a Slinky that was bent out of shape in our hallway, and realized it had been there for quite a while. I noticed that my young children knew it was there, but they didn't disturb it, instead, they just moved by, not playing with it, but not disrupting it, either. I wondered how Slinky dynamics worked in other families.

What I found was that if I brought a Slinky into a family meeting and started playing with it, that I had the full attention of the young child, and could talk their language. When I bent the Slinky, they knew exactly where I was going. Children apparently know intuitively that a stretched and bent Slinky is lonely, in pain, and has reached its limit. They are respectful, but disengaged while hoping for the Slinky to "heal." They like stretching the Slinky, but don't quite know what to do for the Slinky when it has been bent out of shape—except to leave it alone.

When I ask *who* is the Slinky in a family, the most common response from children and parents is that it is obviously the mother, stretching herself in all kinds of directions to meet everyone's emotional needs. Young children understand that when the mom/Slinky reaches their limit and bends out of shape that it stops being fun, and instead becomes a source of tension and confusion. It is relatively easy for a child to learn from a family session with a Slinky that they have some control over whether mom gets too stretched, as they do already understand what makes her feel stretched and do want to know where that limit is. The parents leave these sessions with simplified language they can use with the child ("Watch out, you're stretching the Slinky!") and the child has learned about self-awareness, attention, and self-control. This is usually a good start when a family needs to communicate better and reduce the helplessness they are all experiencing.

Talking a child's language, emphasizing their assets and resources, clarifying the issues, and offering some humor are all good strategies when working with children. Power struggles with children turn out badly. You are important to your child. You already have authority. The artistic and creative part is the way you express that authority. Before you know it, they will be teenagers who *really* are testing your authority.

Growing Pains

Adolescence is a phenomenal and unusual opportunity for growth, and not just for a child. Teenagers are obsessively seeking an identity and can also be making poor, self-defeating choices. Most teenagers seem driven to question everything they have been taught, take risks, and learn about themselves the hard way. I often share some words of wisdom with teens and their parents that were originally composed by Erma Bombeck.

The passage begins, "Someday when my children are old enough to understand the logic that motivates a mother I'll tell them...," and continues with a beautifully stated list of opportunities that children give their parents to exercise direction and love, ranging from bad manners to creepy friends to stolen candy bars to wanting something expensive or going to an unchaperoned party. Bombeck consistently expresses her love as she sets limits on her child, eventually concluding that it takes an enormous amount of authenticity and love to say "no" appropriately and consistently.

A paraphrased and anonymous version of Bombeck's passage ends with this sentiment:

> I loved you enough to let you assume the responsibility for you actions even when the penalties were so harsh they almost broke my heart.
> But most of all, I loved you enough to say NO when I knew you would hate me for it. Those were the most difficult battles of all. I'm glad I won them because in the end, you won something, too.
>
> Author Unknown

When I am discussing the art of parenting with love and discipline, I emphasize that there are different kinds of conflict. We need to know the difference between taking a stand because of a safety concern and taking a stand because we hold certain values that our children are still evaluating, doubting, and/or considering in order to define their own value systems. There are two kinds of arguments here: one about whether behavior is dangerous, and one about whether you can agree on values.

If your concern is truly about safety—and you are *sure* that is true—you need to say "NO" effectively and win the battle. The message needs to get through in a way that teaches your child in the way they learn best. When the difference of opinions is a question of values (which is much more frequent) it takes courage to know you may not win, and that the consequences may be painful for your child. Frankly, it's my opinion that if the issue is not about safety, you're in the middle of a crapshoot, and your best hope is for mixed results, even if you are lovingly saying NO. Remember: if you are thinking about what is "right" or "wrong," or trying to win an argument, the discussion is probably about values, not safety.

One of the goals to keep in mind when you have a teenager is that they need to "leave home well." I remember illustrating this for families with a very plain toy house that I had in my office. I suggested that there were three ways the child could leave home. First, he or she could jump out the upstairs window, escaping a toxic environment at an impulsive moment and getting hurt in the process. My message was both that the family was helping to create the toxicity and that the child needed to be careful when acting on their impulses.

The second option was probably the most common. I showed that the child could probably sneak out the back door at night, not really saying goodbye, and face a dark world with fences, wildlife, underbrush, and no clear paths to anywhere. This would be the result for the family that muddled through, without enough effective communication. This family situation was not so toxic that there was an alarming result, but was not really very connected to the needs of the adolescent, either. Although understood to be quite a common experience, option two indicated that the family leadership had not really grasped the bigger picture, had not thought ahead enough, and had been too expedient for many years.

The third option was for the child to leave by the front door in broad daylight, with parents at the door saying good-bye, while assuring them that they were welcome to remain part of the family. In this scenario, there are all kinds of roads and signs to help the child find their way. This result required hard work on the part of everyone, solid communication, mutual respect, plenty of flexibility, and courage.

The Apple Tree

"The apple doesn't fall very far from the tree." So they say.

When there is a teenager in the home, the tree is the parents and the apple is the adolescent, and they almost always see their situation in very different ways. The tree sees the apple growing bigger, hanging by a little stem, and worries about the safety of the apple that doesn't seem at all ready to fall. The tree doesn't really want to lose the apple and may even remember what it was like to fall when they were going through the process of maturing.

The teenager is extremely aware of being the apple, growing bigger, hanging by a stem, and not feeling very ready to fall. In fact, I have asked many such "apples" what they were thinking about and where their attention was focused, and the immediate response was that they were looking at the ground, not paying much attention to the tree. It is a visceral, obvious statement that the imminent fall to the ground is emotionally consuming. An apple is not listening to the tree. The sobering alternative for everyone, tree and apple, is for the apple to somehow *cling to the tree and not fall*. Everyone tends to understand that a dead brown apple is not a good result, either. There really is no good option.

Actually, the apple is more than just distracted. It can be shown that teenagers do not think the way adults think. I remember Dr. Michael Nerney, an expert on adolescents and brain research, telling an auditorium full of parents: *"They're not thinking!"* He taught that brain scans show that the activity in a teenager's very busy brain is in the emotional areas, and not in the planning, thinking, and avoiding negative consequences parts. It can take until the early 20s for that part of a maturing child's awareness to really kick in.

I do reassure both apple and tree that, once the apple falls, it will not roll very far away, and will still have a relationship to the tree. It may become less dependent and less emotionally enmeshed, but it will still be related. I remind them that it is the rare apple that gets scooped up and made into applesauce in some distant place. Most apples simply experience the scary fall and then settle into developing and growing where they land, just like the tree did.

The art of parenting is very challenging. Here are some pointers:

- Parenting is a special opportunity. Don't miss it.
- Being a parent can be daunting and confusing, but you can find the right balanced formula for success.
- It can be very hard to imagine what your children (or your parents) are experiencing, but it is worth it.
- It is not very easy to put parent/child differences into words. Try, anyway.
- We find it easy to carry our apple experience into our tree experience in ways that *aren't* helpful for the next apple.
- Growth is inevitable, complicated, and messy—and we need to be more ready for it.
- Everyone has better intentions than it seems.

Who Do You Care About?

I distinctly remember a mother and daughter who visited me. Mom was at the end of her rope, feeling disrespected and incompetent in the face of the adolescent "monster" in her midst. They came in together and I asked the daughter to tell me who mattered to her when she was angry, impulsive, and hostile. She immediately told us that her mother mattered the most, even as her behavior clearly stated the opposite. Strangely enough, this didn't surprise me at all.

Is it even possible to see a teenager's fury and opposition as somehow caring about her parents? When we discussed loyalty in families (in Chapter 19), I noted that in my graduate training I was immersed in the theory that we are each driven by a sense of fairness, as well as the feeling of owing our parents for their role in our lives, and caring about their well-being. Parents are dumbfounded when I suggest that their children are using their behavior to say something, and that voice is pleading with the parents to improve themselves by changing something about *their* (the parents') behavior or their attitude toward others, for the parent's sake.

What if a teenager is taking the risk of acting out so that their parents will see *their own* faults reflected in their child and get so fed up with their own failings that they will decide to change themselves for the better? That would be an example of the child being loyal at a high personal cost, all for their parent's wellness. If acting out is the only way a child feels they can express themselves, it is costly for all involved in the conflict. Children need to know that this strategy seldom works (the parents usually don't change) and parents need to know that the child has good intentions that are being expressed in an extremely clumsy way. As usual, *communication matters*.

Step back and consider who your child really is, who they care about, and how their behavior is meeting their needs, including their need to be loyal to *your* needs. They are trying really hard and processing an overload of emotional information. Try to talk about what they feel comfortable talking about. Respect their growth process. It's not easy. Don't you remember?

The Empty Nest

Finally, it is important to note how profound it is for a couple to be faced with the *end* of their direct parenting responsibilities. When the children determine that their parents will be "well enough" if they leave the nest, and so they leave, it is up to *the parents* to live up to that expectation. This is a gradual process that seems to effect couples well in advance of the actual empty nest.

Before the nest is empty, there is a clear and sensible realization that things will be different and you will be just a couple again. It is time to dust off those skills you need to nurture both captains, keep the boat balanced, and keep it moving in a healthy direction. It's not a new boat anymore, but the voyage can still be rewarding and intimate in new ways.

CAPTAIN'S LOG

Parenting is an art and a challenging opportunity for growth for the whole family.

24

What If It Works?

What if we can learn to handle unpredictable weather on the high seas? How are we going to handle the change? What happens next?

> Deep feelings are the voices that need to be heard and expressed to find our transformation. The only feelings that don't change are the ones we don't let go of.
>
> > - Anne Brener
> > author of *Mourning and Mitzvah*

A favorite phrase of mine, intended to teach church leaders that organizations work better when you concentrate on relationships and communication, jumps out of me on occasion when I'm working with couples:

"Surprised people behave badly."
- Rev. Dr. Gilbert Rendle

You may disagree with this negative view of people, or even find it upsetting, but it is worth thinking about. All it really means is that when either of you is at your tipping point, it is difficult to handle something you didn't expect. When you are feeling small and things get even tippier, it impacts your behavior. As long as your partner's behavior surprises you, you have the capacity to act badly. You are familiar with behavior you are used to, and you may rely on automatic behaviors when you are upset. When something changes, however, that can be just as upsetting as the original problem, and you may behave accordingly.

Let us revisit the couple who came to my office one weekend morning for a full day of counseling (which, on the surface, was a very courageous thing to do). They brought with them an indication that they really wanted to work together to change their relationship.

They came in and immediately made it clear that they had tried counseling before and it hadn't really made any difference, suggesting that they didn't really expect anything to change. Remarkably, given their prediction, as the day went by, they took off their shoes, faced each other calmly with their feet up on the sofa, and talked very intimately about themselves, their emotional lives, their families, their needs, and their desires. From what I could see, this was turning into a model session.

What made this couple memorable, however, was that at the end of the day, a switch seemed to be flicked off. They put their shoes back on and they sounded just like they had when they entered in the morning, as they were telling me in that same initial voice that the session hadn't made any difference and nothing was going to change.

I never met with them again. Evidently, for some people it can be that important to avoid change. Even if they did make adjustments because of that session, I got the feeling that they would always claim that they hadn't really had to deal with change. You may need to ask yourselves whether you will resist change the way this couple did.

Dog Catches Car!

It may well be that one or both of you is not ready for change, and would be much more comfortable if you could complain about what you are experiencing *and* could then have what you are familiar with. What a deal. You can act entitled, justify what you want, and then have your partnership or family or job end up feeling familiar. Imagine how powerful it would be if you could reliably expect things to turn out "the usual way," just like some dogs I remember watching with interest.

In Athens, Greece, there are seemingly lots of homeless dogs, and I had noticed that they seem to congregate at busy intersections so they can chase cars together. It is actually fascinating to watch as the lights change and the dogs charge off after the cars in two directions, and then the lights change again and the gathered dogs chase cars in the other two directions. This seems to be an expected and familiar part of the dogs' lives, presumably offering a sense of community and a sport to play, as well. They eagerly push themselves to catch a car, but they never actually catch one.

What I wondered about is what it would be like for a dog that was part of this canine culture if they actually *caught* a car. Imagine the look on the dog's face if they actually reached their apparent goal and succeeded in tracking down a vehicle. What would they be feeling if they had their teeth around the bumper of a car that was charging through the streets of Athens? My suspicion is that they would no longer be calm, collected, and purposeful, but totally confused, scared, and distraught. Surely, we might have the same reaction if our partner started to change in the way we wanted them to. The change might be surprising, and we could behave badly as a result.

It is normal to expect and desire familiarity. When you also want change, you need to be ready to feel something unexpected when change does occur.

Unexpected Reactions

As I mentioned in Chapter 7, I was struck by an unexpected reaction to change, once, while sitting in an airplane. In essence, the car I had been chasing had seemed unreachable, but I had finally caught the car and firmly clamped down on the bumper.

I had just spent two exhilarating years immersed in graduate school, learning to be a therapist. I had taken fascinating courses, done hundreds of hours of clinical work with families, and written a thesis—all in the minimum possible amount of time. I was going to graduate and move on to the challenge of a new career. I was rewarding myself with a solo trip to Hawaii to visit my sister, relax, and bask in my accomplishments. You would think this would have been one of the happiest days of my life, but I was sitting there in my airplane seat, in tears. What had happened?

I had learned that these emotional 'feeling small' moments were opportunities to ask myself not only what I was feeling, but also *how* my feelings had come to be. I eventually understood that I was experiencing *loss*, when I had expected to be experiencing gratification and joy. I had indeed lost all of the familiar aspects of my life from the previous two years, including the courses, the fellow students, and the thesis (that I had been working so hard to lose). I had reached my goal, and it was bewildering and scary to face something completely new. I was grieving the loss of the familiar—even though I hadn't wanted to keep it.

I was surprised to be feeling sad, but the surprise did not

lead to any negative behavior. Really, what was I going to do? I didn't get mad at anyone on the plane or medicate myself or pretend that I didn't have feelings. I found a healthy route to the next step. I was able to short circuit the pattern that leads from feeling small to regrettable big behavior by asking myself what was happening to me and reflecting on my situation in a deliberate way, avoiding the minefield of automatic reactions to compensate for feeling small.

How hard is it to handle change?

It is remarkable how quickly we expect each other to change and then how unlikely we are to completely *accept* change. We've all spent much of our childhood in classrooms and know that teachers are expected to be responsive when children change. We also know that, even for teachers, it is practically impossible to completely change a perception of someone else. Think about the class star who suddenly bungles a test or throws a spitball. Does the teacher discipline them harshly? Think about the disruptive kid who constantly fails, and what happens if they have a good day and sit in their seat and pay attention. Does the teacher confirm the change and treat them like they can be a star? It's very hard for teachers to do—even though they are *trained* and *paid* to be ready to make those adjustments. Actually, even with that training, they can't really be in the moment all of the time. There is an echo chamber, a doubt, a sense that the child will revert to their standard behavior, and that affects the actual behavior of the teacher.

We all know about school, but we ignore this lesson when our partner changes or when we expect our partner to notice that *we* have changed. It takes time. If a trained teacher who is expected, trained, and paid to adapt can't respond purely in the moment, how on earth can we expect ourselves or our partners to do so? Let's give each other a better chance to notice the changes and be more patient about earning credit before we give up on change. What makes us so uncomfortable about change, anyway?

Handling Ambiguity

It seems that there are some very harsh truths about the way we are built, and they create liabilities when it comes to our attempts to handle change or build meaningful relationships.

Oliver Sachs, in the book *Your Inner Fish*, describes how a group of preschoolers first reacted to an ancient fossil he found among the Inuit of the Arctic, which appeared to be partly a fish and partly a crocodile. The preschoolers first took sides, some claiming it was a crocodile, and some a fish. The stormy impasse was fortunately settled by a four-year-old, who had the presence to say it was really *both.* The ambiguity of the fossil had caused tension at first because predictability and reliability are so important to young children (and us), but the child showed that it is possible to have the courage to see that two answers can coexist.

We are constantly experiencing this kind of irregularity and incongruity in our relationships. Our own life experience tells us what to expect, and then our intimate relationships surprise us. We need to be open to ambiguity.

In the September 2012 issue of *Psychology Today*, Lauren Friedman cites research suggesting that "the greater the frequency of people's *mixed* emotional experiences over time, the slower their age-related decline," and, "the ability to withstand the tension of feeling *both* positive and negative emotions may represent an important human strength." (emphasis added)

If, in your partnership, you find it too jarring that the other person has an opposite sensibility about emotions and situations, then you will not be very ready for ambiguity or change. For instance, if you are chronically expedient and speed up your reactions when your partner slows down, or talk more when they go silent, or get more logical when they get emotional, you are exaggerating the opposite of their sensibility. On the other hand, if you strive to have *both* sensibilities and see the world with both perspectives, as a couple, then you will benefit emotionally from that joint perspective.

Perhaps it is our most intimate moments that inform our emotional responses. Maybe the familiar biological reactions to having sex and reproducing are actually very powerful in forming our expectations about emotions. Maybe some of the most confusing and hurtful dynamics that couples experience are not actually that surprising.

Author Jared Diamond (in *The Third Chimpanzee*) makes it irresistibly clear that our relentless purpose on this earth is to reproduce and keep our species thriving. Our entire existence is about juggling our genes and getting them into the next generation with certainty. What if the way we are built to consummate this innate drive really dictates many of our emotional assumptions about our partners?

As little girls, do women learn that the real action of reproduction happens inside them and that gets translated into how important emotions and feelings are? Does this become the guide for seeking serenity and judging other people? Does it also develop into an assumption that someone who has been inside them knows what they are thinking and feeling all the time?

Do little boys learn that nothing important happens inside them, that the action is external, and the real action is in defending what is vulnerable and exposed? Is it then confusing and strange for feelings and emotions to compete with defensive behaviors, logic, strategies, and impulses? Does that become the guide for establishing who is right or superior?

Does that develop into an assumption that emotions and feelings are foreign and dangerous, while behavior matters?

What happens when you combine boys' and girls' perspectives? Do you delight in the combining, or do you evade the complexity?

Two of the most important family systems thinkers of the early twenty-first century, John Gottman and Susan Johnson, emphasize opposite perspectives on relationships and change. Gottman emphasizes the data that he has collected about relationships, quantifies dreaded responses, and predicts outcomes based on behaviors, and, in that way, is a special resource for couples and families. Johnson, on the other hand, emphasizes that feelings are central and need to be the focus of effective communication, and that our emotions hold the key to creating healthier and stronger relationships. Her message is also crucial to grasp and cherish.

Both of them have ideas with merit and mean what they are saying. There is no point in choosing one over the other, as it is more helpful to find a way to apply both perspectives, using data *and* emotions to help navigate your boat. It would seem that opening our mind to both perceptions is the healthiest option.

Handling Change

Ultimately, you will handle change better if you can be flexible. You are in charge of your familiar perceptions and your imagination, and you are likely to trust them when you are under pressure. If what you experience feels too much like you are a dog who just caught a car you weren't expecting to catch—or if you are relying on familiar experiences to keep you feeling like things are under control—then you will have difficulty when your partner changes, and vice versa.

Johan was one of my favorite visitors, and I remember

him describing how he had handled himself while he was changing his approach to his marriage, his children, his job, and his future. To Johan, the goal was to balance old automatic responses that weren't working with new ones that promised a better marriage, less stress, and a deeper personal life. He told me that it was like "learning to use your other hand"— perhaps as if he had broken his right hand by pointlessly punching a wall, and needed to do more things with his left hand. He knew he could continue to get things done quickly and be more expedient with his usual hand, but he needed to keep finding out what would happen if he used the other hand. Thinking of his life this way was a simple and elegant way to keep reminding himself that he was feeling small, but needed to have the courage to try something new.

I illustrated what Johan was telling me by grabbing my trusty Slinky and holding it in both hands, alternating which hand I was raising. The Slinky flowed from one hand to the other, energizing the situation in a way that it could not have done with only one hand raising it. The Slinky's energy represented the new dynamic that Johan was able to experience—creating a healthier outlook on his life and a more satisfying marriage—while it did not feel threatening to him because it was still contained by the Slinky and his own two hands.

Feeling safe when things change requires an awareness of your responsibility about your own emotions, reactions, and behaviors. It is easier to be upset and it is very tempting to stick with what is familiar, reliable, and predictable. Try to resist the temptation.

How do you achieve this?

- Try not to be surprised by what you experience. Your surprised behavior may not be very attractive. What's so surprising, anyway?

- Change can be threatening—but it can also be an opportunity. Change can be ambiguous, confusing, and exciting. Change can be something to avoid, or to embrace. Change can be what you wanted—or even more.
- Juggling different emotions, and choices for behavior, can be productive, and even healthy.

CAPTAIN'S LOG

Change can surprise us in a good way if we embrace the possibility.

25

Separation and Divorce: Leaving a Tippy Boat Behind

Is there ever a time to abandon ship and start over, despite the obvious costs? How does that happen, and are there ways to make the process less painful, especially for the children?

> In a crisis—when we get divorced, when we lose our jobs, when we have a depression—that's when we find out what is real. We create our own crises in order to become who we already are.
>
> - Paul Hwoschinsky
> author of *True Wealth*

Ben and Julia's voyage was getting stormier by the week. Instead of reconciling, their visits told me that they were becoming more aware that they needed to separate, and that doing so would be best for both of them. It seemed that they no longer wanted to work on improving things. What had happened?

I suggested to them that they were behaving like certain organizations I've visited. When I meet with a board or an important committee, I suggest that they experience themselves "orming" (a term which I'll explain soon). Through an exercise involving throwing a ball around, the group learns about normal dynamics and growth. If our innate responses were more logical, coherent, and more under control, groups and couples would work in an orderly way, but they are more complicated than that.

What do I mean by "orming"? The idea is borrowed from Bruce Tuckman's well-researched model of group development and teamwork (published in 1965), and is based in a set of similar—yet very different—words:

F*orming*: This is the fun, promising, hopeful, fresh part. A relationship starts, or a group forms. It is exciting. It's the "building-a-boat" stage.

St*orming*: You discover that you aren't the same as each other, you have different sensibilities, and are trying to live together. Tension builds. Behavior happens. More tension builds.

N*orming*: You establish norms, which means that there are ways you operate as a couple that you've worked out by forming and storming, and by intending to have a deep meaningful relationship.

Perf*orming*: You accomplish things—together—like establishing your careers, furnishing your home, or having children. These are shared successes.

The problem is that, for a couple, these four things don't just happen in that order and stop. Instead, they circle back around, get mixed up, and don't ever reach an end. Relentlessly, new things tip the boat, your further reactions tip the boat, you negotiate as two captains, and the boat moves on to new places. Change, it turns out, is what is actually predictable and normal.

Storming and norming keep happening, and occasionally do so in surprising ways.

Ideally, a marriage would unfold in the order described above, and then settle down in a secure and satisfying way. But, no amount of planning, religious dogma, grace, or controlling behavior can guarantee that you will experience these four stages, and only experience them once, and then proceed to live happily ever after.

Getting Honest With Yourself

Divorce is a decision that carries long-term personal legal and financial consequences—some of which can be hard to predict. As profound as this decision is, and as complicated and costly as the consequences may be for you and those people dear to you, it is nonetheless an entirely personal and private choice.

As hard as you may have tried, and as much as you've wanted a fulfilling and enriching relationship, you may feel that it has become too toxic and that your troubles can't be resolved. That is what Ben and Julia were discovering. Ben finally said, "It took me ten years to get to the point where I could say I didn't want this marriage anymore. I really don't want to go back through that process again."

My therapy sessions with Ben and Julia were spent ensuring that they had witnessed each other's feelings and perspectives on the marriage, and examining their responses to the prospect of divorcing. Both the internal dialogue that Ben experienced before our sessions and the couple's shared dialogue in my office were important. Apparently, the experience of reviewing and debating the resolution that Ben had made with himself was enough to make him sure about his decision. Julia had little choice but to acknowledge that Ben had made a decision, communicate her own anxiety and despair about the decision, and gradually move forward.

If you have reached the point where it is obvious that divorce is a possibility, you will need to face the situation with clarity and courage. Ideally, you would make this crucial decision as a couple, using some of the techniques I have discussed (especially those from Chapter 21), but that would be unusual. More likely, you will each need to determine what stand you are taking and be prepared to disagree with your partner. If you both decide to stay together, or both decide to divorce, consider yourselves fortunate and trust your decision. If you disagree, you are headed down a path of intense emotions and personal growth.

In order to make such a difficult personal decision, you need to be as aware as possible of your needs, desires, and vulnerabilities. It can be valid to decide that you don't want to be with your partner anymore, even after weighing the impact that such a decision can have on your future, your children, your career, and your other relationships. Remember that you are making a profound statement about what you need, how you operate emotionally, and what works for you. Make sure it is authentic.

Have an honest dialogue with yourself, before you declare that you've made a decision. As off-putting as the language sounds, it's vital to make a "cost/benefit" analysis of your relationship, trying to determine whether the burdens of staying in the relationship outweigh the benefits, or vice versa. It is worth focusing your mind on that level of analysis because of what is at stake. Take your time and do a thorough accounting.

If the boat still seems too tippy to you, despite your best intentions and efforts, try to picture a weighing scale that compares costs and benefits and tells you which is heavier. Ask yourself the questions that are listed below. Take your time to consider what you're doing. There is no timetable for the decision you are making. Imagine pouring positive and negative sand into the two sides of the scale as you answer the questions. The benefits side of the scale measures the positive reasons for staying committed to your partner. The costs side measures the negative aspects of your partnership and reasons for separating.

- Do you feel safe in this relationship?
- What is your legacy as a couple? What have you created together? If you have owned a business or raised children, could the legacy stand for itself, or would it be damaged?
- What meaningful moments have the two of you shared? Do you wish to honor those or move past them?
- Have intimate or sexual moments been authentic, restorative, and fun; or have they been unsatisfying—or even unpleasant?
- Has your partner gone out of their way to support you when you have needed them? Are you grateful for that, or does it not matter to you?
- What have you learned from your partner? Are those lessons that make you more whole, or do they diminish you?
- How much have you needed your partner to compensate for your blind spots or help out in situations in which you simply don't perform well?
- How dependent are you on your partner's presence? Do you still need them or not?
- Are you still in love with each other?

Try to be aware of what you are measuring—and how you measure it. As you work through the list of questions, if you think of more questions, answer those, too. Finally, when you've taken the time to think about and answer all of your questions, look at the scales in front of you. Which scale has more sand in it? Which scale has *heavier* sand in it? Is one half empty and the other half full? Perhaps if you think you are leaning toward separation, the "costs" scale seems half full and contains optimism, hope, and promise about something new along with your misgivings about your relationship; while the "benefits" scale seems half empty and contains equally weighty loyalty, memories, and obligations from a disappointing journey as a couple. This is not your final answer. There are many complex issues to consider. You may want to return to this list of questions when you have read the rest of the chapter.

Remember that you are asking yourself—very frankly— what matters most to you, and comparing the good and hopeful aspects of your relationship to the disappointing ones. What makes a particular issue important to you? What makes a deal-breaker a deal-breaker—if that is indeed what it is? You may be responding to a sense of injustice you feel in the relationship, experiencing disappointment about your level of fulfillment or satisfaction, or perhaps recognizing that you have grown and think differently from the way you used to. You may now be more aware of your emotions, and trusting them more— or trusting them less—than you did before. Think it through. You'll know what the score is for you.

You may also need to weigh your own beliefs, any cultural norms, and the family expectations that are part of your world. You may feel that some of these are so powerful that they create an obligation to stay in your partnership. You may feel that these aspects are not really negotiable and that you do not have an option.

If this is the case, you may want to revisit Chapter 10 and see whether you can give yourself permission to make choices based on your own perceptions and personal history. You are encouraged to claim "the Kingdom of God within you" (as was discussed in Chapter 5), assess what serves your mental health and well being, and allow yourself an internal dialogue about your needs, while remaining aware of your impact on others, especially your children.

You may need to be honest with yourself about your own readiness for change (as we discussed in the last chapter). You may need to consider whether it is the time in your development to change the way you are living, or growing. There are distinct stages of your own—and your family's—life cycle, and it may or may not seem appropriate for you to experience the coming stage *on your own*, even if you feel prepared for a different kind of life.

If you are comparing a new relationship with your current one, keep the following things in mind. It can be thrilling to cheat and keep things secret, but that thrill will go away when you change the basis of the new partnership. It is usually more fun, less serious, less pressured, and generally less complicated to visit with or confide in someone new, but what will happen when the "new" wears off? If you have not understood your part of the dance you're now thinking of leaving, and can't hold yourself accountable now, you are likely to repeat that dance again. If you haven't learned, matured, or taken stock of how you operate, you may not be ready to start a new dance in a new way.

Or, if you're like Ben, you've struggled long and honestly with all of these issues, and still believe you need to move on. If so, you are ready to make one of the most important declarations of your life.

It's Over . . . The "Tearable" Marriage: Considering Children's Needs

It is important that you and your partner share the responsibility for a voyage ending in disruption and that, as adults, you continue to take responsibility for the development of the children you have been taking care of. After all, children are neither mistakes nor reversible.

I vividly remember working in a clinic and being assigned to a family in a classic bind. The parents were divorcing and their ten-year-old son was clearly blaming himself for the divorce, acting out by throwing tantrums and refusing to go to school. How was I going to simplify this situation in a way that would break through their fog of divorcing, trying to parent a difficult child, and visiting a mental health clinic?

I came up with an intervention that I now call the "*tearable* marriage."

I started by showing everyone a *clean sheet* of yellow paper from my writing pad. I said it represented the mom and dad's relationship when they were building their boat—hopeful, happy, full of love, dreamy about the future, unblemished. Then I started to make their beautiful piece of paper more complicated.

By simply scrawling the family's last name across it, I made the page less perfect and more serious. Declaring that the parents were a couple had somehow also changed the piece of paper. Now it was unique, something they held privately, making it more emotional and important, as well as somehow less spontaneous and free. The boat had been built.

Next, I introduced the idea of having children by drawing *three squares* along the edge of the paper, using about a third of the page. The couple's relationship was suddenly much more complicated, as the paper illustrated the splitting up of both their emotional needs and the focus of their energies. I labeled the three boxes "MOTHER," "FATHER," and "CO-PARENTING," explaining that their shared emotional attachment as a couple became more complicated by the need for mom to parent the child, the need for dad to parent the child, and the combined responsibility to make joint decisions about things that a child wasn't ready to decide (such as health care, schools, religion, what money was spent on, and so forth).

With everyone's attention riveted on the changes in the piece of paper, I introduced the issue of the parents divorcing. First, I tore off the three squares and presented them to their son, pristine and unharmed. He was *entitled*, I said, to a good relationship with his mother, a good relationship with his father, and their continued co-parenting for his benefit. Those rights were separate from the turmoil the parents were experiencing.

What was now left in my hand was the parents' relationship. This was what the piece of paper had represented all along. The child was *not* responsible for it. His parents had started their connection before he was born and had eventually mangled it. I started folding it and tearing it and crumpling it, until they agreed it represented the current condition of the partnership. My recollection is that the mother wanted to keep a piece of it and the father wanted to throw it away. Their son, seemingly calmer, more attentive, and more hopeful, held firmly to his guarantees (the three squares) about the future, and bore no blame for the condition of the rest of the piece of paper. Meanwhile, the parents owned the path of their partnership and the way each of them wanted to handle the change that had happened.

I like to say that, like it or not, you have changed the piece of paper as it got more complicated. Living together, sharing your lives, and having children can make the relationship more complex. Chances are that the same confusing complexity happened to your parents. Having children may have resulted in the crumpling or tearing of your piece of paper, but only because you continued to expect—or felt entitled to—the amount of attention or affection you were getting before a child came into your life. I remind my clients: *The child did not tear up your piece of paper. Your behavior did.* You started your dance and you chose to complicate it. It's always been your relationship, to handle your way.

Responsible Co-Parenting

If you have had children together, you've made them. There's no way to get around the biology and the reality of what you did. You've been a child and you know that from a child's vantage point there are two parents, each setting standards and nurturing in their own, often clumsy, way. It is in your child's interest for you to establish a way to keep sharing in the decisions that they are still too young to make for themselves and, later, to be good sports as they age, get married, or have their own children's grandparents over to visit.

It is well understood (among family therapists and lawyers who handle divorces) that your divorce happens in two stages: the legal stage and the emotional stage. It is not simple or automatic to be *emotionally* divorced, and it happens on its own two timetables, one for each of you. Part of becoming emotionally divorced is to disengage from your marriage while you continue to share parenting duties. You need to get to the place where you are not in your marriage but are "simply" parenting. That is not an easy change to make. It means you are not fighting each other anymore, but you are still advocating for your own idea of your child's needs, your financial needs, and your own integrity and dignity. You do this *for your children*— yes, including the "not fighting about your marriage" part.

I once was observing a family therapy session that featured parents who had divorced, and their two kids. The kids sat in the middle. At exactly half past the hour, the kids spontaneously stood up and traded places between the parents, showing a balanced loyalty to both parents, with the children being central to the parents' interaction. Their movement was their statement, and was not related to the content of the session or any direction by the therapist. It struck me as an elegant way for the kids to express exactly the dignity, fairness, and balance that they needed. It is up to parents going through divorce to live up to that standard.

Getting to Know Yourself

Leaving the boat behind is the beginning of a whole new voyage—whether on sea or on land. It is hard to know what to expect. It may help to expect the unexpected. There will be unanticipated costs, both emotional and financial. You may experience emotions you didn't expect (ranging from relief when you expect to be sad but aren't, to loss and sadness when you are reminded of a shared experience). Everyone in the family will respond to the change in his or her own way, and those responses can get confusing and complicated. And don't forget that, because of the stress associated with any major change, your health may be affected as well.

The next thing I'm about to say may not be easy to hear, but it's important. If you are the leave-*er*, you are *abandoning* your partner—even if you feel that they emotionally abandoned you, first. You have made a personal decision, decided what your limits are, and are trying to meet your own emotional needs in a new way. You have tried to measure how much toxicity you are already tolerating—and how much is too much to take. You will need to hold yourself accountable for the impact of your behavior, and *trust yourself* as you move forward.

If you are the leave-*ee*, it may have come as a surprise that your partner is actually leaving. Give yourself a grace period to handle the anger and hurt, and whatever else you may be feeling about your loss. You will need time to recover. You can assess things when you are ready.

Later, *both* of you can take a close look at your behaviors, expectations, and values so you can hold *yourselves* accountable in a useful way. Keep in mind that throughout a relationship, abandonment often leads to "sliming" and that sliming often leads to abandonment.

When you are ready, take a good look at how you were co-captaining the boat, and how you were reacting whenever the boat felt as though it was tipping away from you. Chances are, your behavior was making things seem tippier to your partner.

If you've gone through a divorce, you know that everyone feels the loss—and there are no winners. We would all prefer to avoid the agony, despite the potential for personal growth. That is one reason you are reaching out for the ideas in this book.

Whatever you decide to do, in the future you will still want to get that familiar crazy normal big/small distortion under control. Because you are still responsible for your actions and their impact on those around you, you need to remember that both of you have felt small and both of you have looked big. Learn to remember that the other person feels small, too. Learn how to say that you feel small—and that it matters. Learn how to modify your own behavior so it doesn't look so big. Learn how to be in the present moment so your mind isn't making things look bigger than they are as they happen. These are skills you'll need on *any* relationship voyage—including your next one.

CAPTAIN'S LOG

Divorce is a profound choice that can be handled well.

26

FOG!

On a boat, our relationships and families can be very confusing and we can get lost in the fog. This is actually an opportunity. What does it take to seize the opportunity to take care of our selves and those around us?

> Enlightenment is to hold the entire experience—pain and joy, agony and happiness—in one nondual, eternal embrace, and to escape nowhere, because there's nowhere to escape to."
>
> - Andrew Harvey
> author of *Hidden Journey: A Spiritual Awakening*

You may have been thinking that this process of becoming a better partner and establishing a more meaningful relationship was about your own personal growth and mental health. In fact, much of this process has been therapy *for you*, dressed up as a way to improve your partnership. You are, after all, the reader and the person trying to learn and change. A relationship won't change much unless the people develop and change. You are the agent—through your reactions, thoughts, and behavior—for creating new outcomes. It can't be any other way.

As we've noted, relationships are a series of transactions, and it can seem like you have established an ongoing account with your partner, full of giving and taking, loaning and owing, unbalancing and rebalancing. You are, then, *accountable* for your contribution to this account and share responsibility for the current balance.

How do you engage in this accounting? When are you giving and when are you taking? What balance remains in the account until the next issue comes up? Does it feel fair? What is driving these dynamics for you and lots of other couples?

George and Diane have very different public lives, she as a teacher and he as an artist. Diane wants George to speak perfectly in public about his art and organize his presentations. George wants Diane to be more spontaneous and less rigid about her teaching. Neither wants to change how they do their job, both want to be understood and appreciated, and both want the other to benefit from their advice. These desires for change can overflow into other aspects of their lives.

Unfortunately, George and Diane have constant arguments about cleaning up the kitchen. After cooking dinner, she expects him to clean everything up quickly, but he sees the kitchen as a space that is always being used, and prefers to take his time tidying up after a meal and doing the dishes. When this topic comes up in one of their therapy sessions—and it quickly reaches a level of quick defensive and sharp responses—I tell them to stop discussing it because *I* am the only one listening. Although the content might be useful, I stop them so they notice what frame of mind they are in when they are having unproductive encounters.

George tells me he feels justified in being relaxed about

the kitchen, and that he also wishes that Diane would relax. She, unsurprisingly, feels justified in wanting the space to be clean and also wishes that George was a less lazy person. Something very personal is making each of them take the stand they take—and it isn't just about the mess in the kitchen. What I discovered is that both of them are picking this topic to take a stand and get listened to. Both of them also truly want something better for the other person.

The argument, when it is taken apart, serves to express: 1) a deep need for control; 2) a frustration about not being important or persuasive enough; and, 3) a deep caring for the other person. Both people are accountable for *all three* aspects of the interaction. It may seem like a safety issue for both people, an opportunity to get noticed and acknowledged, and also a time to express what each person wants for the other person's growth. In this case, George wants Diane to be less emotional, clean-minded, and anxious for her mental health because he presumably likes being the way *he is*. Diane wants George to be more organized and take fewer risks, because she presumably likes being the way *she is*. The arguments escalate mostly because both people want to be respected and passionately want the best for the other person.

If this sounds familiar—and you are projecting your own needs onto your partner and really want *yourself* to relax or to get more organized—then the dynamics can get even more complicated. In their case, Diane would suddenly accuse George of being rigid, distant, or thoughtless, while he would respond by pointing out things that she always forgets. Each of them are seeing their own insecurities, inadequacies, and exaggerations in the other person. To move forward, they must each realize that they are accountable for these motivations and actions.

Growth

You may recall (from Chapter 11) that we pondered the importance of encountering FOG on your voyage together. When things are baffling and complicated, happening too fast, putting you on edge, or not feeling like they are under control, you are experiencing FOG. We have defined any of these experiences as an "F---ing Opportunity for Growth." These are actually moments that give you an opportunity to learn, to try something new, to take a risk, or to catch yourself—even though they are uncomfortable.

Is growth actually a good thing? Actually, whether it is or isn't doesn't matter—you don't have much choice. You have a capacity to seek a better understanding of your world, and a competing capacity to be afraid that the world is an unjust or unsafe place, but on balance, the urge to improve and grow is really hard to extinguish.

In fact, I would argue that we have an innate capacity to use our curiosity, to take risks, and to optimistically seek personal growth and development, in spite of the fog.

I once put this idea to the test by asking very troubled people to picture some *stairs*. I didn't elaborate on what kind of stairs to imagine, where they led, or how they were to be used. I just wanted each person to describe their gut response to the idea of stairs, and a description of what they imagined. I was inspired by their answers. Most of these people—many of whom were hospitalized for their disorders—visualized a stairway going up to the next, brighter level, and not a dark stairway heading to a basement. It was remarkable, because life had been brutal and abusive to many, and although there was little hope in their stories, they were refusing to get any smaller, or go down the stairs. They were all choosing to go up—to grow.

Actually, I think it is this refusal to give up or get any

smaller that probably triggers our quick reactions when we are cornered or feel threatened when the boat is tippy. We compensate with large behavior, in a hurry. We are trying to stay safe, not disappear, and especially to take care of ourselves. That is the impulsive way we try to grow. But, there is a more intentional and deliberate way to grow, too.

Climbing the Steps

An opportunity for personal growth is embedded in each challenging and tippy moment on the boat. It takes courage to see challenges as opportunities, however, and to take advantage of those moments in an inspired and healthy way. Everyone handles their own impulses to grow in their own ways, and this can be compared to facing a very large stairway, full of opportunities, choices, and rewards.

This idea hit me one day when I was teaching a group of graduate students about family systems. They were from a wide array of universities, and were preparing to be very dignified and respected professionals as psychiatrists, psychologists, and therapists. They were enrolled in excellent programs with talented teachers. Despite all of that, I found them, one day, in a funk, complaining to each other about their shared experience as graduate students—feeling like they were being treated like children, not sure if they would succeed, feeling out to sea. I told them it felt like I'd just walked into a class full of third graders who were suddenly realizing that teachers gave grades, that they might not make it to fourth grade, and that adults weren't always nice to them. I asked them what had happened.

We talked about their plight (which, by the way, is nearly universal in graduate school) and I drew the side of an ancient pyramid on the board—a series of *huge steps*— and suggested that the third graders and the graduate students were actually experiencing the same thing from different places on the pyramid.

Each step on the pyramid feels the same. You are on one of the steps, and driven to keep moving up the pyramid, but the closer you get to the next step, the bigger the wall in front of you looks. If you take care of yourself and slow down, then you lose momentum, have doubts, and start slipping backward toward where you started. Before you know it, you are back at the cliff behind you that you just somehow climbed, you catch yourself, and point yourself back in the direction of growth. We experience these stages of growth as frustrating circles, moving toward our goal, slowing down to avoid hitting the wall, slipping backwards, and catching ourselves before we fall off the cliff, with new energy to move upward. When we are faced with these obstacles and complain, we sound like the students in my class (or third graders), blaming others, feeling sorry for ourselves, and unsure if we can make it.

The next time you sit down in a room, imagine that room as a giant step on a giant stairway or pyramid. The wall facing you represents the next step and the space *above* it is where you are trying to go. Imagine the wall growing as you stand up and move toward it, then imagine slowing down to keep from getting hurt, and drifting backwards toward the cliff behind where you've been sitting before you catch yourself and start moving toward your goals again. That's the way I think the graduate students—and third graders—were experiencing the process of growth.

Since that day with my graduate students, I have thought about these growth circles and wondered what strategies can help us grow effectively. I have come up with five ideas:

1) Look around when you achieve a new growth stage. Take a seat after you arrive and get acclimated, enjoy the accomplishment, and dream a little. When you are ready, look up *over the wall* that represents the next

step, and imagine what that might look like. Where, what, how, and with whom do you imagine your future circumstances? Drink it in and remember it because you are not going to be able to see it anymore as you move forward toward the wall. You will need the picture in your head as a reminder and an inspiration.

2) Think about how you have climbed steps before. What is your style? Do you wait for the wind to blow you? Do you meticulously build a beautiful stairway? Is it more like a climbing wall with a few hand- and foot-holds? Do you grab a ladder? Do you wait for someone to lend a hand, either a push from behind or a pull from above? Do you tie a rocket to your back and hope to land on the next step? Consider how you have gotten where you are. How did you emerge from your family or start your career? How did you get yourself educated in either a street-smart or book-smart way? How did you get yourself involved in the unpredictable world of having an intimate relationship? Keep in mind what your assets and skills are so that you can use them again as you move forward.

3) Imagine the wall in front of you is a traffic light. When you are driving ahead, trying to grow, the light turns yellow, because it is a wall. Do you slow down and lose your momentum, or do you speed up and risk hitting the wall? What are the benefits and risks of what you do automatically? Notice the cliff behind you. Imagine that it is lined with tacks that will puncture your tires—like the spikes in a parking lot warning you to not back up. Do you catch yourself and avoid falling, even without that prompt?

4) How big is the wall looking to you? Don't let it look bigger than it really is. You are just embarking on

another stage of your natural growth.

5) You need lift. That wall is tall and you need to be as light as possible. Is this the time to shed something that keeps weighing you down? Is there a personal burden you have been carrying that keeps thwarting your personal growth? When you are focused on growth, it is also your opportunity to take stock, look at your garbage, and, with a sense of dignity and purpose, put aside things that don't serve you well. Be honest with yourself. Streamline yourself for the journey upward.

Again, this process seems to be predictable. There is nothing wrong with trying to do it well. You have overcome these walls before, and once you've circled around for a while, you'll be defining a new step to try to get over, assessing your strengths, picking up cues, and perhaps reducing your load. Try to do all of these things, or think of more.

Both/And

What if you are embracing your own growth opportunity, but you're still in the fog?

One of the key themes of this book is that opposing things happen together. This is a journey that emphasizes the power of BOTH. To improve your life, to experience personal growth, and to make your partnership more satisfying, you need to develop a frame of mind that allows you to hold opposites in your hands at the same time.

Emotionally speaking, we don't have much time to separate opposites. Feeling small *and* looking big both seem to happen at the same time. Giving to your partner and receiving from your partner happen together. Expressing yourself and listening happen all at once. The boat feeling tippy and you trying to keep it from tipping happen simultaneously. Feeling attacked and defending yourself happen in tandem. Being challenged by your child (or partner) and trying to parent well (or be a good co-captain) occur together. Looking after yourself and trying to be a considerate caretaker seem to happen at the same time. Through your partner's eyes, your caretaking and a sense that you are overwhelming them can happen together— and even seem arrogant to the person you care about.

Simply slowing the process down enough to hold more *confusion* in your mind will help you connect with your partner and feel like you have gotten this play of opposites more under control.

There is a stereotype about marriage counseling which says that the clever therapist always intervenes and says "Ah, you see, you are both right." But—although it may be a cliché— that viewpoint is worth considering. For example, going back to our earlier discussion:

Diane says that George is not only ignoring her needs about the kitchen, but is also paying too much attention to one of the children. This leaves Diane feeling isolated, and it makes her jealous and reactive toward the child. At the same time, he says that her behavior toward the child makes him want to defend the child and be dismissive of Diane. They are both feeling small, they can both justify what they are doing, and they are both stuck in a dance that keeps reinforcing itself. If George and Diane can see that *both* perspectives are valid, and remember the kaleidoscope (or the two sides of the boat, or how men and women intuitively respond to each other), they will have the tools to catch themselves and see that they are going down a dark alley.

It can seem like only half an enchilada to get your own perspective under control, but it is the half you can control. Focus your potential and your energy on ways you can hold more than one perspective in your mind.

Actually, when you are both applying your talents to our familiar distortion (of both of you feeling small and both of you looking big), you are making two things happen at the same time in each quadrant. When one of you is trying to reduce the size of your behavior, the other is trying to be more mindful about how big he or she looks. When one of you is looking for ways to say you feel small, the other is trying to remember how small you are feeling, and listen for the words you are looking for.

What we have been talking about are the basic tools for a healthier relationship. It takes courage and strength to accept more than one truth at a time or work as a team. When you do, you are developing a more balanced and stable view of the world. You are integrating and synthesizing parts of yourself and your immediate surroundings.

Improving your relationships in a lasting way is not really about fixing *your partner*. Actually, it is about handling *yourself*. If it is daunting that personal growth and integrity require this degree of flexibility, acceptance, curiosity, and creativity, you may want still more visual cues to help you achieve that level of growth. Read on.

CAPTAIN'S LOG

Opportunities for growth are constant, confusing and challenging.

27

Fourth Interlude – Checking the Horizon

Taking an opportunity for a final "interlude," let's step back again from the voyage and see what it looks like from a distance.

> Attention is what allows us to perceive and act upon the information that comes to us. If we're not paying attention, we're not going to get it. Attention is the coin of the realm; attention is what we pay.
>
> - Nicki Scully
> author of *The Golden Cauldron:*
> *Shamanic Journeys on the Path*
> *of Wisdom*

Looking objectively at the voyage, let's gather some more wisdom to help with the rest of the trip. Remember not to rush, but to read at your own pace and notice what strikes you before you move on.

Ahoy, Mate!

One of the challenging things about a boat is that there is *weather.*

Why not ask yourself, did you dress the best way for this weather? Are you ready for the weather to change? Is that umbrella you are carrying going to get somebody hurt?

Feeling powerless without a weather forecast?

Feeling powerless about the climate?

Maybe there are ways to change the climate on your boat:

Are you careful about your impact on the emotional climate? Do the two of you have policies and agreements that keep the climate healthy?

**

Do you ever wish that the world would just stop so you can feel like it is really under control? It's not going to happen.

You—and the world—are alive and constantly changing. Even the fact that our body's cells replace themselves every seven years should alert us to the change around us. Growth is an ongoing and constant process. Get used to it.

**

What Kind of Boat? Sloop? Dinghy? Yacht? Junk?

As I got to know myself at a young age, I knew that I was aware of the emotional impact of my behavior on others. I was told that "having a conscience" was a good thing. Actually, this was a mixed blessing, as it made me a shy and hesitant boy and created constraints on my behavior, but—as a therapist—I still advocate having a conscience. I still think it is better than being

255

unaware of our responsibility for our behavior, or our impact on the people we care about.

**

We need to feel significant, needed, worthy, important, and desirable. It is better to discuss these needs and *not* use a familiar measure, like whether a) we have sex, b) we make a lot of money, or c) others automatically comply with our wishes. It's more complicated than that. We do need to measure how we are expressing our needs and how our behavior looks and sounds to the person we are hoping needs us and desires us. Be aware of *what* you are measuring. It may be misleading you.

**

At The Helm
In a nutshell, this is what I learned from Ivan Boszormenyi-Nagy in graduate school:
I'll often feel like the world owes me, things aren't fair and I'm entitled.
I also owe the world something in return.
Will I be constructive or destructive in paying my debt? It depends on how I respond to my entitlement.

**

I ran a department once, full of fascinating people, one of whom loved to play with language the same way I do. He would call computers "confusers."
He would also point out that someone was "climbing out on a limb with a saw, and cutting on the *wrong side* of the limb."
We can all get as self-destructive as that person cutting the

wrong side of the limb, and I have always liked to use that image to illustrate how determined we can be about how right we are—and how blind we can be to the consequences.

**

Heads Up!

Imagine how disarming it is for your partner to say that something "triggers their insecurities and vulnerabilities." They are telling the truth and you can't argue them out of it. Remember, they are not accusing you of anything, just telling you their reality. You can try it, too.

**

I'll stop a couple when they are making each other reach their tipping points. I tell them that *I* am the only one listening and if this dynamic happened at home it would be a waste of their time because nobody would hear them. I stop them so they notice what state, or frame of mind they are in when this is happening. If Eb is getting stiff and Flo is beginning to spin, this is the wrong moment for that, and they need to change gears.

**

As a therapist and writer, I am offering you half an enchilada. When the process has helped, you will be more able to handle your pains and problems, communicate about them, and manage your situation—leading to measurable changes in your mental health and the quality of your intimacy.
Even so, the pains and problems will not completely go away.

**

Getting Our Bearings
healthy self = heal thy self!

**

My daughter was involved in competitive ice dancing for several years. I had a chance to observe very young couples work on a beautiful form of collaboration—having each other's safety in their hands, needing to respond to the music in a coordinated and productive way, handling pressure with maturity. These were teenagers.

Surely, grown couples can find the rhythm and excellence that these young couples achieved.

**

Before we all had computers, we had judgmental parents, kids, siblings, and partners, and that was all we knew. We would make mistakes and others would be upset at us in a *judgmental* way.

Now we have found that we can have a companion who shows us our mistakes but just doesn't seem to take them too seriously. Have we started to want and expect that detachment from our human partners just because computers are so nice to us when we are spellchecking?

**

Turning Hard-A-Lee!
One sage professor of mine stated one day that 70% of us

marry our mothers . . . and the rest of us marry our fathers! Sure looks like *familiarity* matters, even when we are building a boat, stretching ourselves, and risking a grand adventure.

**

If we have an automatic emotional response to unfairness and perceived injustice, is it any surprise that we *justify* our actions and reactions so much of the time? How about *owning* our feelings about injustice, instead?

**

It is refreshing to have couples solve their own problems as they
take the helm of their distinctive craft.
One day, two different couples decided that it would be very productive to actually talk on the phone instead of texting each other.
It is striking how it can improve things when you need to be clear about what you are saying and you can hear *how* your partner is saying what they are saying.
Distortions may be normal, but some of them can be avoided.

**

Staying Afloat

With a partner, if our first words are spoken in a caring, thoughtful way, the conversation has a better chance of turning out well. The research by John Gottman shows that it matters what percentage of our communication is positive, and *what we say first* matters. We can have negative moments and do well as long as we have more positive moments than negative. Choosing to initiate a discussion with words and a voice that are considerate will, therefore, give you a better chance of feeling good about the outcome.

**

When speaking with your partner, imagine standing on a rock and declaring the importance of what you are experiencing, thinking, and feeling.
Say what you mean about yourself.
This serves to anchor you so you can handle your partner's reaction and stick to what you need to say.
(If your partner's reaction upsets you, remember that it is the reaction *they* need to have.)

Speaking from that solid place also serves to give you the stability to find words for what you need your partner to understand. That rock solid stability will feel good and make you a more desirable partner.
(Others want that sense of reliable strength *for you*. Show them you can do it.)

Stand still. Hang in there.

**

Storm Clouds Ahead

If you are a *plus/and* thinker and your partner is an *either/or* thinker, then each time you hear their ideas—and add one of your own—you are contradicting and diminishing their ideas. If you are an *either/or* thinker and your partner is a *plus/*

and thinker, each time you make a comparison between their idea and yours you are confusing them because they weren't *comparing* the ideas. They were *adding to* the ideas.

**

It has become clear to me how absolutely crucial it is for us to keep from feeling any smaller when things feel like they are *not* under control. We simply can't—and don't—risk disappearing into some sort of invisible, meaningless, worthless state. Instead, we act to keep from losing control and disappearing. How big does that action look to others, and does it make someone else feel small?

**

Full Steam Ahead

What if it is not that complicated, and we do gravitate to a straight-line sensibility or a circular one? Computers "think" in zeroes and ones, right? Don't we often resort to circles and arrows to communicate? Aren't lines and circles two basic building blocks for our man- and woman-made environment in which we define ourselves? Maybe it really is simple and we need to be able to integrate the two as an act of love.

**

Feeling Seasick

When someone personally significant in our life dies, we are likely to experience a profound turning point, as my family did when I was a teenager.

It is my observation from that experience that there are two basic responses. One is to be determined to be alive and "lively" for as long as possible, and the other is to avoid dying by slowing down and protecting ourselves from risk and danger.

A major change or loss could trigger these very different responses in each of you and make the boat seem tippier. Your partner's (or family member's) response may seem exaggerated and alarming to you, and your opposite response might seem that way to them, too.

**

Have you thought about the similarities between gardening and raising children?

If you believe that there is too much oppression in the world and your seedlings just need the freedom to express who they really are without interference, what happens?

If you believe that there is too much danger in the world and that your seedlings must be protected from all dangers, both natural and man-made, what happens?

When you get impatient for them to grow or become upset at the results, what happens to you?

Try to balance the amount of work you are doing, the potential for enjoying the process, and the possible results. (Will you end up with weeds? prized but lonely plants? a garden that delights and disappoints? slightly imperfect plants with solid roots sharing the sunlight and the water?)

Weed the garden, do some pruning, give the plants some sunlight and room to grow, enjoy their distinctiveness and growth.

Pay attention, but remember, you *can't* totally control what happens in your garden.

**

When you are waiting for your plane to take off and you are
reminded to use your oxygen mask for yourself *first*, what does
that mean?
Remember that if you don't take care of yourself, you will not
be worth very much to the people you care about.

**

The Boat is Rocking

Ted Williams, one of the most famous ballplayers of all time,
was also a fisherman. Evidently, reaching the pinnacle of
the baseball world made him assume he could catch fish. He
crossed the line between going *fishing* and going *catching*,
thinking he had more control than he really did. Those who
went fishing with him found him unbearable when he didn't
catch fish, as he angrily vented his frustration about his lack of
control and, in the process, made himself an impossible person
to spend the day with.

**

Flo is upset and jittery about a violent thunderstorm that is
looming. She and Eb have had multiple power failures lately
and she wants to be better prepared. She asks Eb to buy a new
lantern that will provide more light during a power failure. Eb
goes out and buys the lantern, but Flo doesn't seem grateful.
Yes, Flo wanted the lantern, but she also simply needed to
express how worried she was about the storm, how she dreaded
being unprepared, how she didn't want a tree to fall on the
house, and so forth. While Eb wanted Flo to be grateful, he

needed to first understand what Flo needed—and it was not just the lantern.

**

Seeking A Harbor In A Storm

When our behavior seems unfair to our partner (withholding affection or credit or gratitude, for instance) we look big.
When we feel entitled to our wishes, impulses and freedom, anyone who applies constraints, criticisms, limits, or rules looks big to us.
That's a lot of looking big which produces a lot of feeling small. Don't be surprised.

**

I suspect that power and control are experienced differently in relation to the Internet. A pre-Internet person experiences control by writing things down carefully, making a phone call, looking at a map, and deliberately planning things. To that generation, using a computer for these tasks feels like a loss of control, as there is potential for error and there is no familiar concrete record of the work that has been accomplished.
To a person who is Internet savvy, there is a tremendous feeling of power and control from quickly planning a route or sending a note or paying a bill. There could be a sense that things are *not* under control when they slow down, when there is a delay in finishing a task, or when there is a need to write something down or think something through more slowly.
It could give both generations the same level of discomfort if they are faced with the other way of doing things.

**

Lost At Sea

Flo makes coffee for Eb early every morning. Eb drinks the coffee, even though it is burnt by the time he wakes up. Flo sees herself as being thoughtful and generous, while Eb is on edge, drinking lousy coffee, and dreading how she will respond if she thinks he is criticizing her if he says something about the coffee. Flo feels unwanted when Eb tells her, with evident contempt, to stop making coffee, and ignores him.

This isn't just about coffee. It is about feeling important, feeling safe, wanting a better connection, and communicating effectively about what each partner needs. Talking without defensiveness or contempt would help.

**

I urge you—as I urge those I treat—to try something quite profound: If you can identify an emotional "tipping point" that constantly triggers your impulsive, quick reactions that are shameful or costly, I suggest using *the same trigger* to produce the *opposite behavior*.

I ask that an emotional "feeling small" moment be cherished, embraced, and accepted—*not* feared or avoided. It *is* reliable and important. It *is* a signal to wake up and do something, just not the automatic, default behavior you have been using.

Make it your signal to remember that you are on a boat,
it is your cockroach moment,
you have a gumball,
or that you are feeling small, while your partner is looking big,
and vice versa.

**

Between The Devil And The Deep Blue Sea

Many people are insecure enough to acquire "love insurance" by confiding in somebody who might step into the void if their partner is not satisfying their needs. It is much better for our partnerships if we are *our own* love insurance, and we can identify and meet our own needs well.

**

It's worth repeating that Valentine's Day (note Chapter 19) is a notable day in the world of marriage therapy. It seems to be a day when couples open a checking account, emphasizing every deposit and withdrawal. (What was the gift? Was it sincere? What did they say and when did they say it? Was it thoughtful, considerate and fresh?)

The day is a mixed blessing. It is really hard, because so much rides on that day's current account. It is also full of kindnesses and questions we could be focused on all year.

(How much do we mean to each other? How deep and solid are we? Are we considering each other?)

Couples learn about their dynamics by looking at their long-term savings account, the way they withdraw and deposit, and what their dance is in relation to their ledger. (Does somebody owe a lot? Is the other person charging interest and keeping someone in debt? Is somebody borrowing heavily and promising to pay interest on the loan? What kind of binds does all of this accounting create? Are the imbalances and expectations being spoken about?)

**

Shiver Me Timbers

Slick technology that increases the amount of information we are bombarded with raises emotional and psychological issues. If, as individuals, we reach some kind of limit to the amount of stimulation we can handle, what happens to our behavior? My sense is that we simplify our responses and react in a more primitive way when technology over-stimulates us. This may manifest itself in self-defeating behaviors—both individually and collectively.

We may act against our own best interests, just as we sometimes sabotage our intimate partnerships when we are overwhelmed by the complexity of what is happening to us.

**

I have found it useful to describe *how* I am a professional and healthy co-dependent. What I mean is that I care about the people I treat and invest in having a connection, but also must keep a boundary so they can still find a way to help themselves. I had to learn how to do that with dignity, giving others space to grow, catching them if they are falling over, but not costing either of us too much by letting their issues or their needs take control of me.

The more power their emotional needs have, the thinner emotional ice I am walking on. I need to be a healthy and considerate caretaker without falling through the ice.

You can learn this, too.

28

Integrity: Being A Pendulum

The sports that we play, in addition to sailing, offer plentiful examples of ways to handle awkward stressful moments with your partner. The goal for both captains, really, is a personal integrity that feels balanced, even on a boat.

> There are two fundamental diseases, and they are really only one: anything that doesn't allow change to happen, and anything that causes change to happen too quickly.
>
> - Richard Moss
> author of *Radical Aliveness*

After Harris and Dot had weathered the storm of infidelity in their marriage, Harris told me how he had experienced the beginning of his therapy journey. He said it was like "being in a little submarine" by himself, seeing his wife and I comfortably communicating and adjusting to our emotions, while he was afraid to reach through the window and test the water because it could all suddenly cascade into the submarine and drown him. He eventually found a way to get wet and not actually drown, but it was a difficult journey. It was something like learning how to play a sport and trusting that you could play the game, and that your coaches would be able to teach you.

Perhaps, by now, you have accepted the idea that your journey as a couple is something like sailing a boat, handling tippiness, sharing responsibilities, seeking understandings about challenges, listening to your co-captain, and experiencing the journey. But other sports also offer lessons in how to be a healthy partner in a relationship.

Athletes speak of attaining real success when they can "slow the game down" enough to make better plays, using better judgment. Real intimacy can be found the same way. You need to catch yourself and risk slowing down your emotional and behavioral process in order to behave better in the context of your partnership. Each challenging moment is an opportunity to remember a visual cue from this book, such as your planet, a cockroach, a boat, a fish, a gumball, a kaleidoscope, a squirrel, or the crazy distortion of both feeling small *and* looking big.

Sports offer constant movement and attention, combined with enough uncertainty and unpredictability to give us important lessons about intimacy and relating. In many sports, it is the ball that determines what happens, just as it is the fish when you are fishing. The ball has power and what happens to it counts. Remember: you can only control the way you handle the ball when it comes your way—not when someone else is holding it.

In order for any game to be fair and satisfying, there are rules. Mostly, they are designed to limit dangerous behavior so that it is safe to play the game. Rules are also designed so that all of the players experience shared limits and constraints that make the game better. There is a sense of community, faith, and trust developed around a game that makes it meaningful for all of the players.

What Sports Teach

I think I learned from playing tennis as a child that I needed to be quick on my feet, to be prepared for change, and to not take my eye off the ball. I learned that if I get ahead of myself, I'm not going to hit the ball well. If I concentrate on positioning myself well, I'm going to hit the ball the right way, and keep the ball in play. I also learned to enjoy the game—not just the score.

One father I talk with wants his boys to learn from basketball that "turnovers"—mistakes—happen, and that the opposing players can sometimes make a good play that makes a difference. He wants his sons to understand that things get confusing and messy, and that other people have good intentions and skills.

I remember when, meeting a couple for the first time, they clearly stated their differences and the tensions they had experienced because of them. They were frustrated with each other. At the end of the session, the wife explained that she likes baseball and he loves football and they can't stand the other person's seasons. As a sports fan who can appreciate how absorbed we can get with sports, I wondered what this might mean about expectations and emotions.

Perhaps men are "from football" and women are "from baseball," and what matters is our relationship to the ball. Perhaps men like having the ball, being strategic, having a plan, and, importantly, *expecting* to be powerful part of the time—and completely powerless the rest of the time (in the face of an angry parent, a confusing partner, a boss, a customer, or a myriad of frustrating moments) because they don't have the ball. Perhaps women start with the ball but *expect* to let go of it and need to be able to handle the immense variety of things that can happen next. Power is relinquished. A team is needed. Flexibility is needed. Unpredictability is normal.

As I thought more about this, I realized that the circular nature of cricket—where the ball can go in any direction at all and there is no foul territory—may be even closer to what women expect. I also realized that men really exaggerate their expectation for scoring and winning, and that they will moan about their powerlessness and helplessness caused by the fact that they will *not* have the ball half of the time. One young woman remembered that the men in her family constantly had a "pissing contest" to determine who was getting the worst deal. It is seemingly just too disturbing to not have the ball.

Aside from whether you have the ball or where it is, how does your physical performance inform you? Could an understanding of your reactions when an activity is at a turning point offer help when your relationship is stressful? Are there lessons to be learned from the ways you compete— or from your favorite sport? What is your most graceful act? When are you most awkward? Does your way of performing at a crucial moment relate to your expectations and perceptions about intimacy?

Golf

Cooper is a very loyal client who has had therapy with and without his wife, and travels a long distance to see me. In many ways, we are from different ends of the universe. Our lives are very different, our political views clash, and we would make an odd couple.

Nonetheless, he sees that he has needed a lot of help with personal growth in order to manage his marriage—or get married at all—and he is one of the most authentic people I have known. We have developed a good understanding and plenty of mutual respect. In fact, Cooper took the idea of a marriage voyage so seriously that he rented a yacht on Lake Tahoe to get married on.

Somehow, along the way, we began to talk about golf in a useful way. Clearly, I'm always seeking metaphors that help simplify emotional complexities, and Cooper had a thorough understanding of the mysteries of golf. He began to compare the journey toward his personal growth to a game of golf. To him, golf is subtle but manageable, a test of self. To succeed, he needs endurance, flexibility, sportsmanship, and grace.

Making golf useful began with a broad view of the course and the game. To Cooper, golf offers an opportunity to compete without conflict. It is really the challenge of getting the ball to behave in nature that is the challenge. The unpredictability and constant hazards supply the drama and the risk. You can play a "parallel" game with someone of a different skill level and *both* feel a sense of accomplishment and success when you've reached the hole.

This sounded like the frame of mind I was advocating for couples. It is important, in a relationship, to visualize a parallel journey that is not about dominating or hurting each other. There are unpredictable hazards and risks to intimacy. Feeling success and worthiness matter. Moving toward a mutual goal matters.

As our sessions progressed, it became clear that choosing the right club for hitting the ball in a particular situation was a key to the mental and emotional aspects of golf. He would joke that he had been in a stressful situation, grabbed a powerful club, and hit the ball into the woods a very long way. He knew he had done the wrong thing. He knew that his resulting score would be poor. He knew he had reacted impulsively and with too much power. He knew he needed tools for making a better choice of a club when the tension was high.

At times, Cooper's back swing was too fast (he was not thinking), he was swinging too hard (showing erratic behavior), or he was choosing his club poorly (showing poor judgment). At other times, his back swing barely began as he was paralyzed by feeling small—and at those moments he needed to loosen up and somehow stay in the game. Cooper recognized that he was relying on one club that was not always the best choice. He decided to find a set of old golf clubs and put them in his office with labels that you will recognize from this book:

Pause, Breathe, Cockroach!, Listen, Kaleidoscope, Slow down, Wait, The other captain, Catch yourself, Get oxygen, Gumballs, Feeling Small & Looking Big. . .

Cooper knew, as he had also been a football quarterback, that to excel in sports it is invaluable to be able to respond under pressure, and that he would also need to do that in his cherished relationships. One way he looked at this was to say that on a *public* golf course you can be loose and easy, while on a *private* course the game is different: expensive, exposed, responsible, important, and conditional. To him, trying his best in Guantanamo, Cuba—where there are landmines, no grass except on the greens, totally unpredictable bounces, and no expectations—was significantly different from paying a lot of money to play at Pebble Beach in California, where it is beautifully groomed and there are high expectations for all who set foot there. Golfing at Guantanamo where you "never know what will happen" struck Cooper as an excellent place to condition himself for the surprises and disappointments of partnership. The intimacy of Pebble Beach makes the game different, creates tension, and demands a more careful performance, like the real thing.

We went on to discover that there were rules embedded in the traditions of golf that were parallel to the rules and norms we were talking about for his marriage. There is a golfing tradition of politeness, etiquette, and consideration for your opponents and for other players—that is helpful to remember. The social norms of golf are passed with care from generation to generation, and are central to the tone of the golf game. A round of golf has a special atmosphere of mutual regard and respect for other golfers that can be carried into other moments and relationships.

In golf, the players take particular care to be quiet when another player is hitting the ball, to wait their turn, and even to make sure they do not step on the invisible line between their opponent's ball and the hole when they are on the putting green. This takes conscious self-control and it is gladly applied for the sake of the game. Couples could do the same. You and your partner are both finding the game to be challenging, are entitled to a moment of concentration and respect, and a chance to succeed in trying to reach your mutual goal, even if it seems like you are competing. You may need to control your impulses to help your partner achieve this. This is what I mean by being captains and developing a "climate" that is safe on your private boat, derived from your history of mutual regard and consideration.

We have also pondered how golf offers a chance to learn about balance. In golf, you play the whole game in a balanced way, playing the ball with deliberate intensity between slow, breath-gathering walks of emotional and tactical preparation, hitting the ball hard off the tee and, later, barely hitting it at all to make it roll slowly into the hole. Like learning any worthwhile sport, it is not easy to develop these contradictory skills of power and finesse. Football, for instance, has both its brutality and its cerebral time of planning and strategizing, not to mention the crucial split seconds at the line of scrimmage when no movement at all is allowed. Soccer, basketball, and hockey have dizzying speed and moments of tiny deception.

Baseball championships are won both by slugging homeruns and doing many little things consistently. Relationships need the same range of skills and flexibility.

The Pendulum

Cooper also attends the men's group that I lead twice a month. On one visit, he said he had been thinking about his own difficulties in finding balance, and had found that he felt like he was on a pendulum. He described one end of the pendulum's arc as very self-absorbed, just wanting things his way, setting limits, making demands, etc. At the other end, he felt he was letting go of all of his needs, complying with the wishes of his partner, capitulating to what she needed and wanted, accommodating her demands and perceptions. Another man said he was always either going too fast or too slow, while yet another said he couldn't find the mid-point between quick, loud responses and long-winded, quiet responses. All were realizing that they wanted to find balance between two extremes. The same week, in my office, I had a woman describe her thoughts about this as a swing between narcissism and co-dependency—or the focus on "self" and "other."

It so happened that another member of the men's group still played very competitive baseball in Florida at age fifty. He and I had the same reaction to the description of the pendulum. Surely this is the same thing as a baseball swing, a tennis swing, a soccer kick, or a golf swing—as an athlete, you *are* the pendulum.

Cooper can now see *himself* as the pendulum when he handles the obstacles, "rough," and sand traps of everyday life, just as the baseball player is when he swings the bat. For both men, it is important to understand the impact of the two ends of the swing on their performance. They can't ignore the feelings and impulses involved in the narcissistic and co-dependent ends of their swings, but the real consequences happen in the middle, when they hit the ball. It takes real concentration and purpose to consistently hit the "sweet spot" in the middle of the ball at the middle of the pendulum swing. If you and your partner can both do that in your practice as a couple, you will really be in the game—and it will be very rewarding.

If you can balance your needs with your partner's needs, your self-caring with your empathy and consideration for your partner, your talking with your listening, and your giving with your taking, then you will be synthesizing the opposite ends of the relational pendulum. You will be integrating the two ends of the kaleidoscope, the two weather reports on the boat, the perspectives of the two captains, or the sensibilities of two cultures or genders or families of origin. You will be creating a special kind of intimacy.

Integrity and the Dialectic

What do you suppose "integrity" really is? Doesn't it sound just right as your emotional and personal goal as a relational person? What if *integrating* different perspectives and emotions and sensibilities is the path to integrity? Here is one formal definition of the word:

> Integrity: The state of being complete or
> undivided. The state of being
> sound or undamaged.
> - *Encarta World English Dictionary*

I suggest that if you can find the courage to integrate baffling and confusing forces in your self and your partnership, you can experience integrity.

This is not totally original. I am intrigued by the eighteenth-century German philosopher, Georg Friedrich Hegel, who is credited with innovative ideas about society, economics, and psychology that defined his *dialectical* view of history.

Hegel's famous contribution, the "dialectic," states that a "thesis" (current measurable reality), forges the creation of its opposite, or "antithesis." The interaction of these inevitably creates a "synthesis" of the two, which becomes a thesis in it's own right—and an antithesis follows—and so forth through more stages of integration. He felt that historical, economic, and social trends could be explained this way. I imagine that Hegel understood his own *internal* mental and emotional process as a dialectic and applied it to his understanding of society simply because that was his particular passion.

I suggest that this pattern happens constantly inside of us as we balance our emotional and psychological memories from our family and parents, contradictory impulses, and/or questions of right and wrong. We grow, emotionally, as we forge our individual path through our various confusing relationships and situations. We have a smorgasbord of levels and signals in our brain, and the different parts are chirping differing and sometimes conflicting ideas. Much of the time we are seeking an integration (or *synthesis*) of opposites, just as the men in my men's group are seeking the best baseball or golf swing that hits the sweet spot. It is through this process of synthesizing our own experiences that we grow naturally and try to remain healthy.

Perhaps you approach your partnership with fascination about the risks, a need for both drama and structure, and a reliance on knowing the final score. To find the sweet spot, you need to slow the game down, let the ball come to you, appreciate the rules, and enjoy the experience. If you try to control too much of the game, you may be skating on thin emotional ice. Ultimately, it's about hitting the sweet spot as often as possible and emerging from that emotional trap in the submarine. A healthy personal journey welcomes the noise, is grateful for the variety, and has the courage to stay in the game, seeking balance, synthesis, and integrity.

CAPTAIN'S LOG

Having integrity may require slowing down the game you are in.

29

Reaching the Lighthouse
and the Harbor

How do we know that we've reached our goal? What does that
look like and feel like? What will have changed about us? Will
we know it when we see it?

> There is a security; it is your connection with
> the higher power of the universe, your higher
> self. It never fails you. It always knows exactly
> what you need to do, and trusting it means that
> you'll always be taken care of. The paradox is
> that this is what we're most afraid of.
>
> - Shakti Gawain
> author of *Creative Visualization*

Imagine a lighthouse on the edge of the ocean, and a full moon.
I try to take notice, dig deep, and forget about time when I
encounter any of these powerful symbols. I find that the ocean
represents the relentless action and variety of our lives. The
moon is a friend, encouraging dialogue and reflection. The
lighthouse is an inspiration, spurring me on to seek meaning

and direction in my life. If I hit the trifecta and encounter all three at the same time, that is my definition of a heavenly time and place. When I need guidance, comfort, balance, and truth, I welcome these symbols, just as you may seek meaning and direction from a book, a church service, or your partnership.

As a young man, I also learned to trust myself on nights when I walked around my neighborhood, down the hill to the bottom of our street, engaged in a very focused dialogue with myself, discovering that I could believe in my own internal process. I was charting some sort of middle ground between the thrust of my first impulses and the paralysis of over-analysis, trusting that there was a light within me that was also going to be my guide. I was discovering a lighthouse within me.

In her book, A *Return to Love,* spiritual activist and author Marianne Williamson captured the power of this inner light:

> Our deepest fear is not that we are inadequate. Our deepest fear is that we are powerful beyond measure. It is our light, not our darkness, that most frightens us. We ask ourselves, who am I to be brilliant, gorgeous, talented, fabulous? Actually, who are you not to be? You are a child of God. Your playing small doesn't serve the world. There is nothing enlightened about shrinking so that other people won't feel insecure around you. . . . We were born to make manifest the glory of God within us. It's not just in some of us; it's in everyone And as we let our own light shine, we unconsciously give other people permission to do the same.

These are powerful words. Many people have imagined them being spoken by Nelson Mandela at his inaugural speech in 1994. (It is a fascinating thought, but apparently only that, as it is not in the transcript of his speech, but actually Williamson's words.)

We all have dignity. There is something sacred, precious and fragile in all of us. It is noble and powerful to own it and express it.

Perhaps you have been captivated, or even invigorated, by the whole idea that your journey as a couple is like building and sailing a boat. My best guess is that you intuitively know that tension and danger matter to you emotionally—and that when you feel small you instinctively seek control. Safety matters deeply to us, and being a couple involves much that is complicated, unpredictable, and hard to control. Hopefully, as we near the end of our travels together, you've picked up some ideas that you can use to make your trip feel safer, more purposeful, and more worthwhile. Let's declare that we have reached a safe harbor with a beacon or a full moon that offers a calming clarity about your emotions, where you can reflect on various journeys (reading this book, being a couple, your personal growth) within your life journey.

Hopefully, as you've been reading this book, certain words have begun to disappear from your vocabulary, such as "winning," "justifying," "blaming," or "defending." I hope you've been replacing them with concepts like curiosity, consideration, teamwork and self-control.

Defining Change

Something very important is at stake. Your attitudes, behaviors, and ideas are creating your legacy to the people who are dear to you, including your partner and your children. You have permission to make choices that affect that legacy. You can be remembered as angry, distant, uncaring, thoughtless, or harsh. Or, you can be remembered as being emotionally available, a good listener, considerate, or having integrity and dignity.

Let's say you feel you've gotten somewhere on this relationship journey. How do you know if things have really changed? Maybe you don't feel like a whole new person, but somehow your partnership is less stressful and you're feeling better about yourself.

There was a memorable member of our men's group who had worked very hard in therapy to get his anger under control and overcome his difficult, tumultuous childhood in Holland. One evening, Britt announced merrily to the group that he and his wife had planned a vacation, but one part of it seemed like a disaster waiting to happen—the perfect storm.

The plan was for Britt to go to a conference in London for a week and then meet his wife and two kids at the airport in Amsterdam. They would then rent a car and visit his dreaded family, where he had learned too much about anger, deception, and pain.

We understood immediately that all of Britt's work on managing himself would be put to the test at the airport. He would be well rested, but his wife would surely be exhausted. After a solid week of single parenting, she would have had to pack up three kids, close up the house, and then fly through the night to Amsterdam, presumably arriving in a flurry of stress and resentment. Britt, meanwhile, would be trying to deal with the details of collecting baggage and renting a car, while trying to welcome his tired, grumpy wife and kids. Add to the mix his sense of dread about visiting his parents. How could he possibly handle all of this with dignity and grace?

The group helped Britt prepare for the storm, gently questioning the plan and then helping him think about how he would process everything that was going to be happening. After a few weeks, it was time for the trip.

When he returned, the group was eager to hear the full report. What Britt reported was that he "stayed on top of things a few minutes at a time." He would feel stress hitting him and make "small adjustments" to his perceptions and awareness that kept him from losing his balance. To everyone's relief, everything had gone well at the airport. Making those little changes when he needed to manage himself had made a big difference.

What had Britt done? For one thing he had clearly focused on his *internal* journey, rather than thinking that he could invent expedient excuses, or fix everything later. He had disciplined himself to stay in the moment and be accountable for his reactions. This is what he meant by making "small adjustments" as things were happening that day.

During his years of hard work in therapy, Britt had learned that "chance favors the prepared mind." He wasn't going to just take his chances. He had done the work, over years, of preparing his mind for a perfect storm.

Britt had recognized that his relationships mattered. He knew there was real value in maintaining what philosopher Martin Buber called an "I/Thou relationship" with his wife, kids, and parents, and that meant being intentional and devoted about those relationships while he was under stress. With these concepts in mind, Britt was able to help his family through the storm, rather than being angrily reactive to the circumstances.

Britt had also understood that he needed to take care of himself—he needed to grab the oxygen first in an emergency. One of the adjustments he made was that he simply kept telling himself to connect and communicate with his family in the present moment. Doing so made him more available, confident, and healthy. If he took care of himself, his relationships would turn out better. In fact, the more self-control he could muster, the more satisfied he would be emotionally, and the more attractive he would be to those who relied on him and shared responsibilities with him.

Finally, Britt had grasped that effective communication could help to keep things under control. Remembering to inform and listen could get him through stressful moments, because dialogue increases understanding and reduces tension.

He made all of these adjustments during the perfect storm, and they calmed the waters. That was how Britt could measure the change in himself. He was the same man, fundamentally, but he was a man in charge of himself.

The Power of Blending

As we experience our personal journey, we have the capacity to balance opposites and combine pieces of information in order to achieve serenity, a sense of control, and mental health. Utilizing this capacity is an important theme of this book.

We observed, in Chapter 28, that Georg Frederick Hegel embraced the idea of a dialectic, which illustrates how we naturally synthesize information. I have also called this process "integration" and suggested that *integrity* is a measure of our ability to combine information about different ideas and feelings. At various points, I have also called this process "blending," "balancing," or "finding the sweet spot" when we are the pendulum. We have explored how executives who are trying to be innovative are open to debate, and call this process "plussing." It's not that whatever we're feeling or thinking about is good or bad, right or wrong. There is a creative and innovative middle, and to get there you need to be combining things, using the word "and," instead of "but."

Throughout our lives, we receive and process information from multiple sources. We continually take in information from two very different sides of our brain, one more creative and the other more logical. Psychologists now rely on a technique called EMDR to emulate the balancing act taking place in our minds as we process different kinds of information.

We embody this process of balancing in familiar physical activities. When you type with two hands, or juggle a Slinky, you are using both of your hands to create something new. When you are reading this book, you're simultaneously recording the content of the book in your mind while also experiencing the process of reading it. Most sports involve two sides, and the interaction between them is what makes it a game.

And, of course, in our relationships we are faced with the puzzling duality of both of you feeling small *and* looking big at the same time. This crazy normal distortion has been central to our journey together. The contradictions inherent in all of these processes are vital opportunities for growth.

When I was teaching television production at the college level, I became the "blender" of opposite approaches for my students.

Seniors were expected to propose a project to a committee of three faculty members, and then spend the entire final year of college trying to execute the project. There were three principal teachers of television production skills, so students would typically approach the three of us with their projects, knowing that they would not graduate unless all of us approved their work.

One professor wanted everything to be completely organized and consistent. He wanted the original script to match the plans for editing the tape and the finished product to be consistent with both plans. He demanded evidence of preparation, planning, and consistency for any student to graduate.

The second professor advocated for just the opposite. He

felt that the best product was one that had *not* been constrained by planning or training or scripting. To him, the most creative product was spontaneous and natural, originating in the most creative part of the student's mind. He told students that they needed to just grab some equipment when they had an idea, tape their content with as much freedom of expression as possible, and be innovative when they were editing their materials. Planning would only constrain them and reduce the quality of the tape, and their grade. The implication was that if they got stuck thinking too much about the product, he would have difficulty graduating them.

The students, slightly boggled by the prospect of pleasing both of these professors, came to me, wondering what on earth I would expect from them. I told them that I wanted them to take *both* approaches. I wanted them to make a script for their tape, be trained in using the equipment, and line up the right people to be in the right place at the right time. Then, when they were creating their tape, I advised them to be spontaneous and creative. I told them that if they could do that, their finished product should have enough integrity to please all three of us.

In many ways, this is what I tell couples: First, learn the skills for communicating well, take the time to listen, and take your relationship seriously. Then, when an important moment arises, take the risk of being intimate in a way that is new and challenging for you. Your integrity will shine through and your relationship will grow stronger.

The Basics

When life's indignities come your way, I believe that your thoughts and your imagination *can* respond to your feelings in a healthy and productive way. That is what my stand as a therapist represents. The odds are with you if you are ready to sense your feelings and use your mind.

The conductor I mentioned in the segment about the string quartet, Benjamin Zander, proclaims to the world in his book, *The Art of Possibility*, that *complexity* is wonderful. It's an important message—one that I've intended to convey throughout this book. Your automatic, or *default*, responses may not be serving you well. Perhaps you have developed what I call "visual literacy" while we've been on this journey, and recognize that new images help you handle complexity in a new way. To review, here are some of the images you may want to remember at that familiar emotional tipping point when smallness rushes in and a deceptive certainty takes hold of you:

- Claim the kingdom within you, master it—and your relationships will improve.
- You are more than a squirrel. An expedient answer is fast, but not usually the best.
- If you are being accused of being clueless from Mars or spinning from Venus, then you may be. Getting in touch with how emotions work is a good start.
- If your response is large, the cockroach you are handling is large. Get to know your own insecurities and vulnerabilities. When you miss the cockroach, admit that you missed it.
- There are always two ends of your kaleidoscope. Even when they are both distortions, they are *real* distortions and both people see what they are seeing.
- It is intoxicating to build a boat, wonderful to launch a boat, and very serious and responsible to sail a boat that you own. Boats feel tippy, and the way that you try to keep your boat from tipping over will probably make it feel tippy to your partner. Your boat requires two captains who work as teammates.
- You and your partner have small, precious, colorful

gumballs. You have both developed warning systems to keep your gumballs from getting harmed. Know the difference between a warning system alarm and an actual gumball attack. One is only the alarm that wakes you up in the morning. The other one is a fire alarm.

- You are a pendulum. At one end of the arc you could be self-absorbed and very defensive. At the other you are caring, generous, and possibly co-dependent. Try to hit the sweet spot in the middle.

- You are climbing a growth staircase. Keep your dreams in mind, use your personal resources in your best way, and let go of burdens that may be weighing you down.

- When it is risky to reveal how you're feeling because you can't predict the outcome, take the risk to start verbal foreplay by talking authentically and listening well. If you don't take this opportunity, you'll never know what you missed.

- When your partner sounds like they are attacking you, play soccer. Get your hands out of the way and hear what they are saying. Tell them what you hear them *say* they are feeling and what you hear them say they care about. They'll behave better.

- Don't forget, "it's up to the fish" whether you catch anything. If you try to control things you can't, you may be on thin emotional ice and there could be a cost for you.

- If it seems foggy, it is an opportunity for growth. Take advantage of it.

- When you can't solve a problem, imagine that you are hungry, go out for dinner, advocate, and listen—and then be creative about solving the problem. Debating is healthy. Plussing works well.

- Over your lifetime, you have collected and absorbed

"garbage" that creates your thoughts, feelings, and behaviors. You have permission to make choices. Throw some out. Tell your partner what is precious about you. If it's non-toxic and used up, recycle it.

- You may be treading water in a swamp and afraid of drowning. If you try to run, you may slip and slide and become more exhausted. Try letting yourself "drown" and see what happens.

- If you use your imagination to try to picture what your partner (or a newborn baby) is experiencing emotionally, it will calm you down and make you more able to handle the situation.

- Take a cue from the dialectic within you. Combining and integrating and synthesizing are the most inspired and innovative things to do as a couple—and for your self.

Feeling Small AND Looking Big

It's all about our need for control. The premise of this book is that you need to feel that things are more under control, and experience yourself getting that to happen. When you are at your tipping point, remember that there is a crazy normal distortion in place and four predictable and reliable things are happening.

- Remember the other person is feeling small. Empathy calms you—and reassures them.

- Claim the way you are feeling small. "I statements" make situations more clear and don't feel too threatening to your partner. Ask *yourself* about you.

- Manage the way you are looking big. If it looks big to your partner, it's big. Get your behavior under control.

- Recognize that you are making the other person look big through your associations and memories. Be more in the moment. The only indignity happening "right now" is the one happening right now. It may not seem fair, but it is all that is actually happening.

- Be conscious of how you are getting yourself under control. That will meet your emotional needs for safety and serenity.

The most precious relationship you have is the one you have with yourself. Ask yourself if you want to have dinner with someone acting like you. You are going to have dinner with that person—and sleep with them, too—whether you like it or not. If you don't like that person very much, you better have a productive conversation with yourself, or you'll have a lousy time. Your partner also needs to take care of their own self. Your partner may not be able or ready to acknowledge what you need to be appreciated for. They may be too preoccupied or distracted to celebrate the good parts of who you are. They are doing what they need to do to take care of themselves, too. How could it be any other way?

You have arrived at a lighthouse in a harbor. Take stock. Take a deep breath and appreciate the journey. Try to notice how you have grown and give yourself credit.

You and your partner are on a voyage that keeps changing. Get used to it.
It's a fascinating dance.
Enjoy the complexity. Get to know yourself. Travel well. Bon voyage!

Captain's Log

- You didn't expect to be on a boat. It is complicated and disappointing.
- As captains, you are both entitled to say your side *and* have your side heard.
- If you listen well, the other person will behave better.
- We respond to increased tension in predictable ways that *increase* tension.
- We need an alarm system that tells us when we are *really* in danger.
- It is "crazy normal" for two people to feel small and look big at the same time.
- We can control something about ourselves when we want control.
- Things aren't always the way they seem, and crutches may be needed.
- You have permission to make choices that clean up your thoughts, feelings, and actions.
- When you're trying to change your reaction to tension, there are lots of opportunities.
- Intimacy can mean a balanced response to each other, I to I.
- Having too much control is confusing, and can be just as disabling as having too little.
- Feeling and facing your fears can bring you the security you crave.
- How we gain control when things feel unfair matters.
- Slow down and say what you want for climate control.
- You have cheated if your partner feels cheated. Face the music together.
- Intuitive family investments can cause more debt in your current account.
- When a problem makes you hungry enough, you can fix

it.
- It's a distortion. Both of you are feeling small AND looking big.
- Parenting is an art and a challenging opportunity for growth for the whole family.
- Change can surprise us in a good way if we embrace the possibility.
- Divorce is a profound choice that can be handled well.
- Opportunities for growth are constant, confusing and challenging.
- Having integrity may require slowing down the game you are in.
- You and your partner are on a voyage that keeps changing. Get used to it.
- Enjoy the complexity. Get to know yourself. Travel well.

Reflections and Acknowledgments

"OK, let's talk about garbage, then."

I reached for the wastebasket and discovered only a piece of chewed up chewing gum, a gum wrapper, and an empty metallic gum package, the kind that had contained five slices of gum. I lifted them out, and started to talk to her about feelings, thoughts, and actions. The hospitalized teenage girl who had never met me must have wondered what I was up to. Frankly, at that moment I was inexperienced, wasn't really sure what to do, and was just needing to come up with something.

From that moment on, I realized that I could choose a sense of direction when I felt lost, would take occasional risks as a therapist, and would think constantly in metaphors and analogies as I worked with couples and families.

A few years later, I was working with a couple and suddenly grabbed the office telephone and asked them what happened when they talked. Were they really hearing each other? Several times, I've used a pillow or a pad of paper or a picture hanging on the wall to illustrate the distortion that provides one of the central concepts of this book. I've been known to use a whole room to illustrate personal growth or escalating tension. I want my visitors to experience moments that get their attention, and store a visual memory of them that they associate with personal growth and change. I believe this stimulates imaginative ways of thinking, new ways of behaving, calmer emotions, and peace of mind.

My perspective comes from sixty-two years of life experience. I've been learning the whole time—and I've needed all of the guidance and wisdom I could get. There have been several losses: My brother died when I was eighteen; my father when I was thirty-one; my mother when I was forty-seven. I am nonetheless grateful for memories of real joy and awe, have worked with remarkable people, been a custodial parent for my oldest children, played an important role in renovating a church and a television production facility, and eventually developed a method for treating couples as a respected marriage and family therapist. Most importantly, for the purpose of this book, I can blend all of these experiences into a way of thinking and behaving—and try to model that for others.

I take a plunge now and then, and honor my inner wild pony, seeking to grow and be creative. I am energized by the pursuit of that flickering flame of truth, dignity and integrity. Writing this book is an ongoing process, which makes it risky in a bracing way, perhaps even a little too bold, to capture it all at any given moment. This cannot be the final word. Yet, it is time to finish writing and start publishing.

When I was young, and an only child in a large-enough home on a hill on a dead end street, I would spend hours playing a major league baseball board game. I would manage both teams, keep the records, and play endlessly. It turned out to be good preparation for marriage counseling, as it demanded that I give equal effort to both sides, quickly balance loyalties and perspectives, and see the game two ways at once. In my office, I strive to pay attention to the process, hear both sides, and advocate winning values for both people. I try to get everyone comfortable with the unpredictability of the process. Couples are usually terribly stuck in some way when they enter treatment, and it can be calming, hopeful, and optimistic to view the process as a vitally important game between equals.

I've experienced sailboats in interesting ways, and I communicate through images. I thank my father for this inspiration. He loved sailboats and also painted wonderfully, as did his mother. The result is a visual literacy that has helped me translate my experiences into helpful stories for couples.

Acknowledgments

I am extremely grateful to my children, my mother, my sailor/artist dad, and many friends for inspiring me and for believing in me unconditionally, while I'm also thankful for my ability to believe in myself in a feisty, sometimes mischievous, way.

I am grateful to my wife, Linda, in a different way, for helping me to understand the dynamics of marriage in a very personal way, and motivating me to use my visual literacy and my teaching sensibility to create interventions for couples and establish a career for myself that has meant so much to me. Linda is a writer, too, and she has inspired me to strive to find a courageous voice that matches my most authentic self.

I am very grateful to a personal potpourri of writers who have paved the way and waited patiently for me to follow: Dick Waters, Lawanna Campbell, John Brendler, Dan Collins, Dan Gottlieb, Linda McMeniman, Dick Smyser, Lynne Baker-Ward, Paul Clement, Doug Marlowe, Richard Lenski, Alan Proctor, and Sue Sugarman, to name those who come to mind first.

I have been inspired by the many clever writers and thinkers who I have never met, but whom I wish to emulate. M. Scott Peck, Carl Whitaker, Benjamin Zander, David Schnarch, John Gray, the legendary *New York Times* commentators, Dan Brown, Khalil Gibran, Jayson Stark, Susan Jeffers, Michael Pollan, Benjamin Hoff, and many, many more. In addition, there are luminaries in the field of marriage and family therapy who taught me so much as a graduate student: Ivan Boszormenyi-Nagy, Steve Treat, Dan Gottlieb, Lee Combrinck-Graham, and Harry Aponte.

I have shared the content of this book with many, and appreciate their input. Marion Sandmaier contributed stellar and professional support, while an entire "editorial board" of friends, colleagues, and family demanded clarity and meaning from my words. I am grateful to them all: Linda McMeniman, Emily Schwab, Jeremy Schwab, Laurel Schwab, Elisabeth Gibbings, Dan Collins, Ted Glackman, and Jonathan Harmon have all prompted me and made this book better. Actually getting the book published required a village, indeed, including Dan Collins, Elisabeth Gibbings, Amiram Elwork, and a host of talented and patient people from Hillcrest Media. Also, a special thanks to Jon Lin for all kinds of support and advice, and Chris Gutshall for his hard work and inspirations.

The thoughtful quotes that begin each chapter, unless otherwise noted, are from a collection of statements made to Michael Toms during "New Dimensions" radio interviews that his organization has made into a calendar I use in my office.

Finally, I am eternally grateful to the couples who have allowed me into their lives and taught me so much. It is their wisdom and integrity that I am simply passing along to more couples.

About the Author

H. Laurence Schwab has practiced as a Marriage and Family Therapist since his graduation from Hahnemann University (MFT) in 1987. He has worked in mental health clinics, inpatient and outpatient hospital settings, and private practice, treating individuals, couples, and families. He co-leads a men's group twice a month and has also taught and supervised other therapists.

Before training to be a therapist, Larry worked as a television producer/writer, a teacher, and a college administrator. He is also involved in helping church leaders determine best practices for governance by leading board retreats and making presentations to congregations and groups.

Larry has three children and two grandsons, and lives and works in suburban Pennsylvania while also maintaining an office in Wilmington, Delaware.

Resources and Works Cited

Quotations to open chapters 1, 3, 4, 7, 9, 11, 13, 16-29: *Wise Words: Perennial Wisdom from the New Dimensions Radio Series*, by permission from the New Dimensions Foundation.

CHAPTER ONE
Boszormenyi-Nagy, Ivan, and Barbara R. Krasner. *Between Give and Take: A Clinical Guide to Contextual Therapy*. New York: Brunner-Routledge, 1986.

CHAPTER TWO
Bernard Guerney (of the National Institute of Relationship Enhancement) is author of *Relationship Enhancement* (Jossey-Bass Publishers, 1977).

CHAPTER THREE
Kaleidoscopes To You offers brushed brass or chrome "Wedding Kaleidoscopes" designed by David Kalish at www. kaleidoscopestoyou.com.

CHAPTER FOUR
Gray, John. *Men are From Mars Women are From Venus*. New York: HarperCollins Publishers, 1992.

Schnarch, David. *The Passionate Marriage: Sex, Love and Intimacy in Emotionally Committed Relationships*. New York: W. W. Norton & Co, 1997.

CHAPTER FIVE
Garrison Keillor is creator and host of *A Prairie Home Companion*, a radio program broadcast since 1974 on public radio stations, which is produced and distributed now through Prairie Home Productions and American Public Media.

Waters, Richard D. *The Son of Man*, A Dramatic Sermon, 1970.

American theologian Reinhold Niebuhr is credited with including the *Serenity Prayer* in a sermon in 1943. It is a cornerstone of Alcoholics Anonymous and other twelve-step programs. The original version was actually longer, and there have been numerous versions and alterations in the last 70 years.

CHAPTER SIX
Chapter-opening quotation from: Verghese, Abraham. *The Tennis Partner*. New York: HarperCollins Publishers, 1998.

CHAPTER SEVEN
The television show *Thirtysomething* was broadcast on ABC and created by Marshall Herskovitz and Edward Zwick for MGM/UA Television Group. It aired for four seasons from 1987-1991.

John Gottman and his wife, Julie Schwartz, head the Relationship Research Institute. Gottman's latest book is *What Makes Love Last* (New York: Simon & Schuster, 2012).

Stephen R. Treat, is the former director and CEO of Council for Relationships, Philadelphia. He and Gerald Weeks coauthored *Couples in Treatment: Techniques and Approaches for Effective Practice* (New York: Routledge, 1992).

Boszormenyi- Nagy, *Between Give and Take* (see above, Chapter One).

CHAPTER EIGHT
Pollan, Michael. *The Botany of Desire: A Plant's-Eye View of the World*. New York: Random House, 2001.

Terry Fralick, L.C.P.C., lectures about mindfulness. You can find further information at www.mindfulnesscenter.org.

CHAPTER NINE
Carl Whitaker and August Napier wrote *The Family Crucible* (New York: Harper & Row, 1978).

Isaacson, Walter. *Steve Jobs*. New York: Simon & Schuster, 2011.

Boszormenyi- Nagy, *Between Give and Take* (see above, Chapter One).

CHAPTER ELEVEN
"Another Fucking Opportunity for Growth" is modern slang attributed to Dossie Easton and Janet Hardy in the book *The Ethical Slut* (Greenery Press, 1997).

CHAPTER TWELVE
"Eyes Open Orgasm" is attributed to David Schnarch in *The Passionate Marriage* (see above, Chapter 4).

CHAPTER THIRTEEN
Berman, Jennifer. *Adult Children of Normal Families*. Simon & Schuster/Pocket Books, 1994.

CHAPTER FOURTEEN
Kabat-Zinn, Jon and Thich Nhat Hanh. *Full Catastrophe Living: Using the Wisdom of your Body and Mind to Face Stress, Pain and Illness*. New York: Random House/Bantam Dell, 2009.

Friedman, Thomas. *Hot, Flat, and Crowded: Why We Need a Green Revolution and How It Can Renew America*. New York: Farrar, Straus and Giroux, 2008.

CHAPTER FIFTEEN
Dan Gottlieb, has been the voice of *Family Matters* and *Voices in the Family*, on WHYY radio in Philadelphia since its inception in 1985. Dan is also the author of the book *Family Matters: Healing in the Heart of the Family* (New York: Penguin Group, 1991).

Jeffers, Susan. *Feel the Fear and Do It Anyway*. New York: Random House/Ballantine Books, 1987.

CHAPTER SIXTEEN
Boszormenyi- Nagy, *Between Give and Take* (see above, Chapter One).

CHAPTER SEVENTEEN
Skutch, Margaret, and Wilfrid Hamlin. *To Start a School*. Boston: Little, Brown & Co., 1971.

The "Slowskys" are a devoted turtle couple in an advertising campaign for Comcast's Xfinity broadband service. The characters were created by Goodby, Silverstein & Partners of San Francisco.

Benjamin Zander and Rosamund Stone Zander are the authors of *The Art of Possibility: Transforming Professional and Personal Life* (Boston: Harvard Business School Press, 2000).

CHAPTER EIGHTEEN
Pat Love is co-author (with Steven Stosny) of *How to Improve Your Marriage Without Talking About It* (New York: Random House/ Broadway Books, 2007), and (with Jo Robinson) of
Hot Monogamy: Essential Steps to More Passionate, Intimate Lovemaking (CreateSpace, 2012).

CHAPTER NINETEEN
Boszormenyi- Nagy, *Between Give and Take* (see above, Chapter One).

Rivlin, Gary. "The Chrome-Shiny, Lights-Flashing, Wheel-Spinning, Touch-Screened, Drew-Carey-Wisecracking, Video-Playing, 'Sounds Events'-Packed, Pulse-Quickening Bandit." *New York Times Magazine* (May 9, 2004) (includes excerpts of interview with Nancy Petry, Professor, University of Connecticut School of Medicine).

CHAPTER TWENTY
Schnarch, *The Passionate Marriage* (see above, Chapter Four).

William H. Masters and Virginia E. Johnson are the legendary researchers into human sexual response and the diagnosis and treatment of sexual dysfunctions. Their first publication was entitled *Human Sexual Response* (New York: Bantam Books, 1966).

CHAPTER TWENTY-ONE
Susan Johnson is the founder of the International Centre for Excellence in Emotionally Focused Therapy (ICEEFT) in Ottawa, Canada, and is the author of *Love Sense: The Revolutionary New Science of Romantic Relationships* (Little, Brown and Company, 2013).
Article quoted is *The Power of Emotion in Therapy: How to Harness this Great Motivator,* Psychotherapy Networker, (May 2012).

Charlan Nemeth has published numerous articles about organizational dynamics, including *Managing Innovation: When Less is More* (The Regents of the University of California, 1997).

Lehrer, Johan. *Imagine: How Creativity Works*. New York: Houghton Mifflin Harcourt, 2012.

CHAPTER TWENTY-THREE
Bombeck, Erma. "You Don't Love Me," from *If Life is a Bowl of Cherries, What Am I Doing in the Pits?* New York: Ballantine Books, 1985.

For Our Teenagers, a paraphrasing of Bombeck's work, is anonymously written.

Nerney, Michael, *What Are They Thinking? The Adolescent Brain: Substance Abuse and Risky Behavior*, a live presentation offered to groups of parents of adolescents.

CHAPTER TWENTY-FOUR
Gilbert Rendle writes about the dynamics of church congregations, including the book *Holy Conversations: Strategic Planning as a Spiritual Practice for Congregations*, (The Alban Institute, 2003).

Sachs, Oliver. *Your Inner Fish: A Journey Into the 3.5 Billion-Year History of the Human Body*. New York: Random House/ First Vintage Books, 2009.
The reference used in the text is on page 25.

Friedman, Lauren. "Mind Your Body: The Perks of Feeling So-So." *Psychology Today* (September 2012).

Diamond, Jared M. *The Third Chimpanzee: The Evolution and Future of the Human Animal*. New York: HarperCollins, 1992.

Gottman (see above, Chapter Seven).

Johnson (see above, Chapter Twenty-one).

CHAPTER TWENTY-FIVE
Bruce Tuckman, published "Tuckman's Stages" in "Developmental Sequence in Small Groups" (*Psychological Bulletin* 63, 1965).

CHAPTER TWENTY-SIX
The phrase "A(n) F-ing Opportunity for Growth" is believed to have originated from Easton, Dossie and Janet Hardy, *The Ethical Slut,* Celestial Arts, Berkeley, CA, 1997.

CHAPTER TWENTY-SEVEN
Boszormenyi- Nagy, *Between Give and Take* (see above, Chapter One).

Gottman (see above, Chapter Seven).

CHAPTER TWENTY-EIGHT
Hegel, Georg Friedrich (1770- 1831) was a German philosopher, and the author of *Encyclopedia of the Philosophical Sciences* (1817).

CHAPTER TWENTY-NINE
Excerpt from Williamson, Marianne. *Return to Love: Reflections on the Principles of a Course in Miracles.* (New York: HarperCollins, 1992).

Zander, Benjamin   (see above, Chapter Seventeen).

Index